THE PE
ME

Maurice Hugh Keen was born in 1933. His father was Secretary of the Oxford University Chest and a Fellow of Balliol. He was educated as a scholar at Winchester (1947–52), after which he did his National Service in the infantry, commissioned in the Royal Ulster Rifles. He took a degree in Modern History at Balliol College, Oxford, and received First Class Honours (1952–4). After graduating he spent four years as a Junior Research Fellow of Queen's College, Oxford. He returned to Balliol as a history tutor in 1961, and has been there ever since as Fellow and tutor in Medieval History. He was awarded the Royal Historical Society Alexander Prize for an essay on *Treason Trials under the Law of Arms*. He has also published *The Outlaws of Medieval Legend* (1961), *The Laws of War in the Later Middle Ages* (1965), *England in the Later Middle Ages* (1972) and *Chivalry* (1984). Dr Keen married Mary Keegan in 1968, and has three daughters.

THE PENGUIN HISTORY OF
MEDIEVAL EUROPE

*

MAURICE KEEN

PENGUIN BOOKS

PENGUIN BOOKS

Published by the Penguin Group
Penguin Books Ltd, 27 Wrights Lane, London W8 5TZ, England
Viking Penguin, a division of Penguin Books USA Inc.
375 Hudson Street, New York, New York 10014, USA
Penguin Books Australia Ltd, Ringwood, Victoria, Australia
Penguin Books Canada Ltd, 2801 John Street, Markham, Ontario, Canada L3R 1B4
Penguin Books (NZ) Ltd, 182–190 Wairau Road, Auckland 10, New Zealand

Penguin Books Ltd, Registered Offices: Harmondsworth, Middlesex, England

First published as *A History of Medieval Europe* by Routledge & Kegan Paul 1968
Published in Pelican Books 1969
Reprinted in Penguin Books 1991
1 3 5 7 9 10 8 6 4 2

Printed in England by Clays Ltd, St Ives plc
Set in Monotype Times

Contents

CONTENTS

List of Maps

Preface

THIS book has been written with the needs in mind of an ordinary, intelligent reader, who does not know much about what happened in the Middle Ages and would like to know more. I have tried to tell their story in as short a compass as seemed reasonable, and as far as possible as a connected and continuous record. I have done my best at the same time to explain what seems to me to distinguish the civilization of medieval Europe from that of Europe in the times that went before and that came after. In the hope of maintaining a continuity of theme, and in order to avoid overcrowding of factual detail, I have probably often been guilty of over-simplifying things, and have certainly left a great many matters undiscussed. The history of medieval Byzantium is so different from that of western Europe in its whole tone and tenor, that it seemed wiser not to attempt any systematic survey of it: in any case, I am not qualified to undertake such a survey. I have said nothing about the history of medieval Russia, which is remote from the themes that I felt it important to pursue: and I have probably said less than I should have done about Spain. Those whose special interests lie in these fields will no doubt find other books that will serve them better. I shall simply ask their pardon for concentrating on the matters which have seemed to me personally to be most interesting and significant, and which I feel least unqualified to write about.

I have received much help in writing this book, which I must acknowledge. My greatest debt is to Professor R. W. Southern, who read the whole book in draft, and made innumerable helpful suggestions for improvement and revision. It would have been hard to find a guide and critic more generous of his time and attention. I am also grateful to Professor E. F. Jacob for much advice and wise comment. I have a debt of a special kind to Dr J. H. Plumb, at whose suggestion the book was written.

I must also thank very warmly Miss Margaret Bamford, who typed the manuscript. I am very grateful too, to Mr A. Grant

of Worcester College, Oxford, who read the proofs, and has
helped me to eliminate a large number of errors which appeared
in the hardback edition. The publishers have been unfailingly
courteous and helpful, as I have always found them to be. All the
faults and errors in the book (and I have no doubt there still
are many, both of fact and interpretation) are of my own making

M.K.

1

The Middle Ages and Their Heritage:
The Idea of the Unity of Christendom

IT was the men of the Renaissance who first called the period which preceded their own 'the Middle Ages'. For them this was a term of opprobrium, a label for the centuries of ignorance, barbarism and obscurantism, which they saw as intervening between the end of the classical age and the revival of classical learning. Unjust as their verdict was, its revision has raised problems. History, it is said, is a seamless garment: it is nevertheless convenient to divide it into periods. Historians, though they no longer see, as the men of the Renaissance did, a clear break in the course of history when the last classical emperor in the west lost his throne in 476, still write about the Middle Ages. Most of them, however, find it hard to say when these ages began, let alone when they ended. Just where the limits are in fact drawn depends very much on the standpoint of the individual historian. Advances in social, scientific and religious ideas seldom keep even pace with each other; those who view this or that change as of special significance will divide their periods of history differently. The problem of defining such a period as the Middle Ages is not that of finding limits which can be justified on all grounds, but ones which are justifiable. My first task, therefore, is to say what limits I am going to use, and why I am going to use them.

On Christmas Day in the year 800, Charlemagne, the king of the Franks, was crowned emperor by Pope Leo III in the church of St Peter's at Rome. 'Him the catholic Church of Europe took as its emperor,' wrote the biographer of his contemporary, St Willehad. That is one limit. The other is in 1449, when, after twenty years of sessions, the Council of Basle was finally dissolved. The council had come together as a body representing the whole of Catholic Europe, both its churches and its kingdoms, and claimed powers to judge orthodoxy and to oversee the quarrels of

11

princes. No single assembly or institution was ever again recognized as exerting such extended authority throughout Europe as, in its heyday, men had acknowledged to belong to it by right. At the time that it was dissolved, few can have been aware that a radical change was taking place. But within a little more than a lifetime this was obvious: in the 1530s one could no longer speak of a Catholic Europe in the same sense as men had done in 800 and in 1449.

These dates of course do not mark sharp divisions. Charlemagne's family had ruled over much of Christian Europe before 800; after 1449, the possibility that another council would again bring together the representatives of European Christendom continued prominent in men's minds for more than a generation. There are no sharp frontiers in history. It remains true, however, that the period which these two dates very roughly divide possesses a certain unity. Within this period western Europe (or Latin Christendom, the terms being more or less analogous) regarded itself, and can be regarded, as a single society, in a sense in which it was not before, and has not been since. Of this the outward and visible sign is the fact that Europeans were prepared to recognize in their society some sort of common authority. At the core of this unity was the acceptance of a common religious teaching, but there was more to it than that. Latin Christendom, they believed, formed a united republic, the kind of republic which can go to war, as it did when it sent its soldiers on crusade. At different times within the medieval period different views were prevalent as to where the ultimate authority in this republic lay; some believed it lay with the emperor, others with the Pope, others again with a general council. Many were prepared to fight for their views, yet the sense of unity remained.

> The Christian republic is a single kingdom, a house undivided: the wars which are waged between its subjects are a matter for great shame: they should not in truth be called wars, but base sedition.

Jacob Meyer, who wrote these words, lived in the sixteenth, not the thirteenth century. The belief in unity was deep-seated and died hard.

This belief could not have been achieved without the sense of a common heritage and common objectives, and without them it could not endure. Where did they come from? Before trying to answer this next question, it will be well to take a look at a map of Latin Christendom, to see what this Christian republic could mean in terms of geography.

If one compares the empire of Charlemagne with the Europe which sent representatives to the council at Basle, the boundaries are not so very different. Charlemagne's empire stretched east and west from the Elbe to Barcelona beyond the Pyrenees, and north and south from the channel coast to the country south of Rome. The Slavs and Avars who inhabited what are now Czechoslovakia and Hungary acknowledged him as their overlord; the British Isles alone, in the Christian west, never formally accepted that he had authority over them. A map of 1449 shows these boundaries extended, but it is still essentially a map of the European land mass. Beyond Germany to the east lie the Christian kingdoms of Bohemia and Poland, and the lands ruled by the Teutonic knights stretching into modern Russia: to the north must be added the kingdoms of Denmark, Norway and Sweden. In the south, southern Italy, Sicily, and nearly all of the Iberian peninsula have been reconquered from the Greeks and Moslems who ruled there in the time of Charles, as also the Balearic islands, Corsica, and Sardinia. The boundaries have extended to comprise most of what, until the Iron Curtain fell, people thought of as modern Europe.

These changes of frontier do not however imply a story of steady expansion. If one were to look at a map of Latin Christendom in, say, the thirteenth century, it would include a much wider area. One would find that a French duke ruled at Athens, and a Latin emperor at Constantinople; between them, the prince of Antioch and the king of Jerusalem controlled Cyprus and most of the coastline of Palestine and Syria. It looked further as if Tunis and other towns on the north African shore, which were heavily dependent on supplies of grain from Sicily, might soon fall permanently under the sway of her rulers. There would be a marked contrast, moreover, in terms of wealth and standard of living, between southern and northern Europe, in favour of the former. This contrast would not be so marked in 800, or in 1449.

This map of Latin Christendom in the thirteenth century is reminiscent not so much of modern Europe, as of the Roman empire. The Romans called the Mediterranean 'our sea' because their empire included its entire coastline, and their prosperity was based on its commerce. In the thirteenth century, Latin Christians controlled a very large part of the Mediterranean coastline, and the merchants of the Italian towns, who controlled its trade, were collectively the richest men in Europe. Of course, all this did not last. Even before the coming of the Ottoman Turks it had become clear that the Latins would not maintain their control of so much coastal land. Although Mediterranean commerce remained of great importance until after Columbus, the towns of Flanders and the Baltic were already in the fourteenth century coming to rival the prosperity of the Italians. The comparison holds for a certain point in time only.

It is interesting that it was in the thirteenth century, when the boundaries of Latin Christendom approached most nearly those of the Roman empire, that the spirit of Christian universalism seems to have reached its climacteric. For a moment Rome once again seemed to be the 'head of the world', when a council, whose members were drawn from a Christendom much wider than that of the fifteenth century, assembled at the Lateran in 1215 at the bidding of Pope Innocent III. Here, I believe, one can find a clue to one of the forces which helped to give Latin Christendom in the Middle Ages a sense of unity more real than that of Europe in succeeding times, and can mark off the one age from the other.

To the peoples of the Mediterranean basin the Roman empire had in its time provided a great measure of political, cultural and commercial unity. Under its rule, peace and prosperity had accompanied a high standard of civilization. The men who lived in Europe in the Middle Ages were well aware of this, and knew too that a comparison between this Roman past and their own times would not be in their favour. Hence the Roman past for them appeared to set a standard, which it should be their object to re-achieve. Everything which they rediscovered about the classical world, about its knowledge of philosophy and of natural science, about its systems of law, about its literary achievements, tended to underline this attitude. The restoration of the world-wide dominion of Rome was the dream not only of medieval popes and emperors but also of many of their subjects and servants. It was a very natural desire, given the blessings which had once followed in the wake of Roman peace.

This attitude was fortified by the fact that most men were unaware of how radically things had altered since the time of the Romans. This again was not unnatural. For, contrary to the belief of the men of the Renaissance, the deposition in 476 of the last Roman emperor in the west was no cataclysm. It merely marked a step, and not a very important one, in the progressive barbarization of the western provinces of the old Roman empire. Their urban and commercial prosperity did not survive the crisis through which they passed in the third century A.D. In Gaul, Spain and Britain, and to some extent in Italy too, men were driven more and more to depend on their own local resources. The defence of their extended frontiers, moreover, outpassed the resources of the Roman army. This problem the Romans solved by entrusting the task instead to the warlike barbarian tribes who lived on the borders of the empire, making them in return their allies or 'federates', and granting them lands on the boundaries of the empire, the privilege of association with it, and the promise of assistance against their own enemies. If these enemies proved too difficult to deal with, the simple answer was to make them 'federates' too. This was the peaceful beginning of the barbarian invasions.

Most of these federate tribes were by origin Germans, of the same stock, that is to say, as the great body of tribes which inhabited the lands east and north of the Rhine and the Danube, which the Romans called Germania. Soon after the year 400, the whole Teutonic world was shaken by the pressure of tribes fleeing from the onslaught of the Huns, a savage nomad people from the steppes of Asia. A whole series of tribes, Goths, Vandals, Bur-gundians and later Franks, spilled across the frontiers of the Roman empire, seeking food, pasture, and the privileged position of 'federates'. These tribes were not very large, but they were good soldiers and the pressures behind them were strong: they did not stop at the boundaries, but penetrated far into the provinces. The Vandals even reached north Africa, where they set up a kingdom which lasted for one hundred years. Since they could not resist them, the wealthy Roman landlords of the provinces which they reached agreed to share the lands with them. The most important of these invaders, those whose influence lasted longest, were the Lombards, who settled in northern and central Italy; the Visigoths, who established a kingdom in Spain which the Arabs overran at the end of the seventh century; and the Franks, who established dominion not only over most of Gaul but also over many of the tribes who still lived in Germany, east of the one-time Roman frontier of the Rhine.

The effects of the barbarian penetration of the western provinces were not cataclysmic. They served rather to accentuate and greatly accelerate already inherent tendencies, the progressive decline of urban prosperity and the reduction of commerce, the retreat of the wealthy to their great landed estates, the breakdown of internal and external communications. Above all, their arrival and settlement deepened the gulf which already existed, in ways of life and thought, between the eastern provinces of the Roman empire and the western ones. This however was a gradual process. So, when in 476 the western emperor was deposed, no one supposed that the empire in the west had ceased to be. For centuries past, though the empire continued to be regarded as a single whole, there had usually been two emperors, one ruling the west from Italy, and the other the east from Constantinople. Now there was only one, at Constantinople, who thus became, in theory at least, the sole ruler of both halves of the empire. The barbarians did, it is true, set up kingdoms in the western provinces, but they did not question the continuing authority of the empire in the lands where they had settled. Kingship denoted leadership of a barbarian people: such leaders looked to the eastern emperor to grant them titles which would give them authority over Roman citizens. Theodoric the Goth became patrician of Rome, and Clovis the Frank was hailed as Augustus. They used the emperor's image on their coins, and continued to enforce the Roman law, not the barbarian laws by which their own people were bound, on the old inhabitants of the provinces. The empire never exactly ended; and though its influence became progressively more remote, deep respect remained for the unity it was supposed to enshrine.

This background must be borne in mind if one is to see the coronation of Charlemagne in 800 in its true perspective. 'Thus the empire, which had had its seat in Constantinople among the Greeks, was transferred to the Franks,' one contemporary remarked. Though the motto which was inscribed on Charlemagne's imperial seal read *renovatio Romani imperii* – revival of the Roman empire – men saw no real break as having occurred in its continuity. In another and a very important sense, however, there truly was a revival. There was a great difference between an imperial crown worn by a little known Greek, and one worn by a king of the Franks, the most powerful and successful of all the barbarian tribes. It provided the respect and the sense of unity with which the name of Rome was associated with new force. The unity of empire ceased to be a nostalgic memory, preserved in name only: it became something worth striving to restore to its fullness.

Other factors further enhanced the significance of this coronation. In religious as well as in secular affairs a deep gulf had grown between the eastern and western provinces of the old empire. It was not just that in the Greek-speaking east, rites were conducted in a language virtually unknown in western Europe; the religious ideas of the two areas were separated by their different levels of culture. Nice problems of theology, which the west could not understand because it had developed no vocabulary to convey them, agitated the Church in the eastern empire. There was a problem, too, of religious authority. In the time of the late classical empire, there had been five patriarchates, those of Rome, Antioch, Alexandria, Jerusalem, and Constantinople. Of these Rome, as the see of St Peter, prince of the apostles, had been recognized as coming first in terms of honour. By the end of the seventh century, three of these had ceased to be of real importance, for Jerusalem, Antioch, and Alexandria had all fallen under the sway of the Moslems. With the decline of the empire in the west, the patriarchs of Rome, more independent than they had been before, began to claim that theirs was not a primacy of honour only, but of authority in the whole Christian church. 'The apostolic see is the head of all the churches,' claimed Pope Gregory I. In the east, the emperors claimed the same universal primacy for the patriarchs of Constantinople, because they presided over the see which was also the seat of empire. In the west, the abandonment by the Lombards in Italy and the Visigoths in Spain of their Arian heresy for Latin orthodoxy, and the close connexions which Gregory and his successors formed with the most powerful of the barbarians, the rulers of the Franks, had enhanced the significance of the papal claims. The Pope's coronation of Charlemagne consequently associated his new imperial office with the religious unity of Christians in the west. It also demonstrated that this unity extended to more than purely religious affairs.

To appreciate the full significance of this, one must bear in mind what the Roman empire meant to educated men in the age of Charlemagne and after it. Here some brief explanation of certain ideas which coloured the historical outlook not only of his contemporaries but of the whole of the Middle Ages becomes necessary.

Instead of separating their views about the classical achievement and biblical history, historians and thinkers of the Middle Ages saw the two together. This approach was one of the most important legacies of the early fathers to medieval Christian thought. The Christian religion had made its first appearance as an obscure oriental sect, the significance of whose claims rested on the interpretation of certain historical events (the Gospel story) in the light of the Jewish scriptures. The early Christians soon found themselves obliged to defend their teaching from the criticism of the educated pagan world, that this did not provide a basis which was worthy of acceptance. They did so by carrying the war into the enemy's camp. The whole achievement of the classical world was, they claimed, no more than a part of the same story as the achievements of God's chosen people, recorded in the Old Testament, and was besides less important and less antique. 'We who are habitual readers of the divine histories,' wrote Tertullian contemptuously,

are masters of the subject, from the nativity of the world itself. If you have ever heard of one Moses, he goes before the fall of Troy by a thousand years: our other prophets, even the last of them, are to be found not later than your first philosophers and law givers.

Plato owed his inspiration to Hebrew traditions preserved in Egypt, the lawgivers of Rome their inspiration to the Jewish decalogue. Thus the Christians answered criticism with an uncompromising assertion of the superiority of their sacred writings, the Old and New Testaments, over all the history and philosophy of the pagans. Their view was strongly defended in the last days of the classical empire by St Augustine in his *City of God*.

Though the learning of Greece still warms the world at this day, yet they need not boast of their wisdom, it being neither so ancient nor so excellent as our divine religion, and the true wisdom.

The *City of God* was probably, after the Bible, the book most widely read in the west in the Middle Ages. About the same time, Augustine's disciple Orosius put together a history of the ancient world, from the creation to his own day, which, with the earlier *Church History* of Eusebius, came to be regarded in the medieval period as authoritative universal history.

The study as history of the Old and New Testaments, taken together, suggests a specific historical interpretation. In them, the whole story of the Jewish nation is seen as part of a divine scheme, preparing the way for the central event in human history, the incarnation of Christ. From this watershed, history looks back to the creation and forward to Christ's second coming at the end of time. This second coming, like the first, is foreseen and foretold by inspired prophets. This was the scheme of things into which the history of the Roman empire was fitted in the Middle Ages. Though it found no place among the seven periods or ages into which men believed that human history was divided (of which the fifth had ended with the coming of Christ, and the sixth would end with his return), its part in the scheme was recognized clearly. 'In references by the fathers to the power and dominion of Rome we see,' writes Professor Coopland,

the pride of Roman citizens, citizens of that empire which had been chosen to bring peace and unity to the world; which should provide a fitting field for the spread of the Christian faith, a field in which there should be peace, easy travel and security for the journeyings of the Apostles.

The Middle Ages accepted the view of the Roman empire which they found in the fathers without question. Like other human events, its dominion had been foreseen in Scripture. Daniel had prophesied concerning four kingdoms; the first three, Babylon, Persia and Alexander's Macedon, were already passed, and Rome was the fourth, destined to endure till the end of time. Thus in medieval opinion the empire whose active rule was revived in the west with Charlemagne was associated not only with the Church's sacred mission to spread the Christian faith, but with the very endurance of the world in which her ministry had been ordained.

The historical teaching which the Middle Ages inherited from the Christian fathers was of great importance, quite apart from what it taught them about the role of the empire. It was at the root of a good many attitudes which are characteristic of the period. Seeing that the sixth and penultimate age had already begun, men saw no reason why it should last much longer. 'The world is growing old,' wrote the Frankish chronicler Fredegar; and again, 'We live at the end of time'. Throughout the Middle Ages, men watched anxiously for signs of the approach of the *finale*: plagues, eclipses, earthquakes, battles, any or all such events might be signs. How much effect this had on the way people acted is not clear. It does help, however, to explain why medieval annalists and chroniclers so seldom give satisfactory accounts of human motives and historical causes: they were seeking evidence in events not of human, but of divine agency. More important, probably, in its direct effect on men's actions was the study of the Old Testament as a historical source with special significance. In the Old Testament they could read of a

God who was a God of battles, of high priests at whose command men were hewed in pieces before the Lord and of kings who led God's chosen people to victory. The society which it described was much more like their own than the Roman empire was, and its sentiments were more familiar.

This is a reminder that, important as their classical and Christian heritage was, the men of Charlemagne's day and their descendants looked on it through barbarian eyes. One must remember, when speaking of their anxiety to restore something of the peace and unity of the Roman empire, that they had little understanding of the things on which these had been based. Many who obeyed the Frankish emperor lived on lands which had never in fact known Roman rule. Where it had been known, their invasions, as has been said, had accelerated the decline of commerce and communication, and the disintegration of unified government. The Europe which Charlemagne's contemporaries knew was a Europe separated into small, largely rural communities which did not know very much about each other, let alone the world beyond. If their religious and political aspirations owed much to the Roman past, their social attitudes and organization owed quite as much to ancient Germany.

Most of the barbarian tribes had already been deeply influenced by contact with Rome before they entered the empire, and it is often difficult to differentiate between what is of Germanic and what of Roman origin. Perhaps the most striking difference of outlook, however, was the inability of the Germans to think in abstract terms. Notions such as authority or society meant little to them as such: they could only comprehend them when they were viewed in terms of specific personal relationships. This helps to explain the importance of two matters essential to understanding the outlook of these barbarians and their descendants, the importance among them of the kindred and their idea of lordship.

Probably the easiest way to explain the importance of kinship to the Germans is in terms of the vendetta. If an individual German was injured in his person or his property, if he was wounded or had his cattle stolen, the way he sought redress was through his own kindred, from the kindred of the man who had wronged

21

him. Redress could be achieved in two ways, by composition between the two kins, preferably before a royal judge, or by fighting. The former was usually preferable, hence the careful itemization in the barbarian law codes of the composition due for an endless variety of injuries, the loss of hand, or foot, or wife: these are guides to royal officials as to what ought to be regarded as fair compensation. But the threat of force was always in the background. Thus blood relationship was the guarantee of some degree of security and order in a little governed society: fear of the vengeance not just of one man, but of a whole kin, was the force on which men relied to deter wrongdoing. It was a rudimentary way of achieving this object, and one obviously which could as easily promote disorder as its opposite. The crime of homicide engendered the most serious of all feuds: the kindred of a slain man had no right to rest until they had avenged him or obtained blood money in turn. It was not easy to limit the bloodshed consequent on such a feud. Dangerous as it was, however, the brand of social responsibility which the vendetta inculcated was of lasting importance. To the French lawyer Beaumanoir, who wrote in the thirteenth century, it still appeared to be both a right and a duty for those of gentle birth to take up arms in the quarrels of their kinsfolk. In France in the fifteenth century, the terrible feud between the dukes of Burgundy and Orleans and their followers showed that the spirit of the vendetta was still a living force.

It would be wrong to think of the kindred of the barbarian laws in terms of pure blood ties. The invasions undoubtedly scattered and divided many kins. A man could leave his kin and join another. In practice, the kinsmen of a chief and his unrelated followers were probably not carefully distinguished. The importance of kinship was the emphasis which it laid on close personal attachment, for this was something which coloured social relations throughout the Middle Ages. In centuries long after the invasions, churchmen thought of themselves as members of the 'family' of the saint to whom their church was dedicated, and knights as 'brothers' in orders of chivalry to which they had been admitted.

Kinship and the vendetta help to explain the Germanic idea of lordship. In a society in which these were so important, noble birth and military prowess were the natural qualifications for a leader. It is not easy to say which was more important, but probably the latter: the frequency of feuds made it the prerequisite of survival. It was therefore the object of every chief to count fine warriors among his followers: 'This is reckoned the sign of rank and strength,' says Tacitus of the Germans, 'to be surrounded always with a large band of chosen youths, which gives glory in peace, in war protection.' To join the following of such a leader was to acquire status, to become as it were his kinsman. If the follower were killed, it would be the leader who claimed blood-money from his slayer, and the follower was bound to stand by his lord even against his own kin. A lord who wished to keep his followers together needed to reward them with rich gifts, outward signs of their rank and prowess. Hence, as Tacitus put it,

You cannot keep up a great retinue except by war and violence, for it is to the free-handed chief that they look for the war horse, for the murderous and masterful sphere: banquetings and a certain rude but lavish outfit take the place of salary. The material for this open-handedness comes from war and foray.

Though Tacitus wrote in the second century, his description tallies closely with the picture given in the eighth century of a great Germanic king, Hrothgar, in the Anglo-Saxon saga *Beowulf*: he is discovered in his great wooden hall, feasting with the heroes whom he has rewarded with treasure. Protection and generosity to his followers were what the barbarians expected of a ruler, not efficient administration: in return, he had a right to demand their loyal personal support. It was only natural to believe that the kindred of such a ruler had some special distinction of blood. The Frankish kings were supposed to be descended from the union of a princess and a sea god, the Anglo-Saxon kings from the god Woden. Who their ancestors really were is far from clear, but it is not very important.

The ethos of the Germanic invaders was military and aristocratic. Courage, generosity and loyalty, especially on the battlefield: these were the kind of virtues they prized most highly. Magnificence, both of strength and riches, they expected to be displayed. This association of fighting prowess and wordly honour took deep root; it lasted much longer, certainly, than the Middle Ages. It is not without power now, but it was much more powerful then. 'The calling of arms ennobles a man, whoever he may be,' wrote Jean de Beuil, a French king's councillor in the fifteenth century: those who adventure their lives in just quarrels, he adds, will gain salvation just as surely as those 'who live in contemplation on a diet of roots'. Admiration for the martial virtues may not be an essential of Christian teaching, but it is easily reconciled therewith. The descendants of the barbarians in the Christian Middle Ages did not question the validity of this reconciliation. A society in which martial prowess is held in such high social esteem is not likely to remain long at peace. It is wrong, therefore, in the Middle Ages, to regard the peaceful condition of things as the natural one; it was not. This had most important consequences. Effective physical protection was a continuous social need. The social function of those who could afford it seemed to furnish abundant justification for their rank and privileges. The direction of events, in so far as it lay with human agency at all, lay with kings and noblemen, with swords in their hands.

This militaristic spirit of the Middle Ages introduces some essential reservations concerning matters mentioned earlier in this chapter. A sense of unity is not easy to preserve in conditions of continuous strife. Unity remained through the Middle Ages an ideal with lasting influence, and the history of the Roman empire showed that it was not impossible of achievement. But how it had been achieved was forgotten. Men could only picture the Roman world in terms of their own, Julius Caesar and Pompey as knights who rode to the wars and performed prodigies of individual valour like the heroes of Teutonic legend. They knew nothing of the commercial unity of the Roman empire, or its system of colonial administration. A common Latin culture and common religious beliefs, both inheritances of the past, brought men together, but martial instinct and local and personal loyalties divided them still more deeply. Ideas can spread rapidly, and often acquire added force in the process. Common social and commercial interests, and territorial neighbourhood in the long run unite men more surely. Both require some degree of stability to have any force at all. In A.D. 800 when the Pope crowned Charlemagne emperor in Rome, western Europe stood dislocated by the decline of its economy since Roman times, by the Germanic invasions and the subsequent internecine feuds of the barbarians. Which was to prevail, barbarian militarism and the facts of geography, or the unity of Roman and Christian ideals?

SECTION ONE

c. 800 – c. 1046

The Restoration of the Empire in the
West, and Its Role in Upholding the Unity
of Christian Europe in an Age of Invasions
and General Insecurity.

2

The Revival of Empire – Charlemagne to Henry III

CHARLEMAGNE'S empire, with the unimportant exceptions of the British Isles and some parts of Spain, was coterminous with Latin Christendom, but its frontier had nothing to do with the coronation which made him emperor. This gave, it is true, a new significance to his rule in lands where it was already exercised, but such political unity as the empire had was due to the achievements of himself and his predecessors as kings of the Franks. These demand consideration, if the nature and fortunes of his empire are to be understood.

Under their great leader, Clovis (d. 511), and his descendants, the Merovingian kings, the Franks conquered the whole of what had once been Roman Gaul. They settled most thickly in the north-east, in the country between the Rhine and Paris; in the south, where they overthrew the Burgundians and the Visigoths of Toulouse, they made their influence felt as masters, not as founders of a new stock. They owed their success primarily to two things, their military prowess, and their acceptance of Latin orthodoxy, which won them a more willing obedience from the Gallo-Romans of the south than these had given to the Arian Goths. In so far as they understood them, the early Merovingian kings adopted the traditions of government of the late Roman empire, but that system, as they inherited it, was already decrepit. With the virtual disappearance of literacy in lay circles, an official class in the Roman sense ceased to exist. What survived was a class of powerful men, many of whom used the Roman official title of count, who were salaried not in money, but in lands. The kings' lettered councillors, drawn more and more as time went on from among the clergy, were rewarded in the same way, for land was the most valuable kind of reward in an age when commerce was being steadily reduced to a trickle. The source on which kings drew to reward their servants was the public fisc, the state property of ancient times which they now as rulers controlled. Here the difference between their ideas and those of the Romans becomes sharply apparent. For the Frankish ruler looked on the fisc not as state property, but as his own, to be divided at his death among his sons in accordance with the Frankish law of inheritance. It was the same with his kingship; his sons became kings in those parts of his patrimony which they severally inherited. These conditions gave rise to two tendencies. On the one hand, accidents of birth and survival in the royal family eroded continuity of government. On the other, the kings tended to become poorer, in terms of landed wealth, their nobles richer.

In the end, the last wretched survivors of the Merovingian dynasty were deposed by Charlemagne's father, Pippin the Short, the head of one of the greatest noble families of the East Franks. Two consequences stemmed from this change of dynasty. Because Pippin's family lands were further east than those of his predecessors, the centre of power shifted eastward: Paris had been a natural centre of Merovingian power, now Aix took its place. Secondly, and more important, Pippin needed some sanction for his arbitrary, if intelligible, action. The sanction he obtained was that of the Pope. This meant that the bonds, traditionally close between the rulers of the orthodox Franks and the patriarch of the west were drawn closer; and it meant more too, for the Pope charged his price. That price was that Frankish arms should defend the Pope's political control of Rome and the country about the city from the incursions of the kings of the Lombards.

Otherwise there was little change, except that it was now from the family lands of Pippin's house that loyal service had to be rewarded. The lack of permanent governmental institutions, the power of the nobles, the drain on royal landed resources through grants made to these nobles in order to retain their fidelity, and the practice of partible inheritance remained threats to the continuity of Frankish rule. These facts deeply affected the history of Charlemagne's reign. His was an empire which in practice was primarily held together by continuous and successful wars, which won new lands for the fisc and provided the nobles and their followers with an occupation fitting to their status and their tastes.

'By his wars he so nobly increased the kingdom of the Franks, which was great and strong when he inherited it from his father, that the additions he made almost doubled it.' This is how Charles's chaplain Einhard summarized the political achievements of his master. These wars, with which the forty-seven years of his long reign were largely taken up, may be considered under two heads. First come the series of wars, as a result of which Christian neighbours of the Franks, who in the past from time to time had acknowledged their overlordship, were brought under effective control. Thus he overcame the Aquitainians (769), the Bretons (786, 799), and the Bavarians (787–8); he made his son Louis king of Aquitaine, and his brother in law Gerold prefect of Bavaria. Of far greater importance, however, were the wars which he fought against peoples who lived further from Francia, and had never really known the Frankish yoke.

It was the link between the papacy and the Frankish kings which had been forged at Pippin's coronation that brought Charles up against the Lombards, whose kings were seeking to wrest from the popes control of the lands in central Italy, which were later to form the core of the Papal State. In 774 Charles answered Pope Hadrian's appeal for aid; he overthrew King Desiderius and was crowned in his place at Pavia. Not only did this extend his rule into northern Italy; he had won the crown of Lombardy as the protector of the patriarch of Latin Christendom, and Hadrian, to remind Charles that this was his role, had made him patrician of Rome to mark the fact. In a sense this was the first step toward the revival of the Christian empire in the west. Two other wars which Charlemagne fought were of equal, if not greater, importance. The war against the Saxons was, says Einhard, the 'most prolonged and cruel' of those Charles ever undertook: he first fought them in 772, and final victory was not achieved till 804. The Saxons were a numerous and ferocious people, who in their lands between the Elbe and the Rhine delta preserved the warlike customs and the pagan religion of ancient *Germania*: it was imperative for Charlemagne to subdue them, if he was to maintain any effective control over Bavaria and the Frisian low countries. Waged against heathens, the war was marked by wholesale massacres, and victory by forcible conversion. His wars against the heathen Avars, a nomad people of Finnish stock who inhabited the Hungarian plain and lived by plundering their neighbours, were still more ferocious: witness Einhard's comment, 'The district where stood the palace of the Khan of the Avars is now so desolate that there is not so much as a trace of human habitation.' These two wars demonstrated the militance of Frankish orthodoxy, and the armed strength of the Frankish ruler as a protector of Christians. By a curious irony, Charles's role as such was remembered later chiefly in connexion with his much less important and successful campaigns against the Spanish Saracens. But later epic was not wrong essentially, in portraying him leading the forces of Christendom against heathen enemies.

Charlemagne's coronation as emperor on Christmas Day 800 was a consecration of this aspect of his rule, by a symbolic act which caught the imagination of contemporaries and later generations. The initiative, it should be noted, came from the Pope, and thus the revived empire was associated inseparably with the religious mission of the Roman church. Pope Leo could congratulate himself on this, for the patronage of the Frankish king had not always been comfortable for papal dignity. 'Your part,' Charles had written earlier to Pope Hadrian, 'is to aid our efforts with your prayers': effective decisions, he implied, were the business of kings. The coronation indicated that the roles were reciprocal, and that Charles's part was to aid the Church with his arms. Even if the Pope's action had its disingenuous side, however, it did in one way mirror the true state of affairs, for Charles's empire had more genuine unity in the religious sense than any other. It had no day to day system of administration to bind it together, as is indicated by the fact that its ruler spent more time in hunting than in any other occupation except war. Its armies were composed of local noblemen and their followers, called out for a summer campaigning season. Charlemagne was probably little aware of the added religious significance which the

**THE EMPIRE OF CHARLEMAGNE & THE
PARTITION OF VERDUN, C. 843**

▬ ▬ ▬ ▬ Boundary of Charlemagne's Empire C.814
●●●●●●● Boundary of Middle Kingdom C. 843

title of emperor gave to his rule, or of any change in his position
as a result of his new dignity. After all, in 800 he was an already
ageing man. Certainly the division which he planned of his lands
among his sons, after the Frankish custom, suggests that he was
not aware of any change. But Louis, the only son to survive him,
clearly to some extent was.

33

The capitularies of the early years of his reign make this quite clear. They stress explicitly and seek to extend the religious unity of the empire. With the aid of his friend, the abbot Benedict of Aniane, Louis promulgated a version of the ancient rule of Benedict of Nursia to be followed in all monasteries in his empire. Benedict of Aniane, in his turn, hailed him as 'Emperor of all the Church of Europe'. This remark reflects the quest of the emperor and his advisers for a unity which, though its roots were religious, should be more than ecclesiastical. Louis, reviewing in 817 the problem of the disposition of his lands after his death, sternly eschewed the promptings of paternal affection to divide his inheritance, 'lest by this means scandal arise to God's Holy Church'. His younger sons should be kings in name, but under the strict control of the emperor. Another of his advisers, Agilbert of Lyons, looked forward to the day when a single, uniform system of law binding all peoples of the empire, Lombard, Frank, Saxon and Bavarian alike, should demonstrate its unity. But despite all this, long before Louis surnamed the Pious died, the empire founded by Charlemagne had begun to fall apart.

*

Louis the Pious had the misfortune that three of his sons survived him. When he died in 840 these three had already begun to fight among themselves and with him, in their anxiety to secure each for himself as rich a portion as he might of their eventual common inheritance. Lothar, the eldest, strove to maintain in his own interest as much as possible of the unity of the empire, his brothers Lewis and Charles to establish independent kingdoms in its eastern and western territories respectively. From their struggles stemmed a series of partition agreements, of which the most important and decisive was the Treaty of Verdun, agreed in 843, a few years after their father's death. This divided the Frankish patrimony into three parts. West Francia, what is now France from the Pyrenees to as far roughly as the line of the Somme, the Meuse, and the Rhone, went to the youngest brother, Charles the Bald; East Francia, Saxony and Bavaria, and the other Frankish lands beyond the Rhine, went to the next brother, Lewis, called the German. The title and dignity (it meant no more) of emperor went to the eldest, Lothar, and with it what now seems a curious medley of lands, known as the Middle Kingdom. It included the lands east and west of the Rhine between the kingdoms of Charles and Lewis, Burgundy and Provence in the Rhone valley, and all the lands that Charlemagne and Louis the Pious had ruled in Italy. It also included most of the important centres of Carolingian rule; Rome, the seat of the papacy and the city where emperors were traditionally crowned; Pavia, the capital of the Lombard kingdom; and Aix, which Charlemagne had sought to make a new Rome in the north, as Constantine had done in the east at Constantinople. When Lothar died, these territories were divided again among his three sons: Louis, the eldest, took Italy and the title of emperor, Charles Provence and Burgundy, and Lothar II the lands in the north which for want of a better name were called after him, Lotharingia. When Charles died the emperor Louis secured his inheritance; but when Lothar II died he was too busy fighting the Saracens to intervene, and in the end another treaty, that of Meersen, divided it between his uncles, Charles the Bald and Lewis the German.

Certain factors accentuated the effect of these ninth-century partitions of the Frankish patrimony. Italy was separated from the northern territories by geography, by the survival in greater degree of ancient culture, and by commercial contact with the Orient. In 843, the Franks of the eastern and western kingdoms already spoke distinguishable dialects; further, each kingdom included peoples who were not Frankish and had no common tradition, Aquitainians and Gascons in the west, Bavarians and Saxons in the east. The boundaries of the Middle Kingdom made little sense in geographic, or ethnic, or linguistic terms. The guiding principle in settling them seems to have been the limits of the estates controlled by noblemen who were followers of Lothar I. There was thus no natural solution, in both the immediate and the longer future, to the rivalry between eastern and western rulers for the lion's share of Lotharingia. And because the kings of East and West Francia saw success not in terms of pushing

EUROPE & THE BARBARIAN INVASIONS
OF THE 9th. & 10th. CENTURIES

	Route of Viking raids
	Route of Hungarian raids
	Route of Saracen raids

forward their boundaries to some natural limit, but of drawing noblemen with great landed estates into their orbit, their rivalry tended to undermine royal control in their several kingdoms. The fidelity, or lack of it, of individual noblemen was becoming a crucial factor in politics at the end of the ninth century.

*

From the middle of that century on, new external pressures on the frontiers of the one-time empire hastened its effective dissolution. As in the fifth century, Europe was again threatened with invasions, and perhaps more perilously, for now they came from three different directions.

In the south, the early years of the ninth century saw a great increase in Moslem naval power in the Mediterranean, and the rise of the powerful Aghlabid dynasty in North Africa. In his later years Charlemagne himself had had to take measures to defend his people from sea-borne Saracen raiders. In 827 the Aghlabids mounted an attack in force on Sicily; by 843 they had wrested most of the island from the control of the Byzantines and established themselves opposite Messina on the mainland. Another Moslem force had taken Bari and set up there an independent sultanate. From these mainland footings, and with flotillas based on the Sicilian ports, they began to raid along the coast and into central Italy: in 846 the suburbs of Rome itself were attacked. It looked for a moment as though all Italy might fall under Moslem rule, as Spain had already. From the hour of his accession, the emperor, Louis II, was as a result almost entirely occupied in the defence of the kingdom of Italy, and that without a fleet against a sea-borne enemy. In the end, in 871, he at last managed to conquer Bari, with the aid of a Venetian flotilla. A few years later it fell into Byzantine hands, and from then on Greek armies more or less contained the menace, though the Arabs still raided along the coasts. But the peril had been grave. Had Rome, the city of St Peter, been taken, the whole history of the middle ages in the west might have been different. As it was, the defence of the city by a Carolingian emperor knit closer the connexions between the empire and the Latin Church.

Before the end of Charlemagne's reign, the raids of another enemy, the heathen Vikings, had already disturbed the northern seaboard of the empire. The great overspill of traders and adventurers from Scandinavia which the ensuing decades witnessed is one of the most remarkable phenomena of medieval European history, and one whose causes have never been fully explained. The secret of their success in their quest for plunder, barter, and lands lay in their skill in shipbuilding and navigating, which was unsurpassed in its time and long after. One Viking band at least, it would seem, even reached North America. Others, from the settlements they had founded at Novgorod and Kiev, in Russia, sailed down the Dnieper and the Volga, to reach the Black Sea and the Caspian, and to establish trading connexions with Constantinople and Persia. In the west, they conquered and settled Iceland, parts of Ireland, and the eastern counties of England. It was the West Frankish kingdom, however, which had to bear the brunt of their attacks over a period of more than sixty years. Sailing up the rivers, the Loire, the Seine, and the Garonne, they penetrated deep into France. Paris was more than once besieged, and countless towns and monasteries sacked. When Viking bands gained temporary footholds at the mouths of the Rhine, the Seine, and the Loire, the whole future of the kingdom of the West Franks began to be in doubt.

In fact, by the year 900 the moment of peril was passed. The Viking settlements on the Breton and Frisian coasts did not last. That at the mouth of the Seine did. In or about 911, Charles the Simple, king of the West Franks and grandson of Charles the Bald, granted Rouen and the lands which were later to be called Normandy to the Viking leader, Rollo. Through these Normans, the impact of the Viking spirit of adventure was to be felt long afterwards far away in Turkey and Syria.

A third group of invaders came from the east. The Hungarians first appeared on the frontiers of the eastern kingdom in 862, in the reign of Lewis the German. Though they did not seem really dangerous till the end of the century, from then on they were for fifty years the first concern of those who succeeded him. Because they arrived late upon the scene, it will be wise to postpone consideration of them for a moment. Meanwhile, something needs to be said of the general effect of the internal disputes and external dangers which disrupted the revived western empire in the ninth century.

In the prevailing conditions, any attempt to maintain a political unity in the empire, such as the early years of Louis the Pious had witnessed, was out of the question. The imperial dignity gave Louis II no more power than he already enjoyed as king of Italy. The petty princes whom the popes saw fit to crown as emperors in the tenth century, Lothar of Provence and Berengar, had very little power at all. The rulers of eastern and western Francia had more than enough to do maintaining sufficient control over their own followers to be able to cope with dangers from outside. All factors seemed to be combined to draw the separate provinces of the empire farther away from each other, with the invasions setting the seal on divisions which fratricidal strife in the Carolingian family had already created.

This picture is true only at one level. In another way the invasions themselves helped to buttress the sense of unity of western Christendom and the imperial ideal. The invaders had one primary motive in common, the quest for loot. In a Europe whose economy was agricultural and where precious metals were scarce, there was one obvious place to look for it. In the treasuries of churches and monasteries were to be found plate, chalices, gold and silver caskets containing holy relics, images in precious metal, often studded with antique jewels and cameos. Churches and monasteries were besides often relatively defenceless, and raiders very soon learned where to go for what they wanted. Their ravages in consequence appeared as a direct attack on Christianity itself and its priesthood. That priesthood in its turn called on all Christians to unite to resist the invader, and very naturally they appealed to the notion of the Christian ruler as the protector of the Church, which had been the inspiration behind the events of Christmas Day 800. Never, as they saw it, had a united effort from the whole Christian empire been needed as it now was. The clergy could not afford to let the empire die. To Hincmar of Rheims, the quarrels of Charles the Bald and Lewis the German were no mere political disputes; they were the cause of 'schism in the Holy Church'. When Louis II died, Pope

John VIII set out to find another warrior king to take up his title, and to make sure he was accepted king of Italy. Charles the Bald, on whom his choice fell, died two years later, at the end of his second unsuccessful expedition into Italy. A few years afterwards, Charles the Fat of Germany was recognized as emperor, again as a result of papal efforts, and for a brief moment the whole empire of Charlemagne was reunited under his rule. His misfortunes and incompetence led to his deposition in 887. Arnulf, the powerful king of the East Franks, was crowned by the Pope in Rome in 896, but the West Franks never acknowledged his lordship in any way. From this time on, they were never without kings of their own. Arnulf's son, Lewis the Child, was the last of Charlemagne's house to be called emperor. The threat to Christendom, however, persisted. All that was needed to revive the empire was that some ruler should demonstrate by victory over its heathen enemies his claim to the title of emperor.

*

It is now time for us to return to the Hungarians. They were a tribe of Finno-Ugrian nomads from the steppes of Asia. Driven off the steppes by other nomad tribes, they crossed Russia and settled in the lands which had been deserted since Charlemagne destroyed the Avars. Cultivation was unknown to them, and they were forced to live largely off plunder and tribute. The brunt of their attacks fell on the East Frankish kingdom, which they attacked repeatedly from about the year 900 on. But to men who had journeyed from central Asia European distances were short. They also raided repeatedly into Italy, and in 926 and 937 far into West Francia; they even once reached the north of Spain. Their raids were devastating. The Hungarians, always mounted, spread out in small groups over a front sometimes as wide as fifty miles, but they could concentrate with uncanny speed when resistance threatened. They never attacked walled cities, but they wasted the land, sacked monasteries and unfortified places, and carried off countless prisoners, whom they ransomed or sold into slavery. The whole of western Europe learned to fear them.

In the long run the Hungarians probably presented a less

serious threat to European Christendom than either the Vikings or the Saracens, but their impact was more alarming. Their primitive habits, their strange Asian appearance, and the bewildering speed of their movements spread terror and wild stories about them far and wide. They were cannibals or vampires, some said: according to others they were the devilish offspring of Gothic witches who had mated with fiends in the wastes of Asia.

Demoralization in face of an unfamiliar foe added to the military problem of organizing resistance which confronted the rulers of the East Frankish kingdom. They had other difficulties too. In 919 the crown of Germany passed to Henry, duke of Saxony. Saxony was the youngest of the four great duchies (Bavaria, Swabia and Franconia were the others) which made up the kingdom, and had no natural frontier to protect her against attack from the east. The native pride of the older duchies meant that Henry could gain no more than uneasy acceptance from their leaders. Moreover, Saxony had less contact than any of the other duchies with the lands that had once formed part of the middle kingdom. The political chaos of northern Italy in particular inevitably attracted the intervention of ambitious leaders of the Bavarians and Swabians. There was real danger that these two duchies might be drawn away into the orbit of some resuscitation of the realm of Lothar, and Henry left to resist the Hungarians with the forces of Saxony and Franconia alone. These circumstances left the Saxon king with little option but to intervene himself in Italy, with whose rule the imperial office was now traditionally associated. But such intervention was not likely to be of much effect until the Hungarians could be held in check.

Henry defeated the Hungarians heavily at the Anstrut in 933. Twenty-two years later at the Lech his son and successor Otto won a victory over them which finally put a term to their great raiding expeditions. The Lech was a battle of European significance. It was noted by chroniclers all over the west, and long remembered. 'He freed the whole Occident from the Magyars,' wrote Bonizo of Sutri a hundred years and more later. In the battle itself Otto carried the Holy Lance of the emperor Constantine. One story goes that after the victory, his troops raised him on their

41

shields and hailed him as emperor. Whether or not this happened, it is incontrovertible that the victory established his title to the imperial dignity, as the deliverer of Christendom from pagan enemies. In 961 he led an army into Italy and was crowned king of Lombardy: in the next year he was crowned emperor by Pope John XII.

Besides this new dignity, the victory at the Lech was the source of other and more tangible advantages for Otto and his dynasty. The place which, as successful resistance leaders, they had earned in popular esteem set them definitively apart from the other ducal families. For the time being, the danger of the disintegration of the German kingdom was passed. It also assisted Otto in his crucial dealings with the Church, with whom it naturally won him special regard. He had seen that the answer to the problem of curbing the independence of the dukes lay in balancing their power with the great landed wealth of the German Church. The problem here was that of getting the right men into the right places, as bishops and abbots of richly endowed monasteries. After the Lech, Otto was able to get men of his own choice preferred, not in Germany only, but also in Italy and in Lotharingia, which since 929 had nominally acknowledged the overlordship of the German kings. For the next hundred years the support of leading churchmen, nominated by the emperor, controlling great landed wealth in their own right and entrusted with administrative offices such as that of count, was the key to successful imperial rule.

Like Charlemagne, Otto I came to 'empire' late in life, and it must remain in doubt how far he understood the implications of a title which made him nominally the temporal leader of western Christendom. They were made abundantly clear in the reign of his grandson, Otto III. Otto III succeeded while still a child, for his father died early. The chief influences in his upbringing were those of his mother Theophano, a princess who came from Byzantium where Roman imperial traditions ran back unbroken into classical times, and of a group of powerful churchmen, imbued with ideas of the Christian role of the empire which had carried weight with ecclesiastics ever since the time of Louis the

Pious. Foremost among these stood Otto III's tutor, Gerbert, the finest classicist of his age, who became pope in 999, taking significantly the name Sylvester, that of Constantine's own pope, the man who had first converted a Roman emperor to Christianity. Before him and the young Otto, just emerging into manhood, rose an impressive vision of the classical empire restored through the partnership of its temporal and spiritual leaders. The emperor began the construction of a new imperial palace in old Rome, on the Aventine: the Pope deliberately associated Otto with him in judgement of ecclesiastical causes affecting lands where the emperor's rule was not accepted. In contemporary circumstances, their ideas were impractical and led to disaster. When Otto recognized the kings of Poland and Hungary, and Sylvester set up independent archbishoprics at Gnesen and Gran in their territories, it did not seem to them to weaken their position: the new kings were liegemen of the universal emperor, the new archbishops subject to the patriarch of Rome. But their actions fatally alienated the leaders of the German Church, who had always consistently sought to extend their authority over the Christians of eastern Europe. Money and men from the estates of the German Church had always been the key to the Ottos' dominion in Italy: now faced with revolt there, aid was not forthcoming and Otto and Sylvester were powerless.

Otto III died in 1002, aged only twenty-two; a year later Sylvester followed him. Otto's successor, Henry II, duke of Bavaria, spent many years fighting the new power of Poland which Otto had helped to build up. During this time Lombardy fell away almost entirely from the empire. But before the end of Henry's reign the Poles had quarrelled with their other neighbours in Russia and Bohemia and he was able to resubjugate Lombardy. Two years before his death, in 1022, he was able to hold, with Pope Benedict VIII, a great synod at Pavia, where decrees for the reform of abuses in the Church were promulgated. Thus the tradition of close partnership between pope and emperor, whose dramatic assertion had been the chief positive contribution of Otto and Gerbert, was renewed. Conrad II, who succeeded Henry, continued his policies, and proved himself a strong and successful ruler in Italy as well as Germany, where the monarchy could once again count on the support of leading churchmen. When Rudolf, the last king of Burgundy, died, Conrad was able to acquire his succession, and thus the last vestige of the Middle Kingdom was absorbed into the empire.

When Conrad died, all that had been imperilled by the over-ambitious dreams of Otto III seemed to have been restored, except control of Rome itself. The city from which their empire took its name lay too far from the real centres of their power for the German emperors to control easily or effectively its proud and turbulent civic aristocracy. On the other hand, it was easy for these aristocrats to control the papacy. This presented a serious problem for rulers who looked on themselves as patrons and protectors of the Church. In 1044 the Romans rose against Pope Benedict IX, who had acquired the tiara through family influence at the age of sixteen, and set up an anti-pope, Sylvester III. Benedict, in his first alarm, sold his right to a third party, who became Gregory VI, but he soon regretted it and reclaimed the dignity he had bartered away. Three *soi-disant* popes were thus contending for office. This was a situation which the emperor, Conrad's son Henry III, could not neglect. He crossed the Alps at the head of an army. In December 1046 in a synod held at Sutri two popes were deposed, and the third retired after another synod held at Rome soon after. Suidger of Bamberg, whom Henry named as their successor, and who became Clement II, was the first of a series of popes who brought the high aspirations and administrative ability of the German clergy to the apostolic see.

At Sutri and Rome in 1046 Henry III played the part of a true 'emperor of the Church of Europe'. Though he had his troubles, with his Slav neighbours and with the turbulent duke Godfrey of Lower Lorraine, his reign marked a new climax in the power of the empire. Charlemagne's military successes and papal policy had revived a 'Roman' empire in the west. Though the barbarian invasions of the ninth and tenth centuries had brought it near extinction, Otto I's victories as a Christian leader, and the ability of most of his successors, had guaranteed its continuance. Of these successors, Henry III seemed the most powerful; his loyal supporters controlled the key positions in the Church, he was king of Lombardy, and the independence of the old German duchies seemed to be fast fading in his time. The Pope was demonstrably his man. But this is to give one side of the picture only: it had other features too, with problematical implications for the future.

The empire over which Henry III ruled boasted no more advanced system of government than that of Charlemagne: if anything, there was less system. It had no capital, no official bureaucracy, and its chief revenues came from the private estates of the emperor himself. Its true power was centred on Germany, and there depended on the ability of the emperor to control appointments to high ecclesiastical office. Herein lay a real danger. True, her great landed wealth put the Church in a position to offset the power and dynastic ambition of lay aristocrats; but the leaders of the Church were themselves largely drawn from the same families as the nobility, and similar ambitions were natural to them. When pagan invasions seemed to threaten Christianity itself, the leaders of the Church had been prepared to rally to anyone who could offer her effective protection. This was Otto I's real title to empire. But in Henry III's time the pagan threat was past, and the Church's first need was no longer for an armed protector, even in Germany. At Sutri, Henry indeed appeared in a still more exalted role, as patron and ruler as well as protector, but it was not clear that it was to the convenience of churchmen to have such a patron and ruler.

Even given the ability to retain control in Germany, Henry's power as emperor was less imposing than that of Charlemagne. The frontiers of his empire were not the frontiers of Latin Christendom. In the east, the imperial overlordship which the Christian Slavs of Poland and Bohemia and the Hungarians acknowledged was purely nominal. In the south, in Apulia and Calabria, Norman adventurers were, in the 1040s, in the act of establishing principalities which did not acknowledge imperial overlordship at all. In the west, it had at one time looked as if the German emperors might re-establish the frontiers of Charlemagne's empire. The tenth-century Carolingian rulers of the West

Frankish kingdom claimed to rule also in Lorraine, which had once been their share of the Middle Kingdom, and this led to frequent interventions into their affairs by the rulers of Germany. But in 987 the last of them, Louis V, fell from his horse when hunting and died, and the assembled nobility of the West Franks chose in his stead Hugh Capet, the most powerful of their number and whose lands were concentrated mostly in the Ile de France. He and his successors had no interest in Lorraine, and ruled their kingdom entirely independent of the empire.

The resulting situation was anomalous. An emperor of the Romans, whose real power rested on his German kingship, seemed to be the highest authority in a Latin Christendom which had a real unity, but of which he was not the universal ruler. Its unity was religious and ideal, not political. As Pirenne put it, the imperial title 'denationalized' his kingship, and gave it the untidy appearance of a universality which it did not really enjoy.

3

Serfdom and Feudalism*

THE break-up of the Carolingian empire and the invasions of the
ninth century gave force to social and economic pressures which
had a profound effect, not only at the time but for centuries afterwards. But these pressures were not new; they were born of the
same conditions as the Carolingian empire itself, of the steady
and progressive decay of the conditions of the late Roman
world.

The key factor here was the decline of trade and town life,
which had begun in the third century A.D. and by the time of
Charlemagne was reaching its nadir. Of course trade had not
ceased; no more had the currency of coin, the medium of mercantile exchange. It had merely ceased to be significant. None of
the great centres of Carolingian government, Aachen, Metz, or
Verdun, were important trading centres. Velvet and silk from the
Orient were, it is true, on sale in the markets of Pavia in the
780s; and a hundred years later, at the height of the Viking
invasions, the monk Abbo of Fleury was able to pour scorn on
those whose manners had been softened by 'eastern luxuries, rich
attire, Tyrian purple, gems and Antioch leather'. The Carolingian
period furnishes plenty of evidence, such as this, of continuing
trade; what is lacking is evidence of trade in any essential of life.
It was on luxury goods, spices and materials for court robes and
church vestments, that trade continued to flourish; goods, it
should be noted, which present few problems of packing and
transport. Here is a sign of the other key factor which went hand
in hand with the collapse of trade and of urban centres, the breakdown of communications, with its inevitable consequence, the
ossification of central government.

These are the conditioning facts underlying the European

* In writing this chapter, I have been substantially influenced by the views
expressed by Professor R. W. Southern, in his *The Making of the Middle Ages*
(Hutchinson University Library, 1953), especially Chapter II.

economy of Charlemagne's day. Towns were too few and too
small to register as a consumer market; trade was largely limited
to inessential luxuries; for essentials, the sparse population of
the countryside had to be self-reliant. To this the units in which
land was measured bear witness; men thought not in mathemati-
cal terms of yards and acres, but of the land which would support
one family, the *mansio* in Gaul or the 'hide' in England, a unit
which varied in size with the fertility of the soil. Two things in
particular could imperil the precarious balance of subsistence in
such conditions, a poor harvest followed by scarcity, and the war
of an enemy who destroyed the crops. The 'great domain', the
typical economic unit of the Carolingian period, came into existence as a social organism which coupled self-reliance with an
ability to respond to these two dangers.

A 'domain' was an estate in land, or a series of estates. At its
head, controlling the whole organization, stood the landlord, the
king, it might be, or a monastery, or some powerful nobleman. The
land of the domain was divided into two unequal parts. One part,
considerably the smaller, was turned over to providing for the
needs of the lord: the rest was divided up into holdings among
his tenants. Since coin was not of much use to him, they did not
pay him in money but in goods in kind, and with their labour
which he used to cultivate his share of the land. Such labour services might amount to two or three days a week through the year,
perhaps more at harvest time. Usually the holdings were in the
form of shares in the large fields around a village, cultivated by
communal effort on the basis of a very simple rotation of crops,
one year plough, one year fallow. With a tenancy went the right to
use of the woodland and common pasture of the domain, in proportion to the number of units (hides or *mansiones*) that each
tenant held. A large domain would contain many villages, in each
of which the lord's rights and the affairs of the community were
supervised by a reeve or bailiff; it was to such men that Charlemagne issued careful instructions for the administration of the
royal estates in a famous capitulary of 802. This gives an excellent
picture of how the system worked in his day. Among other duties,
they were to supervise carefully the collection and storing of the

produce of his share of the land, and its transport to one of his residences, where necessary. For given the expense and difficulties of transport, it was often easier for the lord to come to the estate and reside there for a time with his followers, to consume his plenty on the spot rather than have it sent him. Government, in consequence, became peripatetic, his staff of clerks and courtiers following the king from palace to palace. Inevitably, this reduced the effectiveness of the central authority, and increased its dependence on its local representative.

I have spoken here of villages, but it should be remembered that the real social unit was not the village but the estate. Often a whole village belonged to one domain, but the land around a village might equally include holdings which formed parts of a number of estates. Agricultural methods were crude and simple in this age: legal and social relations could be bewilderingly complex. They were far from being the direct result of economic conditions: like so much else in this period they had developed organically out of the different conditions of an earlier period.

For this and other reasons it is misleading to picture the relations of lord and tenant in the post-Carolingian age simply as those of exploiter and exploited. One must remember what the domain was, a self-sufficing social unit. It produced for its own consumption, not for sale. In times of scarcity, the stores in the lord's barns might be all that stood between men and starvation. It could be in no lord's interest to let the men who worked his lands starve, for land was more plentiful than cultivators. Nevertheless, the lord was the essential pivot of the life of the estate. Because it was self-contained and self-sufficient, relations with people outside were not very important, and internal relations were governed by its own laws, the ancient custom of the estate. If this law was to control effectively the petty arguments and problems of the inhabitants, it needed a guardian. Only the lord, with his social station and his followers, could fill this role. It was the same with external problems: men who wrung their subsistence from a holding which would just support a family were impotent unless someone with superior power would protect them and their interests. In the agrarian community which the estate constituted, the lord played an essential part as the repository of its government and the instrument of protection. This gave him the whip hand. This, however, is no more than a commonplace: obedience to an authority whose decisions may be inconvenient is the usual price which the individual pays for some degree of security and social order.

For the ordinary tiller of the soil, the chaos of the ninth century accentuated the need for protection and for an authority close at hand. In consequence, in this period the outlines of the system we have been discussing set more firmly. This system had evolved naturally out of the economic conditions of the late Roman period, and the tenancies of a Carolingian domain had very diverse antique origins. Some tenants were the descendants of slaves, whose body labour in his household some past lord had found less useful than before, and had therefore settled on some plot of land. Others descended from ancestors who had once been small farmers, producing for local markets, whom the decline of consumer demand and the need for some sort of authority had induced to seek the protection of a lord, by pledging their assistance in cultivating his lands. The commonest figure, however, in the pages of such surveys of Carolingian estates as that of Abbot Irminon of St Maur-les-Fossés is the *colonus*. The *colonus* was, in status, the lineal descendant of the peasant who, in late Roman times, had been given a plot of land from the public fisc, on condition that he and his heirs cultivate it and never leave it. Such a man was called free, but his freedom was strictly limited; he and his descendants were bound irredeemably to the soil off which they lived. This was what in later times made the *colonus* so valuable to a lord, whose position depended in the last resort on men labouring on his lands to support him and his well-born followers. There was plenty of land, and many other lords competing for men's labour, but the *colonus* could not leave his holding because he was bound to the soil by a customary law, whose pedigree stretched back into antiquity.

In antique times, there was a clear distinction between the *colonus*, with his hereditary holding on the public fisc, and the

slave to whom his master had granted a plot of land, for himself
and his family, on condition that he should assist in cultivating
his land. By Charlemagne's time this distinction had become
blurred, at the expense of the one-time freeman. The land on
which he lived was no longer, probably, public land, having been
granted away to some monastery or a lay nobleman, and public
authorities (in effect the king) were too hard of access to give
much protection against the whim of such a lord. The rent he had
once paid had almost certainly been converted into an agreement
to labour, as a serf would, on the lord's land. There were still,
however, as surveys of the early ninth century show, a good
many freemen, holding land in return for labour services but not
bound to the soil; and a fair number of small cultivators who,
however personally bound, owed no service for their holdings at
all. The crisis of the next few generations brought about a social
revolution, in which the class of semi-independent cultivators
virtually disappeared.

In the upheavals of the ninth and tenth centuries the crying
social need was for protection, which only the powerful could
provide. To do so, they needed the labour of men to feed them
and their fighting men, their vassals. The final breakdown of the
state machine further threatened the small man with the fate of
which, probably, human beings are most afraid, absence of legal
and social identity. His only course was to barter with a lord,
offering what he had in return for protection: his labour, his
freedom of movement, and the freedom and labour of his children. He agreed to become, in a word, his lord's hereditary serf.
The story of William brother of Reginald, who 'gave himself up
as a serf to St Martin of Marmoutier; and not only himself but
all his descendants, so that they should for ever serve the abbot
and monks of the place in servile condition,' is consequently one
repeated over and again in estate records of this period. The
granting away of the freedom of a man's descent for all time was
the crucial element in this bargain, for it was the lord's guarantee
of continuing agricultural service, the advantage which he sought
and acquired. Hence arose the practice of the lord charging a fine
(*merchet*) when a serf's daughter married: the lord must be con-

sulted about this, for if she married outside the estate, the labour of all her descendants was lost for ever. This was also the reason why serfdom, as a social institution, long outlasted the conditions of the post-Carolingian age.

The obligation to pay *merchet* became, in most parts of Europe, the test of what remained for ages the most important of all social distinctions, that between the free and the unfree. The unfree serfs were not slaves, it is true, but they were not much better off in practice or in general estimation. Their lot, in accepted social theory, was to till the soil, to which they were bound and which clung to their hands and degraded them, for the benefit of those who followed more acceptable callings, the life of prayer or the life of arms. The social function of the labouring man became confined to the business of sustaining his masters, his mental horizons to the bounds of the estate on which he lived.

＊

In the upheaval of this age of crisis, the same pressures affected the free as well as the unfree. The decisive factors once more were the breakdown of the state machine and the overriding need for protection. The free and their descendants, however, became the beneficiaries, not the victims, of the period of disorder.

Once again, in order to understand the developments which took place, one must start with some description of the administrative system of the Carolingian period. The typical local official of the time of Charles the Great was the count, an official who had been well enough known since the late Roman empire as civil and military governor of a given district. His functions in the Carolingian period were not so very different from what they had originally been. Though he might very likely be a nobleman with local influence, he was still technically an imperial official, named by the king or emperor. On the emperor's behalf he collected such tolls and taxes as were due from the local people. In the county court over which he presided and which met three times a year, he judged all the major civil and criminal pleas of the county (lesser cases went before his subordinates, who supervised the hundreds or *vicarii* into which the country was subdivided). In war, he led the levies of his county. From time to time he would be visited by *missi* or emissaries from the imperial court, who investigated the manner in which he had carried out his commission, and reported on his activities to his master.

Administratively, the count thus discharged important official services. Even more important than those of the count, however, in this Frankish realm which was held together by force and in which the ruler's chief business was war, were the services of the royal vassals. The institution here in question owed more to ancient Germany than to Rome. Originally the word vassal seems to have denoted some kind of servile follower: by Charlemagne's day what it meant was the free-born member of the war band of the king or some great nobleman. Like the warriors of the old Germanic *comitatus*, these men were bound to their chief by a personal oath of loyalty which they had sworn to him: he in his turn had promised them his special protection. The bond was a close and solemn one, creating an affinity similar to that of a kinsman, and as difficult to discard: the vassal undertook to maintain his lord's vendettas, and the lord his. Because he was a free man, the vassal who 'commended' himself by oath to a lord did not, like a serf, bind all his descent. But he did swear, as long as he lived, 'to serve you and deserve well of you as far as lies in my power' – if need be to the death. 'May the madness of infidelity be ever far from you; may evil never find such a place in your heart as to render you unfaithful to your lord in any matter whatsoever.' So wrote the lady Thuoda to her son William, the vassal of Charles the Bald, in 843. It was such sentiments which made the corps of his loyal vassals the key to the fighting might of a Carolingian ruler. On his fighting might depended the king's ability to maintain his realm: this made his vassals very important people.

The vassal of the Carolingian period was, indeed, often a good deal more than a mere fighting man. He needed expensive equipment, arms and a horse, for cavalry was by now becoming a decisive arm in battle. Very likely he might possess estates of his own, inherited 'allodial' lands (as they were called), which he might dispose of as he would. Whether this was so or not, he could expect almost certainly for his services the reward of an estate as a 'benefice', the usufruct of which he should enjoy for his lifetime. Such a benefice was usually carved out of the king's fisc, or from church domains, in which case he would probably have to pay the church some sort of rent from it. The grant of a benefice increased the worth of a vassal, because now he could clothe and feed vassals of his own from its produce, who added to his personal fighting worth. It had the added advantage that it was not a grant in perpetuity, but a 'precarious' tenure: at his death it reverted to the original owner, and could be disposed of to a new vassal. It was thus different from the allodial estate, which if given was lost for ever: the grant of a benefice from the fisc, by contrast with an *allod*, impoverished the king only temporarily. The Carolingians, in consequence, were generous in their grants of benefices, and their vassals became influential men. Very naturally, a good many of their counts were chosen from among their vassals, and given benefices in the counties entrusted to them. Thus the two systems, of comital administration and vassal service, began to fuse.

From the fusion emerged what has been called the feudal system, which achieved its archetypal form in the homelands of the West Frankish kings, west of the Rhine and north of the Loire. During the Viking and other invasions the need for local protection was far too immediate for a peripatetic king to cope with. To commend oneself and one's property to the protection of one of the king's vassals, who had estates locally and men at his immediate disposal, offered for most a far surer security. Such a vassal, though, had his own pressing problems; he was not likely to grant protection except on conditions to his own benefit. His prime need was for adequate followers to defend himself and his estates. The answer was for the client to make himself the vassal's vassal, to hand over his own estates to his newly chosen lord and receive them back from his hands as a benefice. Because his official position gave him added power and status, the local count was the most obvious and desirable choice of master for the man thus seeking protection. From the client's point of view it was the count's power, not his office, that mattered. The count thus found his position much enhanced. Not only was he, in right of his office, judge on the king's behalf over all the men of his county: but besides, all or nearly all of its leading men were becoming his vassals, sworn to serve him and holding their lands from him on conditions, 'precariously'. In his county he was becoming a little king. Not unnaturally, the distinction between his power as a count, and his power as a great landowner and lord of vassals began to be forgotten, both coming to be regarded as part and parcel of the same thing. Thus the old boundaries of counties began to alter; the count became lord and judge not only in the district which the king had committed to him or his ancestor, but in all the lands which he and his vassals controlled.

What has been described here in outline is the process by which a new and immensely powerful aristocracy was born. The acceptance of the principle of hereditary succession to benefices set the seal of permanence on this new order. This was a natural, almost an inevitable step. We must remember we are dealing with a society in which kinship was the most important of all social bonds, and support of a kinsman's vendetta a prime social duty. A man did not commend himself and his land to a lord for his own protection only, but also that of his family and dependents. A lord, be he king or count, who insisted too firmly on his right to grant the benefice of a dead vassal to whom he would was not likely to attract many men to his service. It was not without a struggle that the kings resigned their right to resume and regrant counties and benefices, for this was the key to their control over their followers. But the struggle was hopeless. The way things were going is well indicated in Charles the Bald's capitulary issued at Quierzy in 877, when he was on the point of departing into Italy: while he was away, he declared, if any count died his son should succeed without any question being raised. He knew that any attempt to prevent this happening would cause troubles, which he had no hope of controlling from a distance. A century later the right of the son to succeed the father had become something few bothered to discuss, an accepted part of a system.

Clear traces of the old order survived, it is true. The new vassal still could not enter on his father's benefice until he had renewed for himself the oath his father had sworn to his lord, and paid the lord a sum in money (*rachat*, or relief) for the privilege of being permitted to succeed. The renewal of the oath was a very solemn process. Kneeling, the heir did homage, placing his hands between those of his future lord and declaring, 'Sire, I become your man.' After this he swore to do him faithful service all his life. When this was done he was put into possession of ('invested with') his fee (or *feudum* in Latin, hence feudal), as the benefice was by the eleventh century coming to be called. This could involve a further symbolic act, the granting to the vassal by the lord of a banner, as the sign that he with his followers must serve him in war. In an age when agreements between men were not often written down, these solemn and formal rituals in the presence of witnesses served the purpose of a legal record. They also demonstrated the lord's rights over his man, and over his man's service and land, reminding all present that if the vassal died without heirs, or failed to do his service, the lord could claim back the land he had just given. All these reservations, however, must not be allowed to cloud the essential fact that in the end the lord had no right to refuse investiture, if homage was offered. By the eleventh century, the hereditary principle had established an aristocracy of vassals as securely as it had a proletariat of serfs.

There were plenty of social grades in the free society of vassals. Some fees were more dignified than others, and their tenure carried more extensive rights. Thus, those that were descended from old counties gave their holders much wider rights of justice over their subjects than their own vassals enjoyed on their estates. A man's standing was now judged by the rights he enjoyed in his fee, and the rank of the lord from whom he received it. There was naturally a great deal of pushing and thrusting, as one family tried to make the most of the fortunes or misfortunes of another. There were very few holders of fees, in the eleventh century, who could trace back their tenure to an ancestor of the days of Charlemagne. More settled conditions, however, made the rules of succession progressively harder to dodge by force or fraud. Thus what steadily emerged as the essential governmental unit was the local principality, called sometimes a county, sometimes a duchy, a kind of kingdom in miniature. The distance between the king and the ruler of the county, once his personal vassal, was thus extended immeasurably: all that remained of their close bond was the king's right to demand homage from the count's son when he succeeded. The real power of the kings of the West Franks was thus limited to their demesnes, the lands where they ruled and judged with no intermediary. The last Carolingian kings had so few estates that they were virtually impotent: their Capetian successors did not wield much more power than the average count.

In effect, as a result of the confusion of the ninth and tenth centuries, government had ceased to have much to do with even a rudimentary state machine. It had become part of the patrimony of powerful men. What bound this society together was not a sense of obligation to a common weal, but the personal oaths of individual men to individual lords. The peace of society depended on how far these individuals were prepared to observe their promises, and here force was the moving factor. The system had grown out of the exigencies of a military situation, and bore plenty of marks of its origin. The true centre of a lord's authority was his castle, behind whose walls or palisades he could defy all comers: where too he held his court and judged his subjects. The most essential obligation of the vassal was his service in war: his estate was valued by the number of soldiers it could maintain. And if a man was injured in his right by a rival, or if his lord or his underling broke the sworn agreement between them, what king and count and vassal alike fell back on was the ancient right of the free man, the vendetta. He defied his rival in solemn language, and made war upon him. The wars of feudal noblemen left little peace in many parts of Europe over the four centuries following the year 1000.

The feudal system is often spoken of as if it was the same throughout Europe: it must therefore be made clear that the conditions that have been described here were typical only of northern France. As a result of French and Norman conquests, very similar systems were established in England, in southern Italy and Sicily, and in the crusaders' kingdom of Jerusalem. Elsewhere there were parallel developments, but not an identical scheme. In northern Italy and southern France, which were much less affected by the invasions, many of the holders of *allodial* estates, whose origins went back to the late Roman era, never became vassals, and the dukes and counts never achieved the same degree of local control as in France proper. In Germany in particular the course of events was different to that in West Francia. Much of Germany had never known Roman administration, and Carolingian methods were only half established when, in the late ninth century, crisis struck with the onset of the Scandinavian and Hungarian invasions. The leaders of the great tribal duchies of Germany, as Bavaria and Swabia, did not possess the same wide and defined rights of administration as the Frankish counts. In consequence they never obtained the kind of domination over the other landowners of their duchies, and specially the ecclesiastics, as many counts did in France. The Ottos and their successors, by gaining control over appointments to high office in the church, and by entrusting counties within the duchies to ecclesiastics who were members of their own households, were therefore able to maintain an effective ascendancy. Their ecclesiastical counts were aided by the royal *ministeriales*, landless men of servile origin, much more closely bound to their masters than the free vassal. This was why the German monarchs emerged from the crisis of the invasions so strong, in sharp contrast to the kings of West Francia whom the same invasions had reduced to impotence.

But this contrast between France and Germany must not be carried too far. As with the kings of West Francia, the authority of the German emperors depended ultimately on the local influence of men pledged to them by personal bonds and oaths of loyalty. Neither country could boast anything which could be called a systematic central government: in both countries power in the last resort rested with those who could build castles and maintain enough fighting men to protect the neighbourhood. Certainly it is true that in eleventh-century Germany, with its different social conditions, the men with real potential were a different group: they were not the counts, but those lords, lay and ecclesiastic, who controlled great, free, allodial estates. Having never had, like the West Frankish counts, the experience of delegated authority, they did not yet know their own strength. But they learnt it, in the course of a new crisis at the end of the eleventh century, before the German emperors had found any systematic and reliable method of keeping them in check. Once they had learnt it, they proved themselves no less unruly and no less powerful than the barons of France.

What sort of men were these barons, in whose hands so much power locally rested? To this important but immensely difficult question the careers of three counts of Anjou provide as good an answer as any: Geoffrey Greymantle (*c.* 960-87), Fulk Nerra (987-1040), and Fulk Rechin (1067-1109). Geoffrey Greymantle went down to history as the faithful vassal of the last Carolingian kings of West Francia, a half legendary hero of the invasion times whose loyal counsels more than once saved an imperilled kingdom. Fulk Nerra, the real founder of the fortunes of his house, reigned long and built thirteen castles. He wrested wide territories from his neighbours by force – Saumur and much of Touraine. 'Ever at war, a hard hearted and greedy man': this was how many remembered him. But he also three times made the pilgrimage to Jerusalem, founded two abbeys and gave gifts to many more, and under their shadow little towns began to rise and prosper. Fulk Rechin was a man of letters, the patron of the heretic scholar Berengar of Tours and the author of a chronicle of his house: he also had four wives, two simultaneously, and quarrelled disastrously with his vassals. It would be hard to say which of these three men should rank as the best and most enlightened ruler.

In short, the baron of the new order was no type-cast figure. The conditions of the ninth and tenth centuries certainly put effective power into the hands of feudal noblemen with exalted power and status in their local world. The force of heredity perpetuated their authority and privileged position. What they did with these advantages depended very much on individual character. As always when history comes down to the individual level, it is only in a vague and often misleading sense that one can establish a pattern of behaviour. What these men did nevertheless always mattered, because in feudal Europe key decisions were in their hands.

4

Religious and Political Ideals

A SURVEY of social and economic conditions in the times of the Carolingian and early German emperors has revealed a world driven back on its local resources. The component parts of the secular state of late Roman and post-Roman times had splintered into small autonomous units. As long as one considers these developments in purely secular terms, there will remain a temptation to exaggerate the disruptive tendencies. For men of the time did not and could not so consider them. They were incapable of isolating secular affairs from their supernatural context. To men who saw behind such natural events as storms, famines and eclipses the direct workings of divine providence, any attempt to do so would indeed have seemed the opposite of realistic. Religious belief conditioned their attitude to the whole social framework of their lives, permeating the texture of every institution. The vassal's oath of fealty was sworn upon the gospels or upon holy relics. Serfdom was an estate ordained of God, for the common sustenance of men. The deeds which monasteries preserved, recording men's entry into serfdom, spoke of them 'giving' themselves and their labour to God and the Church, in order that 'he might look favourably upon them'. Thus, at the same time as social pressures and the shocks of invasion were forcing men apart, the bonds of common religious belief and outlook were drawing them together, almost as strongly.

Even in secular terms, it is easy to exaggerate the degree of dislocation. If contemporary conditions rendered large-scale trade pointless, they by no means discouraged individual travel. The cost of carting goods in bulk for even a relatively short distance was almost prohibitive, but no such consideration deterred the pilgrim going to visit a celebrated shrine, or the scholar who travelled in order to acquire wisdom at the feet of some famous teacher in a distant monastery. Such men did not return empty-handed from their travels: they brought back holy relics to place in their local churches, copies of books which they had made from manuscripts of works unknown in their homeland, and endless stories, of amazing miracles, of the learning of foreign teachers, or of the saintly lives led by monks in distant lands. Such wares presented few problems of package and transport. The exchange of ideas was, in consequence, almost as brisk as trade was sluggish. Before he became pope as Sylvester II, Gerbert, born of humble parents in Aquitaine, had studied in Spain and Italy; as his fame grew he was appointed first by Otto II to rule the great Italian abbey of Bobbio, later by Hugh Capet of France to be archbishop of Rheims; later still, he was tutor to Otto III, who made him archbishop of Ravenna. In all these places he had met and influenced people, and experienced their influence in his turn. In learning and in religious standards it was a cosmopolitan age. Because religious ideas pervaded every facet of life, the common culture thus created could touch the lives even of those bound to the soil.

Without any doubt, the strongest religious force in this period was centred in the monasteries. Directly, their influence in the lives of men was greater than that of any other institution in the Church. This may seem strange, when one remembers the purpose with which the rule of St Benedict (the rule followed, in one form or another, in most monasteries all over western Europe) had been drawn up, as a guide for men who sought to abjure the world entirely for the life of the spirit. But there were good reasons for it. The world had changed a great deal since the days when St Benedict of Nursia wrote his rule in the sixth century. In an age in which men consciously saw religious meaning behind every social institution, the flight from the world could not retain its old significance. As against the old ideal of retreat from the world, there emerged a new conception of the monastery, as a stronghold of prayer, of unceasing intercession on behalf of all Christian men. Thus to enter a monastery was not so much a response to a special religious vocation as to undertake a special form of social service. Symptomatic was the spread of the practice of dedicating children, long before they reached the years of discretion, to the life of prayer in a monastery. In our eyes this seems the negation of religious vocation: then it seemed often the most certain way of ensuring that the oblate child led a useful life.

Seen in these terms, the most important function of a monastery was the meticulous performance of an increasingly complex round of liturgical duties. To fulfil this function two things were prerequisite, an adequate endowment of lands, and labouring men to cultivate them. There was thus necessarily a close bond between the life of the monasteries and of the local communities. A new monastery was a concrete projection of the pious feelings not only of the lord who had founded it, but of the little aristocratic nucleus which he and his vassals formed: a long series of foundation charters testify that a lord's gift was nearly always the sign to his followers to emulate his generosity. Their gifts were not made for themselves alone: they created for them, for their ancestors, and for their posterity an intimate and personal association with the prayers of the monks. Their names were recorded in the *necrologies* of the abbey for special mention at the mass for the dead; perhaps they might also hope for burial within its holy precincts, and so to gain at the last day some virtue by association with its saintly inmates. It is no accident that the feast of All Souls, when the Church remembers all and each of the faithful departed, dates from this period.

For the peasant too, even though it must often have appeared as the hard taskmaster, the monastery had something to offer. He too was associated directly and personally with its activities: the man who made himself, or was made the serf of a monastery entered into the family of the saint to whom it was dedicated, and was entitled to his special protection. This could mean much more to him than the ministrations of the priest, whom the lord maintained on the estate. The manner of living of such a man was insufficiently removed from the peasant's own, and his small bare church could not stand comparison with the spacious house of God in which the monks lived. Stone built, housing holy books and relics, and men whose lives were dedicated to the performance of a sumptuous and imposing liturgy, the life of the monastery transcended the limits of a scanty and often unpleasant

63

existence. On its standard of life depended the present and future well-being of both its patrons and its dependents. In a way that nothing else could, its magnificence gave tangible expression to their most important aspirations.

Because so many men travelled for spiritual rather than for material gain in this period, the standards and observance of a particular monastery could acquire rapid influence. This was the secret of the success of Cluny. Founded on land among the hills of Burgundy by Count William of Auvergne in 910, the magnificence of its ritual and the personality of its abbots spread its renown far and swiftly. In England and Lorraine, and later in Spain and Germany, monasteries began to model their observance on Cluny, and to follow its lead in additions to their liturgies: significantly, it was at Cluny that the feast of All Souls was first observed. The emperor Henry II was only one of the great men of his time who visited the abbey and whose name was written in its *necrology*. In the monasteries which they reformed, leaders of the religious life like William of Dijon and Gerard of Brogne modelled their rule upon its customs. Cluny thus became a great moral force. Its two most famous abbots, St Odilo (994–1049) and St Hugh (1049–1109), gave decisive counsel to kings and emperors. They were constantly on the move, accompanied by a following which, men said, was worthy of royalty. In their day, the influence of the abbot of Cluny was greater by far in the councils of Europe than that of the Pope, or of any other ecclesiastic.

We must, however, be clear about the nature of this influence, and that of the monasteries as a whole. It was a moral influence that the monasteries exercised, not a political one. In political and legal contexts, they inevitably looked up to the secular authority. Their very endowments they owed to the generosity of lay noblemen. This much, moreover, remained of the old ideal of retreat from the world, that their spiritual contact with the lay world was indirect. The monk's life was enclosed by the cloister, and he was not, like the parish priest, directly concerned with the salvation of individual souls. The monastic ideal was not, in essence, sacerdotal, and the priestly powers, to confess, absolve, and impose penance, played little or no part in the monk's relations with laymen, intimate as they could be. His prayer had power in another world: in this world the authority even of an abbot of Cluny was bounded by the letter of charters recording what laymen had granted him.

These facts profoundly affected the notion of the lay ruler's role in this monastic age. The monastic leaders did not regard his authority as in any sense a rival one. The legal relations of men in the Christian world were rightly in his hands. It was his duty, by enforcing justice and good laws, to promote Christian living, as the patron and protector of God's Church. If he failed, their recourse was to pray for his enlightenment. In his proper sphere they accepted him as master, as the guardian and landlord of the Church militant.

*

As in the case of other social institutions, the office of the lay ruler and his authority in Christian society were justified in religious terms. This justification had important consequences: to understand it we will need to look not only at what learned men said about the matter, but also at the rituals and iconography which brought their ideas home to unlettered people. But first something general must be said about the cast of thought and learning in the period.

Here an enormous debt was due to the little band of scholars whom Charlemagne gathered together in his palace school. They were drawn from all parts of his empire and from beyond it. Paul the Deacon came from Lombardy, John the Scot from Ireland, Alcuin, probably the most famous of them all, from York. This small group of rather self-conscious *literati* were the founders of what has been called the Carolingian renaissance. By comparison with the more famous renaissance of the fifteenth century this was a renaissance with a difference. It produced few ideas original in their own right. The Carolingian scholars set themselves a humbler object than the propagation of their own views, to wit, the preservation of as much as was possible of the learning of Latin antiquity and of the age of the fathers. They steeped themselves in classical texts (the works of many of the great Roman authors are known to us only through manuscripts of this period). They called each other by nicknames such as Ovid and Homer, and wrote verses to one another in the style of such masters. But much more important in their eyes than classical literature was the study of patristic and liturgical texts. Their efforts here are revealing of a general contemporary attitude. Just as Carolingian illuminators, seeking to decorate new manuscripts, copied faithfully (or as faithfully as they could) classical models, so their object was to reproduce patristic authority and antique liturgy with exact precision. The ancient texts awed them as the products of a higher civilization, and as the legacy of an age which stood closer to the gospel days. This explains what their patron Charlemagne, in whose person the Roman empire was revived, looked to them to do, to assist him in restoring something of the old standards. His imperial authority gave the fruits of their labours lasting importance. Alcuin's edition of the *Sacramentum Gregorianum* became the basis of the medieval Roman liturgy, the text of the canons sent to Charles by Pope Hadrian became the basis of the law of the Roman Church, and the rule of Benedict of Nursia became, with additions and revisions largely due to Benedict of Aniane, the standard rule of life for monks throughout the Occident.

Besides these memorials to their scholarship, the Carolingian scholars bequeathed to the succeeding age a conception of the authority of the ruler which was based, as one might expect, largely on the Bible and the writings of the Fathers, but owed something too to classical Rome. 'All power is ordained of God,' St Paul had written: in the temporal world (the 'earthly city' of Augustine) the ruler was thus Christ's minister, his vicar. The Old Testament story, of how God had chosen first Saul, then David to rule his people, confirmed this attitude. Elsewhere the Old Testament spoke of another ruler, Melchisadech of Salem, who was 'priest and king'. The king's authority, this showed, was not merely secular, nor was obedience to him merely a secular duty. These were the kind of ideas which lay behind the eleventh-century claim of Gregory of Catino: 'Divine scripture admonishes us that we ought to understand that the king is the head of the church.' The Old Testament made it very clear that kings were more than mere secular governors.

Nowhere was the religious element in kingship brought out more clearly than in the sacrament of coronation, first used when Charlemagne's father became king of the Franks. Here again the guide to practice was scriptural precedent. After the manner described in the Old Testament, priests anointed the new ruler 'with this holy oil of unction whence thou hast anointed priests, kings and prophets'. This was a sign that, like David and Solomon of old, the king had been chosen by God to rule his people. The symbolism of the ceremony, the staff and ring which were placed in the king's hands, and the vestments and sandals he wore, all were, moreover, nearly identical to those employed at the consecration of a bishop, thus emphasizing that, like a bishop, it was to a spiritual as well as a secular office that the king was called. The same kind of symbolism appears in the illuminations of contemporary manuscripts in their portraits of rulers. Thus, in a copy of the gospels presented to the abbey of Monte Cassino in 1022, Henry II is pictured sitting crowned upon a throne of justice, wrapped in a garb of state similar to the 'pallium' of an archbishop, while the spirit of God, in the form of a dove, descends from heaven to inspire him. Otto II, in the Aachen gospels, is portrayed with his feet resting on the crouching figure of Earth, but with his head above the veil of cloud which divides earth and heaven. The authority such rulers wielded was accepted as more than merely terrestial: it had priestly connotations as well as kingly ones.

The direct control which kings and emperors exercised over ecclesiastics and ecclesiastical appointments thus had a more serious sanction than that of naked power alone. No one, indeed, supposed that the king could make the sacrament, as a priest could; but his religious office gave him the right to appoint men to authority in the Church and to invest them with the appropriate insignia, as he did other secular officials of his kingdom. It must here be remembered that in fact the authority of a bishop or abbot over the vassals and serfs on his estates was not very different from that which a count exercised: he might indeed also be acting as a count. Thus grew up the system of what has been called the 'proprietary church', under which a ruler disposed of ecclesiastical preferment as if it had been his ordinary feudal property. As has been seen, this system was one of the bases on which the power of the German emperors rested.

As regards what has been said so far, the position of the German emperor does not seem to have been regarded at all differently from that of other kings. They too were kings 'by the grace of God', anointed with holy oil, and like him disposing freely of ecclesiastical patronage. But there was an important difference. In 800, Charlemagne was crowned emperor not of the Franks, but of the Romans. This title had nothing to do with contemporary territorial divisions of Europe; its prestige and significance could only be understood in terms of past, not present circumstances. This significance was no less clear to writers in the times of his Ottonian and Salian successors than it was to the Carolingian classicists. To Hrotswitha of Gandersheim, Otto I was a new Octavian: Otto III and Gerbert took Constantine and Sylvester as their models. There was conscious archaism here, no doubt, but it was an archaism which carried men back not only to the classical past, but also to the Fathers of the Church, and their conception of the religious mission of the historical Roman empire. The antique interpretation of the prophecy of Daniel, identifying the Roman empire with the fourth of the great world empires, destined to last till the end of time, was not forgotten by such tenth-century writers as Adso of Montiér-en-Der. The legend inscribed on the seal of Conrad II expresses clearly the political implications of this traditional view: 'Rome, head of the world, holds the reins of the round earth.' To its religious significance the scene of imperial coronations bears witness: no man could be made emperor except at Rome, and by the Pope, Peter's vicar and the patriarch of the church universal.

This gave the emperor a unique position among the rulers of the western world. True, it knew other consecrated rulers independent of the emperor, but their provincial kingships were not to be compared with his universal authority. 'Do not speak as if there were no difference between Caesar and a mere provincial king,' wrote Cardinal Beno, towards the end of the eleventh century. What he meant, doubtless, was not so much that the emperor had authority over all other rulers, as that he was pre-eminent among them. In contemporary conditions, however, this distinction was not so important as it might seem today. Men did not think of a ruler as the giver but rather as the guardian of law. Law itself rested not on the ruler's enactment, but on custom, hallowed by time, God's gift to men of old. In detail customary law might differ infinitely from province to province, but its principles remained the same everywhere. To safeguard these principles was the duty of every ruler. Among rulers, the emperor's Roman title, divorced from contemporary national and provincial divisions, gave him priority, the first place in the counsels of those to whom God had entrusted the guidance of his people and the maintenance of his Church.

To a society whose religious beliefs and practices were common, Rome, the heart of Church and Empire, provided a visible indication that its unity was social as well as religious. This gave the survival and endurance of the empire a significance, to which the precise boundaries within which individual emperors ruled were in large part irrelevant.

SECTION TWO

c. 1046 – c. 1216

The Struggle of the Empire and the Papacy
for Priority as Universal Authorities in
an Age of Development and Expansion, and
the Apparent Triumph of the Papacy.

5

Empire and Papacy – the Beginning
of the Struggle

It has been said that in 1046 Henry III deposed all three of the popes who were quarrelling for the see of Peter. This is not quite true, but certainly all three were got rid of, or retired. In their place he appointed a German ecclesiastic, Suidger of Bamberg, who became Clement II. Clement and Damasus, who followed him, both ruled very briefly, and the man who succeeded them, Bruno of Toul, was another German of Henry's choosing. He became Leo IX, and his pontificate witnessed the beginning of a great revolution in papal government and policy, of which the emperor had made himself the unwitting author.

Henry's own intentions were, doubtless, conventional ones in a pious ruler, who lived in an age of widespread zeal for reform of the Church. In the years before 1046, the Roman aristocracy had used control of the bishopric of Rome as a pawn in their family feuds. To men who took very literally the description of the Church as the bride of Christ, this represented no mere untidy political anomaly: the church of the chief of the apostles seemed to them to be publicly deflowered and polluted. This was not a situation which a ruler such as Henry III, hailed by admirers – whom he took seriously – as 'head of the Church in Europe', could tolerate. In 1046 he marched into Italy to free the church of the apostles from those who had ravished her, and henceforward his power was the guarantee of her new-found freedom.

The men who became popes under his aegis were inspired by ideas which had a long tradition behind them in Germany. They had risen to prominence among churchmen imbued with the high ideals of the reformers of Cluny and Lorraine, amid a general desire for the quickening of the spiritual life among laymen and clerks alike. The contemporary instinct to look to the past for the highest standards had taught them to take as their guide the ancient canon law, the antique rules governing the lives of clerks and their relations with the laity. The early eleventh century had seen a great revival in the study of these canons, especially in Lorraine: collections of them, like that of Bishop Burchard of Worms, achieved a ready circulation. These collections stressed the high moral standards expected of a priest, whose life should be dedicated, and who should be married not to mortal woman but to the church he served. Insistence on the duty (and hence the right) of clergy to make themselves and their lives free from all wordly entanglement was a constant theme in the teaching of men like Burchard and Wazo of Liege.

How could priests possibly be expected to discharge their mediatory role if promotion to high ecclesiastical office was dictated by local politics? It was natural to the German bishops, in their genuine zeal, to look to the emperor for assistance, not only to impose higher standards on their clergy, but also to protect their own independence from local aristocrats, who were anxious to buttress their influence by advancing friends and relatives to positions of authority in the Church. Thus was born the tradition of endeavour to establish the independence of the clergy from the lay world. In this tradition Leo IX and his advisers had been brought up.

With papal authority behind them, these ideas began to acquire a new importance. The primacy of the see of Rome among the churches of the west was a thing accepted from the long past: the natural objective of Leo and his associates was to use this primacy to establish throughout the western church the standards of clerical life and independence to which they themselves had been trained. Thanks to the emperor's actions they were in a position to employ papal authority with an independence which for centuries no pope had enjoyed. Leo's pontificate, in consequence, was one of tremendous energy. At Rheims, Mainz and Vercelli councils were held under his presidency to decree reforms. Legates were sent out into the provinces to hold more councils, and to judge by his delegated authority any causes which involved churchmen. In 1054, the year Leo died, his legates in Constantinople were demanding that the Christians of the east acknowledge his primacy equally with those of the west. The Greeks bitterly repudiated their demands, but these in themselves were indicative of the new emphasis that was being laid on the authority of the Bishop of Rome, as the emperor's coadjutor in universal rule and final judge in all spiritual disputes.

When Henry III died in 1056, the Pope and his advisers were left to defend their new system and claims alone. The emperor's successor, Henry IV, was a child of six, and his realms were plunged into the political confusion of a minority. When Pope Stephen IX died in 1058, the reformers faced crisis. The Roman aristocracy and some of the cardinals chose Benedict X as his successor, but the majority of the latter, most of them men of Leo IX's choosing, refused to install him. Instead they named Gerhard, bishop of Florence. Imperial approval, won by Cardinal Hildebrand, and the arms of Count Godfrey of Lorraine carried the day for Gerhard, who took his place as Nicholas II. The uncertainties of the minority, however, looked like lasting, and he and his friends were anxious to avoid further risks. In 1059 they took two grave steps in order to protect themselves. At Melfi the papacy entered into alliance with the leaders of the Norman adventurers, who by this time were establishing themselves firmly in control in southern Italy. At a Lateran council in the same year, Pope Nicholas laid down new rules for the election of a pope, which gave the decisive voice to the cardinals. The need for the approval of the emperor or of the Roman nobles, which had hitherto usually decided the succession, was mentioned barely, in passing.

The importance of these events of 1059 must be stressed. To turn to the Normans was a revolutionary step: never before had the papacy sought to preserve its freedom of action in any way but by reference to a titular Roman emperor, either Frankish, or German, or at Constantinople. The decree concerning election was more important still, constituting for the papacy a kind of declaration of independence. It was a measure of how far men's ideas had progressed since 1046. Then Henry III had appeared as the saviour, coming to liberate the Church of Rome from its enslavement to the lay nobles of the city. But the emperor himself was a layman: in principle the same objections could be raised against his choosing a pope, as to the choice of some local family, like the Crescentii. Though few complained at the time, this point was one not likely to be missed by a group of reformers, one of whose chief aims was to inhibit lay interference in matters of church preferment.

The man who really took this matter up was Cardinal Humbert of Moyenmoutier. In his 'three books against simoniacs' he pursued it to its logical conclusion. Simony, the sin by which ecclesiastical office is obtained for money, was a natural target for the criticism of reformers seeking to free the Church from entanglement in wordly affairs. The essence of simony, Humbert pointed out, lay not in the fact that money had changed hands, but in that spiritual office was conferred as a result of wholly material considerations. Whenever lay influence dictated preferment, there was thus a suspicion of simony. This view represented a direct attack on the whole system, whereby the choice of candidates for office in the Church depended on the lay ruler. Ever since the time of the Ottos, the power of the German emperors had largely depended on their ability to control, through men of their own choosing, the vast landed wealth and administrative influence of the Church in their realms. Implicitly, therefore, Humbert's views attacked the very basis of the empire itself.

Cardinal Humbert probably had a considerable hand in drawing up the election decree of 1059. Another decree of the same council, forbidding laymen to invest ecclesiastics with spiritual office, was entirely in line with his views. The challenge was clear, but in the confusion of the minority the empire was in no position to respond. While Henry IV was growing up and learning to aspire to wield the same power as his father had done, the new system of the reformers began to establish itself, in Italy at least. It was the beginning of a great revolution, aimed to turn the Church into the master of the authority whose client it had lately been.

*

In these conditions a clash between the authority of the new papacy and of the German empire was bound to come sooner or later. The man who had to meet the crisis on the papal side was the one-time Cardinal Hildebrand, elected pope as Gregory VII in 1073, and one of the greatest leaders that the medieval church ever knew. The *casus belli* was the proud and ancient archbishopric of Milan, once the see of St Ambrose, but also a key archbishopric in political terms, controlling the passes which connected imperial Germany and Lombardy. The situation there was already very complicated when Gregory became pope. Archbishop Guido, who died in 1071, had sought to resign his office, and during his lifetime a successor, Godfrey, had been invested with the ring and staff of office at the court of Henry IV. But Godfrey was not acceptable either to the Pope or the Milanese, and at Guido's death the latter, in the presence of a papal legate, chose Atto, a cathedral clerk, to succeed him. Alexander II gave his approval to this election, so that Gregory was bound to uphold its validity. In 1073 Henry IV, in a moment of weakness when he was faced with revolt in Saxony, submitted the whole matter to the 'apostolic judgement' of the Pope. The Pope's end thus seemed to be secured, but a year later Henry, now triumphant over his rebellious subjects, went back on his submission. Gregory, on the eve of opening a great synod at the Lateran, was faced with a plain choice. He must either give way to the emperor or seek, with whatever resources he could find, to uphold the principle of the freedom of the Church to choose its own leaders.

The dilemma was perilous. If he gave way, the papacy's dependence on the empire would be made plain to all, and the whole endeavour of the last twenty years would be endangered. If he stood firm, the outlook was no less dangerous. The alliance with the empire, the traditional ally and perhaps the only authority capable of protecting the papacy in turbulent Italy, might be broken for ever. To stand firm besides implied asserting claims of a quite revolutionary tenor. The archbishopric of Milan was not just a spiritual office: it was a position of great political power, and the estates which were inseparable from the see gave its holder control over strategically important passes. If he stood by Atto, the Pope could not ignore these political implications of his position. To do so meant claiming more than that, where spiritual office was in question, recognition by the spiritual superior must be decisive. It meant that the decisions of the Bishop of Rome, as the highest spiritual authority in the western world, must in the last resort override those of any secular authority, even that of the Roman emperor. In Gregory's time the distinction later drawn between spiritual and secular matters was not clear: men had never thought of political authority being divorced from a religious basis. Gregory would have therefore to claim that, in the Roman world, ultimate decisions rightly lay not with the emperor of accepted tradition but with himself as Peter's vicar.

In fact he never hesitated before the alternatives facing him. At the synod of 1075 he promulgated decrees forbidding more stringently than ever before the investiture of ecclesiastics with spiritual office by laymen. When Henry replied by charging Gregory himself with usurpation of the papacy, Gregory proceeded to excommunicate him. This was a momentous step. Excommunication put Henry outside the pale of the Church, whose rite of coronation had made him king: his whole authority was thus deprived of any religious significance. He could no longer claim any right over any man 'by the Grace of God': in effect, he might as well have been deposed. Reconciled briefly in 1077, he was excommunicated by the Pope once again three years later, in 1080. Gregory made the position explicit this time, passing solemn sentence of deposition, as well as excommunication, upon him.

Thus Gregory confidently asserted the superiority of the monarchy of the papacy over the monarchy of the empire. Though it did not stop Henry acting as if he were king, it was a revolutionary step which no one could afford to ignore. It dissociated the Church, or at any rate all who would follow the Pope's lead, from the consistent tradition of the last two hundred years. Nevertheless, the Pope's position seemed to be well founded in canon law. Just before he took the decisive step of excommunicating Henry, Gregory had drawn up for himself a series of articles, a kind of *aide-mémoire* on the canonical authority of the papacy, known as the *Dictatus Papae*. They make remarkable reading. 'No council (or decree) is to be held general without the

Pope's approval'; 'The bishop of Rome, if he be canonically chosen, is sanctified by the merits of Peter himself'; 'He is entitled to use the insignia of empire'; 'It is lawful for him to depose the emperor'. Most of these articles were drawn direct from a contemporary collection of canons, called 'the book in seventy-four titles'; the last-mentioned conclusion, not before explicit, was only a logical conclusion from the others. The canons in the book purported to carry the weight of ancient authority, some of them dating from the sub-apostolic period. In fact, much of what its author included came from documents forged in the eighth and ninth centuries, which he found in the collection of canons now called the 'Pseudo-Isidore'. Among these was the spurious Donation by which Constantine was supposed to have given temporal power in Italy to the popes; and Pseudo-Isidore included a number of very early canons, quite ungenuine, which provided spurious antique sanction to the final jurisdiction of the pope in any dispute involving the Church or churchmen. Gregory and his contemporaries did not know these documents were forged, and took them honestly at face value as ancient witness. As proof positive that the imperial hegemony of the eleventh century was a recent usurpation, these forgeries were a force to be reckoned with in an age which looked to the past for its standards.

Politically Gregory's position was clearly much weaker than it appeared to be in law. But he had powerful natural allies, and that in the heart of the empire itself. Imperial control had always borne hardly on the lay nobility of Germany: the minority of Henry IV had given many an opportunity to assert a long-sought independence. Henry's determination to rule as his ancestors had done threatened new-found privileges, and his excommunication gave men the excuse they needed to defy the bonds of an unwelcome allegiance. Gregory lifted his sentence of excommunication in 1077, after Henry had stood for three days, barefoot and penitent in the snow at Canossa where the Pope was staying, but it was too late to stay these allies of his. A number of them met at Forcheim, in 1077, and chose Rudolf, duke of Swabia, to be king in Henry's place. In 1080, when Henry's actions and attitudes had made it clear that his show of repentance was only a political subterfuge, Gregory endorsed their choice, deposing Henry formally and recognizing Rudolf as king and emperor designate.

After Canossa, Henry wavered no more: he would consider no accommodation except on his own terms. He stood as sternly by the custom of recent ages, as the Pope did by the usage of a spurious antiquity. Neither side made any attempt to distinguish spiritual and temporal authority: Henry claimed what he considered his predecessors to have enjoyed, authority over all churchmen, and Gregory claimed neither more nor less. To Henry and all his followers, Gregory was a usurper – 'no pope but false monk' – and the author of a mighty schism in Christendom. In 1084 Henry's soldiers stormed into Rome, and at his orders Guibert of Ravenna was set up as Pope Clement III. Gregory was declared deposed. What was thus done was less solemn than what had been done in 1046, but the only essential difference was that only one pope, not three, was displaced by imperial arms. A further practical difference however was that Henry IV lacked the power to maintain himself in Rome, with Germany in the uproar of civil war. This was why Gregory's cardinals took no fear, when their master died next year, about electing a successor to him. They did not turn to Clement.

*

Gregory's successors, in fact, carried his programme further still. In 1095, Urban II not only forbade ecclesiastics to receive investiture with spiritual insignia, but he even forbade them to do homage to laymen for land held from them, on whatever conditions. Thus the struggle deepened. The whole empire was plunged into the confusion of simultaneous civil war and schism, and men changed loyalties, which they probably often did not understand, at convenience. As emperor, schism, and civil war all grew older, Henry's son and heir saw his whole inheritance imperilled. Rather than lose all, he decided to break with his father and to seek agreement with the Roman pope.

This move by the future Henry V was astute: his father did not long outlive his disloyalty, and his enemies thus found themselves deprived of any cause in whose name to resist him. His difficulties, however, did not end with his re-entry into the communion of Rome. He might not claim all his father had claimed, but he could not afford to abandon the homage of his ecclesiastical vassals, the vital oath by which they bound themselves and the endless followers who lived on their estates to his service. To do so would have constituted the Church an independent corporation within his kingdom, in it but not of it, the source of endless potential friction in the future and of obvious weakness in the present. The estates of the Church were scattered too widely, too closely interlaced with those of the lay nobility, for any viable kingdom to survive settlement on such lines. Here time served Henry better than his father. The sweeping claims of Urban and Pascal II had threatened the position of other rulers besides the emperor, whose support, in the crisis, the popes could not afford to forego. In England, where they had brought the Church into conflict with the powerful Norman kings, compromise had been achieved which pointed the way for Henry. There churchmen, monks of an abbey or canons of a cathedral, in name chose their leader, in the king's presence: the elect then did homage to the king for his lands, and was afterwards consecrated and invested with the ring and staff of spiritual office by fellow ecclesiastics. Thus his two capacities, as lay subject of the king and spiritual subject of the Church, were kept separate. In 1122, by the concordat of Worms, this compromise was at last extended to the empire.

The word compromise must not be allowed to detract from the importance of this agreement. It did not just end a civil war in which the original objects had been lost sight of. It established a principle of fundamental importance: that there was a difference between the allegiance men owed to spiritual and to secular authorities. In the past this distinction had not been clear. The consecrated ruler had been able to call on all his men, lay and clerk alike, in the name of authority and of religion. Now he could not. Henceforward there was to be a dual allegiance: and if religious considerations could claim formal priority, there were quite enough sceptics in the twelfth century who preferred present and material advantages to future and spiritual ones – and plenty of honestly bewildered men besides. Fruitful seeds were thus sown for future divisions in the Christian world.

For immediate purposes, however, it was the papacy that gained most by the struggle and settlement, by a long margin. Henry V certainly managed to save a good deal from the wreck. He could still command the homage of his bishops, and he was still emperor of the Romans. But this homage no longer secured their only, or necessarily their first, allegiance. Moreover, he was emperor of the Romans not so much because he was his father's son, but for the same reasons as Rudolf of Swabia had been king, because powerful men had recognized him and the Pope had approved their choice. The German monarchy had taken a first step towards becoming elective, which inevitably weakened it as compared with a hereditary kingship. Henry V in fact died childless, and his lands, but not his title, passed to nephews; they were the constant enemies of Lothar, his successor as emperor, who was not of his blood. Worst of all, the struggle with the papacy had shown up clearly how far the proud title, emperor of the Romans, fell short of its pretensions. Throughout, the kings of France and England had acted independently: they had made their own peaces with the Pope. The word Roman still carried universal implications, but they were now demonstrably unfulfilled.

By contrast, the popes had capitalized on the same universalist ideals. They had not gained all they sought, the complete freedom of the Church under the monarchy of the Roman see: bishops and abbots elect still did homage to laymen. But a high religious authority resting in the papacy was recognized now throughout western Christendom, and recognized as one not limited to otherworldly affairs. The primacy of religious over material considertions, on which the popes based their claims to authority in this world, had not been challenged. The contrast between the actual authority of the pope and of the emperor had besides been signally demonstrated. In 1095, while Henry IV was struggling to restore order in his German kingdom, Urban II had summoned a council to Clermont. At that council he had called on the faithful of all the Christian west to take arms for the relief of the Holy

Land from the subjection of the Turk. In 1099 the army which he had launched had entered the Holy City of Jerusalem, and chosen Godfrey of Lorraine as advocate for the Church in the lands newly conquered. While the Roman emperor was fighting to maintain his local German kingship, the Roman pontiff had stood forward as the leader of all Christendom in a great Christian martial endeavour.

The empire, and the ideal it enshrined, were still powerful forces, as events were to show later, in the time of Frederick Barbarossa and his descendants. But things were never the same as they had been before Gregory VII threw down the gauntlet to Henry IV, and could never be so. New powers had arisen, and not only that of the reformed papacy with its revolutionary claim to obedience throughout the 'Roman' world in the name of St Peter. Social and economic changes were releasing new forces, whose consequences we must shortly pursue, and new modes of thought had begun to challenge many traditional attitudes.

6

The Expansion of Europe

IN the ninth and tenth centuries, as we have seen, western Europe stood very much on the defensive, against the forces both of man and of nature. By the middle of the eleventh century these conditions already belonged to the past. A new age of expansion had begun, with revolutionary consequences which were to affect the lives and attitudes of men throughout Christendom. Towns and trade had begun to revive; new lands were being brought under cultivation, and the frontiers of Europe were expanding. Most important of all, the number of her inhabitants was increasing. The rise of new urban centres had something to do with this: in them the increase in the population was at its most dramatic. But until long after the end of the Middle Ages more men still lived on and by the land than anywhere else, and there too there was the same increase. There were simply more people, more mouths to feed. Between the approximate dates of 1000 and 1300, the overall population probably increased at least twofold, and in places much more.

It is difficult to diagnose the causes of this increase in numbers, or to measure its precise extent. Some historians have stressed the relevance of improvements in agricultural techniques, the development of harness for horse ploughing and the adoption of a three-field rotation of crops (cereals, legumes, fallow), which made it possible to use more land more productively. But this explains how more people were fed rather than why there were more of them. Since, in the past, by no means all the cultivable land was in fact being cultivated, it would seem that it was not starvation pressures simply which held down the earlier population. Better nutrition (the result of a more varied diet, based on a wider variation in crops) may certainly have been a contributory factor working toward expansion, but will not serve as a complete explanation of the phenomenon. It does not account for the increase in numbers of people even in areas where such improvements as alteration of the system of crop rotations cannot be traced. It seems to be impossible, in fact, to offer any complete explanation of what was clearly happening almost everywhere. When one comes on to try to measure the increase the evidence is again elusive; the scanty records of estates, preserved often without system, do not furnish the kind of information which can be subjected to statistical analysis. The face of the land, nevertheless, tells a story whose meaning is unmistakable. From all up and down Europe comes evidence of lands which had lain waste for centuries, and some of which had never been cultivated before, being brought into productive use. The phenomenon is widespread and its implication is clear: the land is having to support more people.

Thus in Flanders in the time of Count Baldwin V (1035–67), men who were brought from inland estates, which still prospered, were building dykes and canals to secure for agriculture lands periodically inundated by the sea. At much the same time references in the charters of the archbishops of Cologne to tithes due from 'new' lands witness to a similar process in the Rhineland, where new villages were growing on land cleared of forest and scrub. Clearing was going on in north Italy also, in the great woods along the banks of the Po; here and in the valleys of Tuscany, dykes and channels were cut to drain swamps. Operations of this order varied, of course, in date and scale from area to area. In the eleventh and early twelfth centuries the evidence from Germany of reclamation of land which had been heath and forest is particularly clear. In England, to judge by the records, the thirteenth century was the peak period of clearing and draining. But local variation notwithstanding, the process was general, and the moral is clear. Not only more labour, but many more labourers also were engaged in the tilling of the soil.

Much of this great work of reclamation was evidently due to the undirected initiative of peasants. Lords sometimes gave little enough encouragement to those who with axe and plough won land from the forests which afforded such scope for their favourite relaxation, hunting. William I of England, who 'loved the tall stags as if he were their father', imposed ferocious 'forest laws' to make sure that agriculture did not curtail the freedom of his deer to roam at will. He would have seen eye to eye with the Count of Vendosme who burned the houses of the men who had made clearings in his woods without his leave. Other lords, however, took a different view, above all those great corporate landlords, the monasteries. Indeed, the Cistercians, the new order founded by Robert of Molesme in the last years of the eleventh century, were themselves leaders of the enterprise. In their quest for a greater purity of life, they observed strict rules: Cistercian houses were to be built in waste places; the monks were to accept no settled land, but to labour for their upkeep with their own hands. The lay brothers of the order were its labour force, simple folk, mostly of peasant stock, too unlettered to live the full life of the cloister but aptly fitted to worship God by the work of their hands. In the plains of East Germany and on the moors of Yorkshire they made their order prosperous on lands which no one before them had put to use.

The Cistercian lay brothers, sworn to poverty and chastity, did not found homesteads or raise families. Thus their reclamations did little to satisfy the general hunger for land. This was not the case with the elder Benedictine monasteries. When the Count of Maine gave land to the church of St Vincent of Le Mans to build a daughter house, he gave also 'leave to build a *bourg*'; to build about the new church a little town and rent the houses to country-men who would agree to cultivate the land around it. With its little market, and the better protection which numbers gave against the depredations of feudal brigands, such a *bourg* could well prosper. Not surprisingly, lay lords soon began to imitate the churches. Louis VI and Louis VII of France became famous for the new towns (*villeneuves*) which they founded on their royal estates in the twelfth century. Because they were kings and rich men they were able to offer attractive terms to settlers.

These new foundations of kings and churches are witness to the profound social consequences of land reclamation. Lords had land to offer; they learned to encourage colonization because they found its cultivation made them richer. But there was plenty of land to go round, and they had to make their terms attractive to the colonist. The most inviting prospect they could offer to the cultivator was a greater freedom. The countryman who came to live in a new town was protected and privileged by the charter of its founder. He did not here have to labour on his lord's land: he paid a rent, in money or kind. He and his descendants were not bound to the soil; they could sell their holding, and seek better circumstances elsewhere. Hence the famous principle 'town air makes free'. There were other advantages, too, of living in such a community. In a violent age, the larger a community, the better was its chance of defending itself effectively. In the twelfth century the *razzias* of noblemen could be just as serious a threat to the labourer's existence as bad harvests and famine.

Thus European agriculture came to centre more and more upon the large nucleated village or townlet. In many parts of Germany, men left their hamlets to live in the security of a larger village, coming out daily to farm their old fields. In Italy the process was still more marked. In one year, 1217, ninety-four families from a single village came into the little town of Jesi and took up their abode there. The desire for wider freedoms and greater security was too strong a force to stem: lords of land had to make their terms with it. In this manner the manorial system of the previous age began to decay; at the same time the gulf between those who owned land and those who tilled it grew wider.

*

While enterprising men were clearing waste and settling down to cultivate new lands within the old confines of Europe, others more adventurous still were seeking fortunes beyond ancient frontiers. The crusade to the Holy Land is a part, but only a part of this story. In Spain in the eleventh century Christian reconquest was pressing forward. On the lands recovered from the Moslems, little towns (*fueros*) were set up and peopled, like the French *bourgs*, with men who undertook to cultivate the country round about. From the middle of the century on, there is evidence that a good many of these settlers came from far afield, beyond the Pyrenees. By the year 1100 Alphonso VI of Leon was ensconced firmly in Toledo: the Cid's widow was ruling in Valencia. Thenceforward the Christian expansion into the south continued steadily.

In Germany a similar expansion was afoot. The leaders of the Saxons had fought long wars in the past against the pagan Slavs who lived beyond the Elbe; now the pattern of the struggle was changing, however. Where once overlordship and tribute had been the prime German objective, the settlement of conquered land began to take pride of place. In 1147, when the second crusade to Palestine was being launched, the lords of north-east Germany won leave to discharge their crusading vows by war against the Slavs instead of the Saracens. The devastating campaign of this year seems to have been the decisive blow to Slav resistance. 'Let the God who is in heaven be our God and it will suffice,' declared their Prince Niklot to Henry, Duke of Saxony. 'You may worship whom you choose; we will worship you.' In the wake of the armies came a 'host of men of various nations', from Saxony, Westphalia, Flanders. Carefully organized recruitment and settlement soon bore fruit, in prosperous villages, and towns too. The merchants of Lübeck, founded in 1143 by Adolph, count of Holstein, were, before the end of the century, playing an important part in the trade of the Baltic. Meanwhile, German settlement was being pushed further east again, and south too, into Austria and Bohemia.

Perhaps even more striking than these developments in Germany and Spain was the expansion of a single province of northern France, Normandy. As its story demonstrates, it was not peasants only who felt and responded to the pressures of increasing population. Tancred, baron of Hauteville, had twelve sons: his patrimony could not support them all. In 1038 Drogo, Humphrey and William were all in southern Italy, where experience had taught Norman pilgrims that fortunes were to be won in the service of the Greeks and Lombards who were disputing with the Moslems control of the land. Their brothers Robert and Roger soon joined them. What the Hautevilles taught the Normans was that they could win these lands for themselves. In 1059 Robert, surnamed Guiscard and the eldest to survive, was recognized as count of Apulia and Calabria by Pope Nicholas.

In 1061, with his aid, his younger brother Roger captured Messina, the first step in the conquest of Sicily, which occupied the rest of Roger's lifetime. Before Robert Guiscard died (1085), he and his son Bohemond were already contemplating conquests further afield, in the lands of the Greek empire in the eastern Adriatic. When all the Norman lands in Italy and Sicily passed to Roger's son, Roger II, who adopted the new title of king of Sicily, he inherited these wider ambitions also.

The other great triumph of the Normans was the conquest of England in 1066. Here, as in Italy, it was as a conquering and restless aristocracy that they made their influence felt. No host of peasant immigrants came in their wake. Nevertheless, the Norman conquests and the German colonization in the east are part of the same story. They reflect, at different social levels, responses to identical pressures. Externally, as internally, Christian Europe was expanding.

*

What was, in fact, almost certainly the most important feature of this expansion remains to be discussed, the recovery of commerce and the revival of city life. In the cities which were growing in the eleventh century in Flanders and Italy, the rise in population was more dramatic than it ever was in the countryside. More people emigrated to the cities, probably, than to any newly conquered lands. And it was not only a numerous population that was growing in these urban centres. New forces were born in them which were to influence profoundly the ideas and way of life of medieval Christendom.

In the renaissance of urban life, commerce and industry were natural partners. The secret of a merchant's success was to know where to find the goods that he could sell far afield: wherever production could be concentrated, therefore, merchants would gather. The prospect of a ready market was thus one great stimulus to urban concentration of industry: as always in this unruly period, the artisan's need for security was another. The same went for the merchant also. A native city provided him with a base and potential associates. Association in a group or company of merchants diminished risks, and made available more capital for enterprise on a bigger scale. The merchant's need for security was indeed greater, if anything, than the artisan's. He needed it not only in his home but on his travels too, and in the places where he came to buy and sell.

These principles underlie the pattern of expanding European commerce, as it begins to emerge with clarity in the early thirteenth century. The goods which came from outside which were most in demand in Europe came from the Orient, silks and spices coming via the Red Sea and the Persian Gulf from China and the Indies. Not surprisingly it was Italian merchants who carried most of these goods, which they bought in the markets of the Levant, into Europe. The goods produced in Europe which had the readiest sale in the Levant were cloths. The great centres of the cloth industry were the towns of Flanders, where wool brought from England, Spain and Scotland was woven by skilled artisans. Though already Italians were coming to Flanders themselves, the great meeting place for Italians and Flemings was at the fairs of Champagne. Thither also came merchants from the Baltic, from Lübeck and elsewhere, with valuable wares, furs, honey, and pitch. Not only the fairs themselves and those at them, but all those coming and going to and from them were under the special protection of the king of France, a privilege that was paid for from the profits of the fairs. Flanders, north Italy, Champagne: these were the nodal points of commerce. The cities of Flanders and Italy flourished in consequence beyond all others.

In fact, throughout the medieval period the townsmen of Italy excelled all others in wealth and enterprise. It is to Italy, then, that one must look for the origins of this new civic prosperity. In early times most goods coming into Europe from the east had been routed through Constantinople; on this trade merchants of Venice, well protected by her lagoons from the attacks of Lombards and others, were already growing rich in the tenth century. In the eleventh century, the strength and fortunes of the Byzantine empire were in eclipse: Venice, and other cities too began to make contacts of their own with the merchants of the Moslem world.

The earliest achievements were due, no doubt, to individual enterprise. A well established merchant or a nobleman raised money, on the security of his fortune or lands, to enable a partner to load a cargo: they shared risk and profit. But profits were large enough to encourage the towns early to take a hand, as corporate bodies: such giants as Venice, Genoa, and Pisa had established hostels for their citizens in Levantine centres before the crusades. These marked a great leap forward. The price of the cities' services to the crusaders, advancing ready money, ferrying troops and supplies, was the grant of whole quarters to themselves in newly captured towns. Pisa, Genoa and Venice thus built up wide commercial empires, despite the fact that they were not themselves fully sovereign states.

Adventure and success abroad had powerful repercussions at home. They increased the demand for goods which could be exported, and stimulated the circulation of the means of exchange, currency. The quickened pulse of economic life in the cities began to attract to them men of all sorts from the country round. Noblemen who had seen the potential of commerce left their country homes and came to live within the walls. This was one reason why the Italian cities were able to gain control of the surrounding countryside, the *contado*. It also helps to explain the bitter family feuds among their citizens, for the nobles brought their bad habits from the country with them. The towers of such a town as San Gimignano testify to their warlike ways; they were built to be forts and dwelling places at the same time. Lesser men sought in the cities a living as clerks, butchers and bakers, in those occupations without which city life is impossible; others found work as artisans, for local industry often flourished in the wake of trade, as at Florence and Milan. The rapid growth and the prosperity of the cities enhanced at the same time the prosperity of the countryman, who found in them a ready market for his produce.

In Flanders the same story was repeated, but not perfectly. The great Flemish cities, Ypres, Ghent, and Bruges, started perhaps at a disadvantage, for their sites were not so old as those of, say, Florence. But as in Italy it was round fortified places that cities grew up. As in Italy, too, the inhabitants were largely men drawn in from the countryside by the lure of opportunity. The Bruges which Galbert described in his chronicle in the early twelfth century shows the process actually at work; with the old fortified *bourg* at the centre of a new town, protected at this stage only by a wooden stockade. Years and growing prosperity were to efface all traces of the one-time separation of *bourg* and merchant suburb. But rich as the citizens of Bruges and other Flemish cities became, they never rivalled those of Florence or Venice. In Flanders, moreover, very few of the nobility ever came to live permanently in the towns. In consequence, the Flemish cities never achieved the same independence as the Italians: in the long run their culture was less rich and individual, and depended more on the protection of noble rulers.

The rise of cities and the expansion of commerce had consequences of general importance. A class of citizens engaged in commerce had no place in the social framework of landlords and peasants which had emerged after the invasions of the ninth and tenth centuries. The *bourgs* and old episcopal towns round which the new urban societies grew up had been ruled in the past by bishops or noble landlords, who had little or no understanding of problems which had everyday urgency for commercial men, the judgement of questions of contract and debt, the regulation of wages and prices, and conditions of labour and sale. In the virtual absence of any state machine, there was only one way in which such matters could be dealt with competently, by the citizens themselves. The right to a degree of self-government was therefore vital to them. It was won by long struggle and the common endeavour of citizens who had sworn to act together to obtain the right 'to choose their own laws'. These sworn 'communes' became the government of the cities, when their one-time lords accepted the force of change and granted the privileges sought of them. In effect, their concessions of self-government gave recognition to the existence of a new force in the life of Christian society, the *bourgeoisie*.

The keynote of this new influence was independence. The cities were bastions of liberty: the runaway serf who lived a year and a day in a city won thereby his freedom, exchanging the law of his manor for the city's law in the regulation of his life. But it must be stressed that the freedom of any one city was something peculiar to itself, the fruit of the individual efforts of its own inhabitants. Thus history conditioned the outlook of the citizens. The magnificent buildings, churches, cathedrals, and guildhalls which they endowed, testify to public spirit born of pride of achievement: but their patriotism was as local as it was passionate. They did not think of other cities as natural allies, but rather as rivals. Every trading privilege that Genoa won was anathema to Venice: the Flemish cities feuded likewise. In face of a common danger cities might ally, as the Lombard communes did against the emperor Barbarossa; left to themselves, they made war on one another. Even internally their freedom had its exclusive side. The leaders in the struggle for independence had been the wealthy. These civic aristocrats were not much inclined to share with others privileges they had won for themselves and their families. The *bourgeoisie* was from the start exclusive and privileged: the natural tendency of city government was towards quarrelsome oligarchy.

Two further effects of the civic and commercial revival must be noted and stressed. Increased commercial exchange stimulated a great revival in currency circulation. The long-term result of this was steady depreciation of money, which became the nightmare of medieval governments. For it was not to merchants only that freer circulation of money mattered. 'The power of princes rises and falls as their portable wealth ebbs and flows.' So wrote Richard Fitz Neale at the court of Henry II of England (c. 1180). With money lords and princes could hire soldiers and ships, and pay experts in administration to see to their affairs. Government became more businesslike as money came to count for more than land. The peripatetic kingship of earlier times, when a royal hunting lodge could be the seat of administration, was ceasing to be an effective means of ruling.

Besides, it was not only coin that now circulated more freely. External commerce brought Christendom into contact with other societies and ways of thought: internal exchange assisted the rapid spread and assimilation of new ideas. Cities were natural meeting places for others besides merchants. London, England's commercial capital, became its administrative capital too in the twelfth century. Paris in the same century also became a capital, and Bologna the site of a university with a European reputation. Neither, significantly, was a commercial town. Commercial recovery had generated a wider process, in which human activity was shifting away from its old centres, the manors and monasteries of the countryside, to the towns. In the long run the forces thus generated were probably divisive. More immediately the effect was to bring people from all over Christendom into closer and more regular communication, to promote a more common level of culture, to sharpen men's awareness to problems which appeared general to their society. Thus, as Christendom began to expand, a more solid basis was being given to that unity which men believed to exist in Christian society.

7

New Movements in Thought and Letters

THE same period which witnessed the renaissance in commerce
and in city life which has been described, saw also a great renaissance in thought and letters. This new outburst of intellectual and
literary activity in the eleventh and twelfth centuries was a many-
sided movement, and it generated multiple forces. Here it will
only be possible to mention some of its more important and
influential aspects.

A spirit of curiosity, demanding a why and wherefore for old
values and assumptions, is the hallmark of the new movement in
thought. If we wish to trace this attitude to its scholarly origins,
we must turn our eyes away from the traditional centres of
learning, the monasteries, to the schools which from the eleventh
century were beginning to flourish in the shadow of the cathedrals,
especially in northern France. Though their spiritual life was less
active generally, as centres of study the cathedrals enjoyed certain
advantages over the monasteries. A cathedral chapter, like a
monastery, was a corporate body, similarly immersed in attention
to a round of services, and in the administration of its own
business affairs. In both societies these activities in themselves
demanded literacy among their members. But the rule by which
the canon of a cathedral lived was a much looser one than that
of the monk, and his life was less inextricably involved with that
of the community to which he belonged. A cathedral and its
chapter thus provided a focus round which scholarly activity
could centre, without being cramped by the exacting demands
made by a regular monastic life.* This gave the cathedral schools
the opportunity to develop more freely, on their own lines.

This greater freedom lent their learning a more speculative

*I do not wish to suggest that the monasteries bred no thinkers. Lanfranc
and Anselm at Bec were rightly acknowledged to be the best minds of their
age in the later eleventh century.

edge. Logic was the subject which their masters made their own, a discipline which was uncongenial to the religious, reflective cast of monastic thought. It was not a subject to which the fathers or Holy Writ devoted much attention. Indeed, almost all that could be learnt of it was known from Boethius' translations of Porphyry and Aristotle, pagan philosophers who had expounded a learning apparently wholly secular. It was not easy for a mind trained in the cloister to seize, as the masters of the cathedral schools did, the immense potential of their works. They had no natural place in a monastic course of reading. Aristotle and Porphyry nevertheless relayed a method by which the vast and amorphous body of knowledge inherited from the past, on which monastic attention had focused, could be reduced to order and its truth be tested. They indicated a means by which statements, meanings, and argument could be categorized, classified and valued. The study, revived in the late tenth century, of Boethius' exposition of antique logic, familiarized scholars for the first time in many centuries with intellectual standards which were entirely human and rational, independent of revelation.

Studied for itself, logic tends to become in the end an unproductive exercise: it provides a tool which needs to be applied. This was where the cathedral schools owed their debt to the past, to the monasteries and to the Carolingian scholars. The latter had striven to save what they could of the learning, especially the patristic learning, of classical times. What they bequeathed furnished a later generation with food for meditation. The commonplace books of monks had distilled, from the fathers and Holy Writ, what seemed to them most significant in sacred writing. It was to these collections of hallowed texts that the logicians turned their attention, in the hope of wringing further meaning from them by new methods. It did not take them long to find that the texts themselves were far from consistent.

This attempt to view sacred truths in the light of everyday human reason could seem blasphemous. To the conservative minded, it appeared to question by inapposite standards the whole revealed teaching which Christian society had adopted as its guiding light. Rational inquiry fitted ill with the monastic ideal of obedience, contemplation, and concentration on the life of the spirit, which had been seen as the highest expression of human striving and was still in the twelfth century a vital force. Eremitic movements, which looked back for inspiration to the desert fathers, had been one impetus behind the demands for reform of standards in the Church in the eleventh century. Just how widespread were the impulses to which these movements were a response was shown by the mushroom growth of the ascetic Cistercian order, which could count well over three hundred new foundations between 1100 and 1152. The Cistercians, who threw open monastic life even to the illiterate lay brother, divorced themselves more sharply than any order before theirs from the world and secular learning. The contrasted efforts of monk and schoolman tugged, it seemed, in opposite directions.

This tension lay behind the famous struggle of St Bernard and Abelard, which reached its climax at the Council of Sens in 1141. Abelard was the greatest philosophical teacher in his day. Neither his previous condemnation, by the Council of Soissons in 1121, nor the terrible culmination of his love affair with Heloise, had succeeded in tarnishing his reputation, or in dissuading students from flocking from all over Europe to hear him. Bernard, Abbot of Clairvaux, was the most influential Cistercian of history. The drama of the confrontation of these two men has given it, for historians, an almost symbolical significance, with the champion of mysticism of the old school taking up the challenge against the rising tide of radical speculation.

This imagined confrontation is, I believe, a false one. It is unfair both to Bernard and to Abelard. The asceticism of Citeaux and the intellectual astringency of the schools were not such worlds apart. It is not fair to Abelard, in portraying him as a sceptical genius: genius he was, but a sincere Christian also. It is not fair to Bernard, since it focuses on his human error. Inspired by his own intense religious conviction, he secured Abelard's second condemnation, and broke him, as a man, for ever. He acted because he thought he saw in Abelard's logic danger to the faith. Yet his patronage helped to make the careers of some of the men who had profited most from Abelard's teaching. It was not that monk and logician were essentially at odds, but that they misunderstood each other as individuals.

That Abelard was misunderstood was partly his own fault. He could not resist the gifted teacher's instinct for dramatic presentation. The work for which he was most remembered was his *Sic et Non*, in form a collection of contradictory texts from scripture and the fathers. Taken at face value, its object seemed to be to demonstrate the utter incoherence of authoritative teaching. But this was not Abelard's object, as he himself made clear in the prologue to his book. Here he outlined the means by which seeming contradictions must be harmonized. One must look behind the words of the texts to the meanings that were in their authors' minds. Words are imprecise, and their imprecision gives the colour of unreal contradiction. Logic will show what cannot be reconciled: analysis in terms not of words but of true meaning will open the way to reconciliation. Abelard was not demonstrating that scripture was incoherent, but that its coherence could only be uncovered by stern endeavour. He was asserting that the highest truths need to be established by the highest standards.

Abelard was too fond of academic limelight to make the most of his own methods. This had to be left to more moderate men, among them Peter Lombard, Bernard's *protegé* whom men came to know as the Master of the Sentences. The *Sentences*, his great work, presented systematically the key texts of scripture and the fathers over the range of Christian doctrines. Where it was feasible, he extracted orthodoxy, following Abelard's method, from the apparent conflicts of the texts: where it was not, he indicated the main lines of possible argument and left the questions open. His texts were mainly picked up at second hand. He used the *Sic et Non* extensively, and collections of texts made by earlier theologians and canon lawyers, as Isidore of Seville and Ivo of Chartres. But his work was so inclusive, and touched so surely on every point where controversy could arise or had arisen, that it found no rival. It became, as companion to the Bible, the standard theological text book of the Middle Ages. In this way the Lombard's influence, and that of Abelard were stamped on the curriculum of every medieval university. The *Sentences*, the fruit of their thought and method, became the starting point for all theological study and controversy for three hundred years.

*

It was in the school of Paris that Abelard and Peter Lombard taught. Abelard's method contributed largely also to the achievement of another scholar, in another place. Gratian, the slightly earlier contemporary of the Lombard, taught the canon law at Bologna. This was a subject no less live than logic, perhaps even more so, given the attention which the arguments generated by the quarrel of the empire and the papacy had focused on it.

The problem facing the student of canon law was twofold. His first was to distinguish, in the vast body of materials drawn together in old collections of the canons, between what was authoritative and what was not. Put together in ages when the Church had no real central authority, they included – besides matter based on Scripture, the fathers, and the decisions of early councils – more dubious rulings of local synods and bishops and even of lay rulers. Here the canonists of the Gregorian period established what became the accepted standard: the sanction, express or implied, of papal approval. They were able to justify this view of the decisive effect of papal authority from the Gospel commission to St Peter, 'Whatever thou shalt bind on earth shall be bound in heaven,' and from the doctrines of papal supremacy which they found in the forgeries of pseudo-Isidore.

Their second problem was similar to that of the theologians, to reconcile apparent conflicts within the remaining body of authoritative legislation. This was what Gratian, adopting Abelard's methods, set out to do in his *Concordance of the Discordant Canons*. His success established his work, usually known simply as the *Decretum*, as authoritative. In the study of canon law it came to play the same role as the *Sentences* of Peter Lombard in theology.

Canonical studies exercised immense influence in this period. A sound knowledge of the canons was fast becoming a prerequisite for a successful ecclesiastical career. In consequence, the standard of authority adopted by the canonists was a powerful force in spreading throughout Europe respect for the papal claims to ultimate directive control in the affairs of Christendom. The systematic mode of thought of the cathedral scholars now made it possible to justify these claims in terms quite independent of the canonists' interpretation of the texts of pseudo-Isidore. In their writings John of Salisbury and Hugh of St Victor were able to present a systematic view of Christian society as a whole, based on an examination of its nature, its component parts, and their respective functions. The final goal of the Christian republic, in their analysis, was universal salvation in the next world: to this end all in the terrestrial sphere must be functionally orientated. They saw in the clergy, through whose ministry God's redemptive power was made active, the soul that animated the body politic. This clerical body took in turn its direction on this earth from Christ's vicar, the bishop of Rome. As the soul in man rules the bodily members and activates them, so the spiritual authority should direct the secular arms of the Christian republic. Delving thus behind the names of institutions to find their nature and purpose, these thinkers, whose master Bernard had sought to silence, justified by Abelard's technique of investigation Bernard's claim:

'The Kings of Germany, England, France, Spain, and Jerusalem, with all their clergy and people, cleave and adhere to the lord Pope, as sons to their fathers, as members to the head.'

As the writings of John and Hugh demonstrate, the methodical approach of the masters of the schools enabled them not only to give a new order and coherence to ancient teaching, but also to attempt a rational and systematic exposition of their own society and its institutions. As propaganda for papal claims to ultimate superiority over all temporal rulers their works were immediately influential. But far more important than any conclusions they reached were the means they used to reach them. Their method was one which could be adapted to tackle any problem, whether theoretical or practical. This was where the thought of the twelfth century took its great stride forward. For the moment pious regard for authoritative teaching concentrated intellectual effort in specific directions, but wide vistas lay open ahead. Already in Abelard's lifetime a start had been made at Bologna, where Irnerius and his disciples were studying the ancient civil law of Rome with a view to establishing principles of justice, sound in purely human terms. Here at least learning was beginning to break free from a framework dominated by theology.

*

In a milieu very different from that of the schools, men were making discoveries in the twelfth century which had little to do with either law or logic. There was not much authoritative about the materials from which Geoffrey of Monmouth, writing at the court of Earl Robert of Gloucester, put together his history of Arthur and the kings of Britain. Out of these same materials, deriving ultimately from the fantastic realms of Celtic legend, Chretien of Troyes at the court of the Count of Champagne was to weave romance of a new order, in which the cross-currents of conflicting human emotions, of love, loyalty, and conscience, sustain the interest of the story. More went to the making of this achievement than the bright colours of Celtic myth. The amorous lyrics of the troubadours of Languedoc, extravagant to absurdity though they sometimes were, uncovered to literature a new dimension of feeling. Their cult of woman blended in romance with the traditional cult of military prowess to form a secular, 'courtly' ethos, aristocratic and sophisticated, whose home was in the castles of the nobility. This courtly writing invested with a new fragrance sentiments which men had been taught to believe led along the path to the everlasting bonfire, and this presented another challenge to old ideals, perhaps still more serious than that of the schools. 'I would rather,' says Aucassin in the famous romance, 'follow all the sweet ladies and goodly knights to hell than go to heaven without them.'

This challenge likewise found a response. The development of the Arthurian cycle illustrates this very clearly. The story of the *Quest of the Holy Grail* tells how Galahad, brought up by white monks in a distant land, came to Arthur's court and passed the test of the Siege Perilous. Later it was he who found the Castle of the Grail and cured the Maimed King who lay there, to die after, in the moment of beatific vision which revealed to him the mystery in the vessel which Christ had used at the Last Supper. Therefore, explains the story, his fame outshone that of all the knights of Arthur, whose impure lives foredoomed them to failure in the quest for the cup, above all that of Lancelot, the pattern of lovers. This is the Cistercian answer to the amorous courtly ethos. We do not know who wrote it: but we do know that it was written in a Cistercian abbey, and by a monk steeped in the mystical teaching of Bernard himself.

The story of the quest for the Grail became part of the accepted canon of Arthurian myth. This is indicative: a reminder, once again, that we must be cautious in talking of challenge and response, in contrasting in this period new forces and traditional ones. Men who enjoyed the colour of other stories, and even who found an echo of their own feelings in the tale of the adulterous devotion of Lancelot and Guinevere, did not question that the values which the Grail story relayed were the higher ones. In the twelfth century one can see, it is true, flashes of tensions which were to become important in the future. The implied contradictions strike us now, however, more forcibly than they did men at the time. Just as logic then showed the way to reconciliation of conflicting teachings, so sensitivity to new dimensions in human feeling opened the way to fresh expression of religious as well as secular experience. Uniformity of religious practice, teaching, and standards, remained so basic an assumption (even though it did not always tally with the facts of life) that it coloured and orientated every fresh development. New ideas were at work and had already carried men far from traditional starting points. Yet still the basis of authoritative and accepted Christian teaching held together the ferment, and preserved a unity of purpose.

8

The Twelfth-Century Revolution in Government

THE late eleventh and twelfth centuries witnessed, as we have
seen, a revival of city life and of commerce which gave new importance to money as an everyday medium of exchange. The same
period saw also, in the schools, the development of a systematic
approach to intellectual problems. These developments in combination made possible a third advance, which was perhaps even
more important. This was in the scope and methods of government. Men with a practical bent and a training in the schools
provided a potential corps of professional administrators. Cities
provided potential centres of permanent and settled administration.
Cash salaries enabled officials to take a more professional attitude
towards their task than their predecessors, who had been
rewarded with estates whose management raised distracting
problems.

Here were the makings of a social and political revolution
which had decisive consequences for the subsequent history of
the west. Its outcome was dictated, as always, not by new forces
alone but by their complex interaction with traditional pressures.
For this reason, it is important to remind ourselves about the
political conditions in which new potentialities began to appear.

The social dislocation of preceding centuries had achieved a
kind of 'fragmentation' of state authority. For the ordinary free
man, the government which mattered to him had become that
not of some distant king but of some locally powerful lord. This
lord, on his compact estates or fief, sustained his vassals, faithful
fighting men bound to him by the oath of homage. His castles
controlled its routes: his courts supplied his subjects with such
justice as they got. Time had entrenched his position, making it
hereditary. Even though he himself probably owed homage to
another, contemporary custom stretched his rights so far as to
permit him to make war to defend his own causes or those of his

men. The power of such a petty feudal state, one of the counties and baronies which had grown out of the disorder of former times rested chiefly on three things: the lord's wealth, his castles, and his ability to impress his leadership on his vassals to a degree which would make homage a meaningful relationship. Given these, were he a vassal's vassal twice over, a local lord could be to all intents an independent ruler.

The new forces released in the eleventh and twelfth centuries made possible, within this framework, a radical shift in the balance of power. The efforts of a nascent bureaucracy to establish a degree of system and order in estate management and in the activities of courts of justice made the ruler's personal intervention necessary less often, and enabled him to control wider estates more effectively. Wider estates meant more money coming into his treasury, with which he could build more castles and pay men to defend them. With the great monetary and military resources thus available, he might be able to turn the lip-service of nominal vassals far afield into a real subordination. Especially this might be so if he were a king, whose unction had invested his authority with a religious significance that men were bound to respect.

Such, viewed in purely mechanical terms, was the situation and its possibilities. So far all sounds to the advantage of the superior lord, be he king, or count, or some other noble. No human situation, however, can ever be understood in mechanical terms. Any extension of an overlord's power could only be achieved at the expense of the independence of other, subject lords. Men proud of the ancient prestige of their family, and of the power established by the individual efforts of ancestors, were not likely to resign their inherited freedoms without a struggle. To them their independence was their birthright. The new developments thus raised tensions which other factors helped to exacerbate.

For one thing, these new factors operated at various different levels of feudal lordship: two men, nominally in the relation of lord and vassal, might find themselves advantaged by similar circumstances simultaneously. Also the best means for an overlord to check the growing power of one vassal – the judicious granting of lands and privileges to others – was the one most likely to build up the power of another vassal whose fief was contiguous to that of the first. This temporary solution could easily result in the overlord's descendants having to cope with two formidable enemies instead of one. Other factors often forced his hand in the same dangerous direction. The men he employed to man his castles and his administration had their own ambitions: in a society where his great vassals stood out as the social group whose position was most securely established, that was the natural rank to which new men aspired. Patronage imposed a depreciation rate on gains in administrative efficiency and military power. It constantly replenished the very class of men at the cost of whose independence such gains were made.

In any case, any description of relations between a ruler and his greatest subjects in terms of natural antagonism is misleading. They were his most respected subjects; he had been brought up among them to share their tastes and prejudices: if they absented themselves from his court it could only damage his prestige. His succession depended in part on their assent, for the principle of primogeniture in royal houses was slow to assert itself: to be of the blood royal was important, but, till the mid twelfth century at least, the wishes of the powerful men of a kingdom were almost equally decisive. In consequence royal authority could often only be retrenched and defined at the price of concessions to privileged groups.

If of course a ruler could extend his resources, especially in land, without cost to the rights of others, he was better situated. Since the right to rule over lands and men was accepted to be heritable, empires were more easily built in the marriage bed than by the sword. This made dynastic considerations of primary importance, a factor which dominated secular politics in the Middle Ages and outlasted them. Another means to the same end was for the ruler to establish his right to take over the lands of a vassal who died without heirs, or who failed to abide by the legal implications of his homage. This was a harder way, if surer in the long run, since he might need a sword to enforce such rights.

*

The only way to show how the forces so far described applied is to see how they worked in practice. A start can be made by looking at the two countries which, by about 1200, emerged with the most highly organized governments in the west, the two Norman kingdoms of Sicily and England.

Their precocious development owed much to the fact that both their ruling dynasties established themselves by conquest in the eleventh century. Their vassals, owing their authority to the same conquests, did not enjoy the same entrenched independence as those of, say, the king of France. Both monarchies also owed important debts to the past. Repeated Scandinavian invasions had forced the Anglo-Saxon kings of England to organize their realm efficiently for defence. In Sicily the Norman kings inherited an administration whose framework was Byzantine, and which was based ultimately on the sophisticated practices of the late Roman empire.

This is why Sicily, in the twelfth century, stands out as the kingdom with the most highly developed government in Latin Christendom. As the granary of north Africa and the natural stopping place for shipping bound for the east from Spanish and Italian ports, it was also probably the richest. Roger II, who proclaimed himself king in 1130, inherited all the one time state-revenues: dues from ships which used his harbours, and valuable monopolies of trade in corn and fish (to which silk was added when he set artisans captured in Greece to weave it in factories at Palermo). These sources provided the money with which he paid his Moslem mercenaries, whose efforts wore down resistance to his rule from the turbulent Norman barons of southern Italy.

The consistent theme of the laws (assizes) which Roger established for all his kingdom in 1140, after his triumph over the mainland barons and their ally Pope Innocent II, is the omnicompetence of royal authority. There is not much suggestion here of the fragmentation of power: all matters, feudal and local, are to be ultimately controlled, through royal officials, from the highly organized court of Palermo. Many of Roger's officers were, significantly, of Greek or Arab extraction, trained in traditions of administration older than any known in the west. The multiracial composition of his kingdom's population contributed futher to the exceptional power of his crown; the royal authority was the only one which Greek, Norman, and Arab alike acknowledged. This was also what made Roger's court a centre of magnificent and cosmopolitan culture. The accounts of the royal treasury were kept by Arab scribes who knew more about reckoning than any Greek or Latin. Byzantine models inspired the mosaics in the new cathedral Roger built at Cefalu, but their legends are in Latin, in Roman character.

English administrative development may owe a good deal to men who, like Henry II's clerk Master Thomas Browne, had visited the court of Roger of Sicily. But already in William the Conqueror's time (1066–87) Norman direction, working within Anglo-Saxon traditions of local administration, had produced in Domesday Book the most complete survey ever made of the resources in men and wealth of a medieval kingdom. And in financial administration the reign of Henry I (1100–35), who died when Roger's struggles with his enemies were at their most desperate, saw novel and important advance. Under the guiding hand of Roger Bishop of Salisbury, the king's treasury (hitherto supervised by chamberlains attached to the itinerating court) was organized into a rudimentary government accounting department, the Exchequer. Hither twice a year came the sheriffs, the royal officials who managed the king's estates in each of the old Saxon shires and presided over their courts. They paid in to the king all monies due, and gave the names of all who were for one reason or another in his debt. All the sheriffs' expenses, for the upkeep of castles and manors and payments for the king's service, were credited to him, and the details were recorded at length on the 'Great Roll of the Pipe' by the exchequer clerks. Thus the king had an annual account of all that was due to him and all he paid out, and a means of checking the activities of officials whom he might seldom meet.

Henry's grandson, Henry II (1154–89) restored this system to working order after the civil wars between Stephen and Matilda. His reign saw a great deal more besides. He and his councillors really began the process of knitting together the governmental resources of England into a unitary force. This stands out most clearly in the field of justice. The doing of justice was the primary task which the twelfth century expected of a ruler (most of what we might call welfare was accepted to be the responsibility of the church and the family). Henry's reign saw not only a great drive to detect and control crime, but also a strenuous effort to provide injured parties with swift and efficient means to obtain redress. This was achieved by means of writs, official letters in the king's name, instituting automatically proceedings at law to set right the wrongs of which individuals had complained. One sort of writ, for instance, was in form a letter to the royal sheriff, bidding him see that a man who had allegedly wronged another, by taking his lands or goods or accusing him falsely, take steps to give him redress, or come to the king's court to explain why he should not do so. All that the king's clerks had to do if a man complained of injury was to fill in his name on the appropriate writ and despatch it to the relevant official. To deal with the issues thus raised the king sent justices from his court regularly about the shires, to hear and settle them in his name. Where it was necessary to ascertain the facts of the case, the writs told his sheriffs to swear panels (juries) of men from the neighbourhood who would know the truth, and bring them before his justices to establish it.

Henry's advisers were educated men: their practice shows the spirit of the schools, of the *Sic et Non*, in action in government. Their ready-made writs classified the wrongs which the king might have to set right, differentiating injury to person, to property, to good name, and supplied to each an appropriate means of redress. The use of sworn juries ensured the judgement of cases by a standard all could comprehend, that of human knowledge, which made earlier methods of establishing the truth (as the ordeal of hot iron, or the judicial duel) look primitive. The king's judgements, moreover, were now recorded, like the debts of those who owed him money: there was no forgetting them. A host of litigants in consequence sought the readier and surer justice now available to them, especially lesser men, tenants of others than the king. Royal authority thus began to be something meaningful to a much wider range of people than heretofore: while the protection which the king's writs gave them in his courts began to shape a common law of all the land.

If Henry had been king of England only, there is no knowing where the steady growth of royal power would have ended. But marriage and inheritance had made him master also of a great empire in France: Normandy came to him through his mother Matilda: Anjou, Maine and Touraine through his father Geoffrey: Aquitaine by the right of his wife, Eleanor. Before he died, tension was growing between him and the king of France, his nominal overlord in this motley assemblage of fiefs, who could hardly view his growing power in them with equanimity. As the French king's insistence on his rights increased, Henry's successors Richard and John had to strain at their English resources to defend theirs. By 1205 John had lost all but Aquitaine, and in his efforts to win back what he had abandoned he used his administration to raise money in England in a way which seemed to stretch royal right beyond the point which was reasonable. In 1215 his powerful subjects combined to force him to seal a Great Charter, in which the just limits of his rights over them were set down. Thus the very growth of royal power ended by forcing the king to acknowledge the boundaries beyond which he could not go without some sort of agreement from his subjects.

The ascent of the French monarchy from near impotence to near absolutism began long before this, in the reign of Louis VI (1108–37). The great part of Louis's life was spent storming the castles of robber barons in the Capetian home-land of the Ile de France – only a small beginning. Louis in fact was doing no more than his subject Count Geoffrey was doing at the same time in Anjou, and Count Charles was seeking to do in Flanders. But for all its small scale the operation was important. Until order was established in their own lands around Paris, the French kings had little prospect of making their power felt further afield. What Louis achieved guaranteed to his successors resources in men and money, which, if modest, were at least secure, and capable of improvement.

The first improvement which showed clearly was a more

methodical approach to government of the now more ordered domain. The instructions for the administration of his lands left by Louis's grandson, Philip II Augustus, when he went on crusade in 1190, reveal that there was already in operation an efficient and professional system of administration, modelled on that of the English kings in their continental fiefs. His royal domain was divided into districts, each supervised by a *bailli*, a salaried official appointed by the king and removable at his will. The *bailli* looked after the exploitation of the king's estates, the collection of tolls and dues and the fines imposed in his courts, and recorded them. Once a month he held a court to hear, in the king's name, the pleas of all the king's subjects great and small in his district. Three times a year he came to Paris to pay over the king's money and give an account of his takings and expenses. He also at these times referred to the king's council any matters which he had not felt able to settle on his own responsibility. From the councillors deputed to deal with these matters there developed, in the time of Philip's grandson, St Louis, the professional judicial body known as the Parlement of Paris, the highest court of the French realm.

The fortune which efficient administration helped him to amass enabled Philip to impose his authority on great feudatories who had hitherto been well nigh independent. In his dealings with these great princes he was rather fortunate. During his reign the powerful Count of Flanders was long absent on crusade: Champagne was from 1201 in the hands of a minor in his wardship, and Brittany from 1203 was in those of a woman. This left him very free in his dealings with the most formidable of them all, the king of England, who was duke of Normandy and Aquitaine, and count of Anjou, Touraine, Maine and Poitou. At Le Goulet in 1200 he forced King John, who was disputing the succession to these lands with his nephew Arthur, to recognize the homage that he owed for them. A year later he was therefore able to summon John to his court as his feudal vassal, to answer the complaints made against him by the count of Lusignan. When John did not appear, the court declared his fiefs forfeit to the crown for contempt, and Philip unleashed his mercenaries against them. By 1205 Normandy, Anjou and Maine were effectively his. Philip's domain lands had more than doubled, and his power became in a new sense a force to be reckoned with.

In 1214 Philip defeated at Bouvines the forces of the coalition of England, Flanders, and the Welf emperor Otto IV, which John had brought together in a desperate attempt to regain his lost inheritance. From then on, Philip's mastery was secure not over the Capetian patrimony only, but over everything in France which had once been the patrimony of the house of Anjou, except Aquitaine. The battle marked also the end of the German pre-eminence among the kingdoms of northern Europe, and the beginning of the French. For the moment, it is true, royal authority was a negligible quantity in the south, in Languedoc. It is true also that even in the north the provinces retained distinct customs and administrative practice. Even the Parlement never established a common law in France such as England knew. But Philip's lands were very nearly as well administered as those of the king in England, and they were wider and richer. After Bouvines, the Capetians' claim to be the successors of Charlemagne no longer had a hollow ring.

By this time, in England and France the new professionalism in the administration of ancient royal rights and domains had built these countries into kingdoms, which henceforward can only be regarded as independent powers. Westminster and Paris had become settled centres of effective rule. The kings of France and England had grown rich enough to back their policies when necessary with well trained mercenary armies. A new kind of political force had been created, more formidable than any secular organization medieval Christendom had yet known. Its growth demonstrates the new political potential of the power of money wedded to a professional approach to problems of government.

Sicily failed to develop in the same way, but only because a dynastic marriage linked its fortunes to those of the empire. As this suggests, what we must do to complete the outlines so far traced of the trends in government in the twelfth century, is to see how the forces at work behind the rise of monarchy in France

and England affected the positions of the two older and more
universal powers, the papacy and the empire.

*

In terms of sheer organizational efficiency there was no secular
government which could compare with that of the Church. The
papal judicial system, especially, was most effectively organized.
Experts had worked to shape the canon law into a practical working code, based on principles far more rational than the laws of
secular kingdoms, and the church courts had evolved regular
rules of procedure. Travelling legates, despatched from Rome,
visited the provinces regularly to hold councils and hear cases in
the Pope's name, referring back to Rome any matters they found
too thorny to settle on the spot. By the mid twelfth century so
much business was being referred to papal authority that such
methods became insufficient to cope with it. Hence the practice
arose of settling cases by appointing a small commission of local
churchmen for the occasion, and giving them papal authority to
deal with the individual issue on the spot. This made papal justice
much more easily available, and further swelled the number of
causes in which its authority was invoked. The officials who were
needed to deal with all this day-to-day work grew in number, and
improved their methods of recording papal business and authen-
ticating decisions. Regular synods were held at Rome, at which
decrees were promulgated for the reform of the standards and
organization of the clergy, and relayed with speed to the provinces.

The nature of the matters which the Pope and his officials could
be called on to judge was rich in variety. Breaches of oaths,
questions of legitimacy, cases concerning marriages, testamentary
disposition and church endowments were accepted as properly
within their jurisdiction, as well as matters more clearly spiritual.
Their authority thus did not extend over clerics only, but in many
matters over laymen too. Theirs was besides a universal authority,
not limited by the bounds of any kingdom or the custom of any
locality. For all the complaints made of the venality of the church
courts (and there were plenty), the fact that the Church was
backed by a governmental force which could be seen actively to

work in every part of Christendom inevitably enhanced the prestige of the papacy. Its claims to an authority which outshone that of any lay ruler did not seem unrealistic in these conditions.

In terms of the men and the method necessary to sustain professional administration, the papacy lacked nothing by twelfth-century standards. It was in physical force that it was weak. For the enforcement of its commands in distant places it had to rely on moral prestige and the cooperation of secular authorities, which could often only be secured by politic compromise. In Rome itself, moreover, the turbulence of the citizens and local aristocracy was a constant threat to its security. Innocent II, Eugenius III and Alexander III all spent periods in exile from their capital, and to maintain themselves had to seek the aid of secular princes who disposed of military force which they did not themselves possess. These princes expected advantages in return for their assistance, and in order to retain its political independence the papacy had to avoid too absolute a dependence on any one ally. This sometimes involved purely diplomatic manoeuvres, not altogether easy to square with the spiritual ends to which the papacy was in name committed. There was danger here for the future. In the twelfth century, however, the unremitting efforts of the papacy to raise moral standards among laymen and clerks alike, and to raise men and money for the crusade to the Holy Land, kept its reputation soaring.

No such cheerful picture confronts us when we turn to look at the other universal power, the empire. Certainly the prestige of the emperor still stood higher, in the twelfth century, than that of any other secular ruler; but he was ceasing rapidly to be a serious rival to the pope as the political leader of the Christian west. And at the practical level, the German emperors had to face, in their secular dealings with their subjects, problems which were very acute.

When the great war over investitures broke out, the emperor Henry IV was already at loggerheads with a powerful German nobility. The old threat from the leaders of the tribal duchies had been scotched long ago in the time of the Ottos, it is true. But now new conditions were altering the structure of noble power. In lands where, when they were waste and forest, the emperors had not challenged an aristocratic authority exercised mainly over beasts, a population of settlers was growing. Imperial attempts to control the relations between the nobles and these new subjects of theirs were naturally resented. Why should their hitherto unchallenged authority in these lands be questioned, seemingly simply because they had become a source of prosperity? These were the kind of resentments which activated the men who took the opportunity provided by Henry IV's excommunication to elect Rudolf of Swabia anti-king in 1077. The uncompromising break which they then made with the hereditary traditions of monarchy was reasserted when Henry V died childless in 1125. His successor Lothar was without royal ancestors, and Lothar's successor Conrad was in turn not his kinsman. In consequence in the disordered years between 1077 and the election of Frederick Barbarossa in 1152 the rulers of the empire had no chance to build up a block of family lands sufficient to overawe any vassal, in the way Philip II did later in France. The disorders of the same period gave the dynastic nobility a golden chance to establish its independence: they achieved for the German feudality very much what the ninth century invasions achieved for the feudal lords of France.

Something of the same sort was happening at the same time in north Italy. The slackening of imperial authority during the wars of investiture gave the Lombard cities the chance to shake themselves free from the control of the imperialist bishops. Where in Germany the advantages of a period of radical social change were reaped by the nobility, here the city communes were the gainers. But the effect was similar. When Barbarossa became emperor-elect, these communes were nearly as independent behind their walls as the German nobles in their castles. They were also much richer than any town or prince of Germany.

Barbarossa was one of the most impressive personalities among the medieval emperors. He had a sharp sense of the eminence of the empire and its antique heritage. 'My army is the Roman army, my council its senate,' he told Rome's rebellious citizens and their republican leader, Arnold of Brescia. He was a great patron of the

Roman lawyers of Bologna: his court poet hailed him as a new Caesar, 'destined to restore the affairs of Rome to their pristine state.' But all this pomp and the appeal to antiquity were not enough without a settled administration and powerful resources in men and money. These last were what the emperor sought strenuously through a long reign, and never quite succeeded in winning.

In Italy Barbarossa sought to turn to his advantage the growing wealth of the Lombard cities, by the reassertion of all the ancient rights that the Lombard kings and the emperors had once enjoyed. But this involved the sacrifice of more of their hard won independence than the cities were ready to forego, and in face of external danger they were willing to forget their feuds with one another. In 1167 the communes formed the famous Lombard League, and pooled their resources to fight for their rights. The support and guidance of Pope Alexander III, who saw great dangers ahead for the papacy if the empire were to become strongly established in Lombardy, helped to hold the league together. After some initial successes, Barbarossa was decisively defeated at Legnano in 1176, and it became clear that the attempt to establish direct imperial administration in Lombardy had failed. In return for an annual tribute, he finally agreed by the Treaty of Constance (1183) to leave the cities of the league in untrammelled control of their internal affairs. Like the English Magna Carta, this treaty defined the limits of the emperor's overlordship: it did not in any sense end it. But it gave the cities a much greater independence to control their private affairs than the English barons won from King John, an independence that amounted to a right of internal self-government.

Without adequate local allies in Italy, Barbarossa had to deal circumspectly with the German nobility, in order to win their support for expeditions south of the Alps. Thus he confirmed the Welf Henry the Lion in his inheritance of Saxony and Bavaria, and set up a new duchy of Austria for Henry Jasomirgott, to balance the Welf power. Such actions limited the effect of his genuine efforts to strengthen imperial power in Germany. By judicious exchanges and purchase he extended and consolidated the estates of his own house in the south-west. At his great councils or diets he took pains to stress the personal feudal relation of the higher nobility to the empire. It was as a vassal who had contumaciously refused to abide judgement in his lord's court that he was in the end able to sentence Henry the Lion, whose lands in the east, conquered from the Slavs, were growing into an empire within the empire, to the loss of all his estates. But he was only able to enforce the sentence because other princes besides himself viewed the rising Welf power with envy, and were ready to support him in return for new privileges for themselves. Henry the Lion's lands went to the emperor's allies, not the emperor. By the end of the reign the greatest among the German nobility were beginning to emerge as a recognizable estate of princes, with all but sovereign rights in their own lands.

Barbarossa died on crusade in 1190, drowned crossing a river in Asia Minor. That his empire passed without challenge to his son Henry VI showed how much he had achieved. Even so, the empire had neither the settled and organized central government nor the wealth which were together making monarchy so powerful in England and France. In Italy and Germany the forces which elsewhere made kings formidable worked to the benefit of local rather than central authority. The empire comprised too large and unwieldy a territory to profit by them.

At the end of the century, however, new vistas for imperial power in Italy opened suddenly, as a result of one of those accidents of birth which can be crucial in a world where the inheritance of authority is an accepted part of the political system. William II of Sicily died, and his rich and well organized kingdom passed to Henry VI's wife Constance. The union of Sicily and the empire made another confrontation with the papacy inevitable. It also gave imperial power a new relevance to the affairs of the east and the crusade. To understand the sequel, something in greater detail will have to be said about these last two matters.

9

The Crusades

BEFORE the time of the crusades, the Holy Land was known to the Christians of the west almost solely as a place of pilgrimage. Until the middle of the eleventh century, those who made the journey thither could travel through lands governed by Christians for all but the last stretch of it. East to the Euphrates, and south as far as Antioch in Syria, the sway of the Greek emperors of Byzantium was acknowledged. But by the 1050s their empire was beginning to fall on evil days. In Constantinople court factions were undermining imperial authority. Meanwhile the Asian provinces began to suffer from the inroads of the nomadic Seljuk Turks, who were establishing an empire for themselves in the lands which had once been united under the Arab caliphate of Baghdad. In 1071 the Seljuks won a tremendous victory at Manzikert in Anatolia over the Byzantine armies and captured the emperor Romanus Diogenes. The years that followed saw their advance carried to the eastern shores of the Bosphorus, and Constantinople herself threatened. The Anatolian lands had always been an important recruiting area, and there was a desperate shortage of fighting men in face of rising military crisis. In 1095 the emperor Alexius Comnenus appealed to Pope Urban II to assist him in raising mercenary auxiliaries from the west.

When he heard that the interior parts of Romania (the Greek empire) were held oppressed by the Turks, he was moved by compassionate pity: he crossed the Alps and came into Gaul, and summoned a great council from all sides to gather in a city called Clermont.

This is how Fulcher of Chartres sums up Urban's reaction, which led to the launching of the crusade. At Clermont, in a field in the hills of Auvergne outside the town, the Pope preached on 27 November 1095, to a great crowd of persons, lay and clerical, calling on men from all over Christendom to come to the rescue

117

of their fellow Christians in the east: 'Undertake this journey for
the remission of your sins, assured of the imperishable glory of
the kingdom of heaven.' A great cry went up in response from
the assembled people: 'It is God's will!'

Urban's appeal caught the revivalistic imagination of his time.
At Clermont itself a great number swore immediately to undertake the 'journey', sewing on to their garments red crosses in
witness of their vow. Those who thus took the cross, or who gave
alms in its cause, were promised remission of sins. Popular evangelists, like the Frenchman Peter the Hermit, took up the Pope's
message and spread it far afield. Strange miracles were rumoured
to have accompanied their preaching, demonstrable signs that
the undertaking had won divine approval. Great hosts began to
gather. This was aid on a different scale to the mercenary bands
Alexius had looked for. It amounted rather, as he himself put it,
to a 'great movement of peoples out of the west'. It was the
crusade.

The first 'crusaders' to reach Asia were the peasant bands
brought together by Peter the Hermit and the French knight
Walter the Penniless. As the frightful massacres of the Jews
which they committed *en route* bear witness, their followers lacked
both discipline and a clear notion of their objective. But the very
fact of their gathering, let alone having reached Asia Minor
before the Turks wiped them out, is itself startling testimony to
the response which the preaching of the crusade had evoked in all
quarters. The more formidable hosts, under noble commanders,
gathered more slowly: they began to arrive around Constantinople at the end of the year 1096. One army, led by Godfrey,
duke of Lower Lorraine, and his brother Baldwin, came overland through Hungary. Another, led by Count Raymond of
Toulouse and mainly recruited in Languedoc, came by way of
north Italy and Illyria: with them came Adhemar, bishop of Le
Puy, whom Urban had appointed as his legate to direct the
expedition. Bohemond, son of Robert Guiscard and heir to his
ambitions to extend his dominions into the Adriatic at the cost of
the Greeks, crossed with an army of Normans from Italy to
Durazzo, and marched thence along the coast and across Thrace

to Constantinople. Altogether, these forces formed a host of perhaps fifty thousand men.

Between their leaders and the Greek emperor relations were from the first strained. In the end, Alexius managed to persuade them all to do him homage, and to promise to acknowledge his imperial overlordship in all reconquered lands which had been ruled from Byzantium in the tenth century. In return, he promised them supplies and support, to the limit of his ability, in their march through Asia Minor. In spite of hazard and prolonged privations, that march was accomplished. By the autumn of 1097 the crusaders had reached Antioch, which fell the next year after a long siege. Here Bohemond set himself up as prince of the once Byzantine city, oblivious of his promise to Alexius. Raymond of Toulouse had coveted its government too, and there were long bickerings between them. (Adhemar, who had healed such quarrels before, had died at the siege.) In the end Raymond and Godfrey of Lorraine, under pressure from their followers, marched on down the coast towards Jerusalem. On 15 July 1099, the Holy City was stormed. 'Sobbing for excess of joy,' and with their hands still bloody from massacre in the streets, the crusaders gave thanks for victory that night in the Church of the Holy Sepulchre.

After long consultation, Godfrey of Lorraine was chosen to be ruler of the new kingdom of Jerusalem. The disappointed Raymond was consoled with a county of Tripoli; Tancred, Bohemond's nephew, became prince of Galilee. Baldwin, Godfrey's brother, had meanwhile established himself as count at Edessa, far into Syria on the Euphrates. When Godfrey died in 1100, he succeeded to the kingdom. Within a few years the outlines of the new 'crusading states' had become clear. The Latins controlled a thin strip of coastal territory from Arsuf in the south to the borders of Cilicia, stretching inland to Jerusalem and the Jordan valley, with an outpost in the north at Edessa, much deeper into the hinterland. All the important cities of the Levantine coast, including Acre, Tyre, Tripoli, Tortosa and Antioch, were in their hands.

This rapid success of the crusades at their very inception was crucial to their subsequent history. Victory set the seal on the

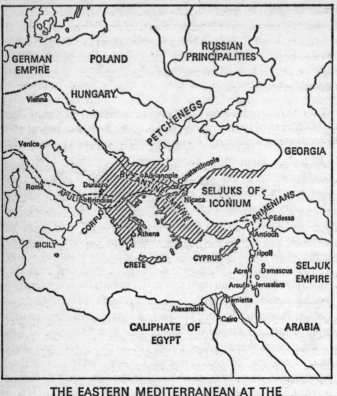

**THE EASTERN MEDITERRANEAN AT THE
TIME OF THE 1st. CRUSADE**

Shading shows roughly territory controlled by Byzantines C. 1100

------- Shows route of first crusade

movement that Urban had put in train. From an episode, crusading crystalized into a Christian activity with a specific nature
and object. Its call was to find a response among Latin Christians
for the rest of the medieval period.

To a very large degree the first crusade owed its success to the
spirit of the men who went on it. The common soldiers had been

120

stirred in a way which would brook no halting: it was they who forced their commanders to lead them on to Jerusalem. The call to crusade had succeeded, for them and others, in summing up and fusing in a single ideal a whole range of aspirations which were contemporarily powerful. They gave expression to a militant tradition which seemed fastened securely in the holy books of the Old and New Testaments.

Take the road to the Holy Sepulchre . . . that land was given by God to the children of Israel as a possession . . . the Redeemer honoured it by coming thither, adorned it by his sojourn, hallowed it by his passion.

It is not clear that Urban II (to whom a chronicler attributed these words) originally meant Jerusalem to be the primary goal of the crusade. But the preachers, running to Holy Writ to give emphasis to their appeal, soon made it so. Their eloquence decked the crusade in the guise of a pilgrimage, a 'seeking of the way of the Lord' and of remission for sins through hardships endured for His sake. It was, however, a pilgrimage with a difference, 'a new way' opening the ascetic road to salvation to the men in arms.

The Church had long been seeking to channel the vigour of such men into activities more pleasing to God than the endless feuding of the nobility. She had given her blessing to wars against the heathen, and especially had sought to organize soldiers for service in Spain against the Saracens. The Church had also endeavoured to orient martial enterprise by associating religious rites with the old ceremonies observed among the Teutons when a young warrior came of age. As early as 950 a liturgy for the blessing of his sword was in use at Mainz. This is the oldest original that has survived of the later elaborate ritual for the making of a knight, with its prayer:

Almighty father, who hast permitted the use of the sword to repress the malice of the wicked and defend justice, . . . cause thy servant here before Thee never to use this sword or any other to injure anyone unjustly, but always to defend the just and right.

Fine words, but it needed more than words and ceremony to

curb the turbulence of a military aristocracy which viewed feuding as its hereditary right. The crusade provided a cause which could instead enlist and consecrate both its martial vigour and its social pride.

This fusion of Christian and martial ideals, which the crusades fostered, is nowhere reflected more clearly than in the organization of the new military orders, the Templars, the Hospitallers, and the Teutonic knights. The Templars, the oldest and the original of them all, were founded by Hugh de Payns in 1119. In its early form theirs was an order of monks in arms. Its members swore to live, according to the rule of Benedict, in poverty, obedience, and chastity, and to 'fight with pure mind for the supreme and true King'. Their asceticism was tempered only by the necessity to be strong in arms at need.

Thus in battle they deck themselves out not in gold and silver, but with faith within and mail without, to strike terror, not avarice, in the hearts of their adversaries.

So wrote St Bernard in their praise, contrasting their stern rule with the luxurious ways of secular knights. The habit of the knights of the order was a simple robe of white, the symbol of purity, with the crusaders' red cross upon it. This robe, of the same colour as that of the Cistercians of Bernard's own order, reflects the same marriage of monastic austerity with the martial spirit of chivalry, which, as we saw earlier, underlay the romance of Galahad and the Holy Grail.

The endowments of the faithful made the Templars one of the richest of all the religious orders. It was privileged too: it had its own chaplains, subject only to the Grand Master, who in turn was directly responsible to the Pope himself. This is a reminder of the extent to which the success of the crusade was due to the organization which the Church could put behind it. The host which won Jerusalem was recruited from all over Christendom. Churchmen preached the crusade, they recorded the vows of the future crusaders, they collected and administered the alms of the faithful which helped to finance it. Acting through her diocesan bishops, the Church took into her special protection the lands and property of all who left for Palestine. Without the unitary papal system of administration behind it, the crusade could never have been organized as a large scale enterprise.

The crusade demonstrated, indeed, what a real unifying force in Christendom the Roman Church had become. To the canonists, the crusade became known as the 'Roman war', 'because Rome is the head and mother of our Faith.' This was not an idle aside of the jurist. The crusade showed Christendom uniting in a single endeavour. It revealed the initiates of chivalry as something more than provincial nobles, as an order in the great Christian society, with common standards and shared concerns. It drew together the secular and spiritual aristocracy of Europe, in a way whose importance was lasting because the inspiration behind it was genuine and durable.

*

Other more material forces worked also for the success of the crusades at their outset. The cramped and confined conditions of life in many parts of Europe made the adventure in the east attractive. Many, especially among the younger sons of the nobility, hoped to find 'beyond the sea' a more ample heritage than could ever be theirs at home. 'It was easy to persuade the men of the West Franks to leave their country,' wrote Ekkehard, 'for Gaul these many years had been afflicted now by civil wars, now by hunger, now by pestilence.' Bible stories of the fertility of the Holy Land encouraged such persons. 'Jerusalem is the centre of the Earth,' Urban is said to have declared, 'its land fruitful above others a like paradise of delights. . . . As scripture says, it flows with milk and honey.' The same forces which led men to seek new lives in lands conquered from the Slav in Germany, and the Moslem in Spain and Sicily, took them also to the Holy Land.

The quest of the Italian cities for new markets in the east was also most important to the crusades. At Antioch and at Jerusalem the timely arrival of Genoese squadrons saved the fortunes of the first crusade: later, in the reduction of the coastal cities, Beirut, Tyre, Jaffa, Acre, their assistance and that of fleets from Pisa and

Venice was again crucial. In return for quarters in conquered cities and for trading privileges, the Italians were willing to support the crusades with ships and, above all, with money, which was vitally important for an enterprise in which soldiers and others needed payment in ready cash. Not the least astonishing feature of the crusades was their haphazard and uncertain finance: the alms of the faithful and the private funds of well born leaders were long their chief resources. Loans from the Italians often tided over their inadequacies, which would otherwise have been fatal.

Conditions in the Orient at the end of the eleventh century were favourable to the first crusade. Like other nomad empires, that of the Seljuks had no intrinsic force to hold it together. The rule of the Turkish horsemen was superimposed on peoples less vigorous but far more cultivated. As under the Arab caliphate, a high proportion of their subjects in Syria and Palestine were Christians. With nothing but the personality of military leaders to unite it, the Seljuk empire rapidly broke up into a number of principalities, whose rulers (usually called emirs), nominally subservient to the sultan of Baghdad, were virtually independent. Like the western feudality, they were constantly quarrelling among themselves. The crusaders soon learned to make the most of their rivalries, and of the discontents of their Christian subjects. The squabbles of the rulers of Aleppo and Damascus weakened Moslem resistance at the time of the siege of Antioch and after. At Edessa, Baldwin gained supremacy as the champion of the local Armenian Christians. Palestine itself was disputed territory, between the area of Seljuk overlordship and the Fatimid caliphate of Egypt. Jerusalem was in Fatimid hands in 1099: the Fatimids had done nothing to help the Seljuks in Syria, and the Seljuks in turn did nothing to assist the Moslem defence of the city.

The other great power in the east was the Greek empire. It was a Christian empire, and should have been the natural ally of the crusaders. Urban II appears to have been at least as much inspired at Clermont by the idea of reuniting the Christians of the east and the west, as by the desire to see the Holy Places recovered from the infidel. There were, however, serious difficulties in the way of such a union, even indeed of successful alliance.

These were largely due to the very different historical experience of the Christians of Byzantium and of the west. Since the time of the Teutonic invasions of Europe, the Byzantine empire had been constantly assailed from all sides. In the east she had to face the onslaught of the Arabs and later the Seljuks; in the Balkans of nomad tribes from beyond the Danube, of Huns, Avars and Petchenegs; her dominions in Italy had been eroded by the assaults of Lombards, Arabs, and finally Normans. The military prowess of her soldier-emperors and skilful exploitation of the rivalries of her enemies had preserved Constantinople; but since the most dangerous threats had always come from the east, her contacts with Rome and western Christendom had in the course of her continuous struggles dwindled to a minimum. Hence from the western point of view Byzantine culture and customs were Greek and alien. Byzantine attitudes were conditioned by her religious and cultural heritage, shaped by the ideas of Hellenistic antiquity and by the theological controversies of the fourth and fifth centuries A.D. Her pride in these traditions could allow no place for the eleventh-century papacy's claims to universal jurisdiction in the Christian world and to final judgement in matters of faith. This was why earlier efforts at reunion of the churches, such as that of 1054, had always proved fruitless.

The new western concept of Holy War could not make much impression on the Greeks, with their different theological tradition, and their habit of thinking in terms of power politics. Guiscard's raids on their Adriatic territories had taught them that western Christians could be formidable enemies. The emperor Alexius in 1096 was anxious first and foremost to get the crusading armies out of the area of his capital, across to Asia Minor. Thereafter he was happy to see them launched against the Seljuks, and to aid them there as far as he could. But once the crusading states were established, in Byzantine eyes they became just another force to be manoeuvred in the complicated web of Byzantine oriental policy. This failure to respond to the call of Holy War shocked the crusaders and roused suspicions that the

Greeks were not good Christians. Their treatment of the Greek Christians in Palestine and Syria roused reciprocal suspicions among the Byzantines.

Norman ambitions and duplicity above all ruined good relations between the Greeks and the crusaders. It was common talk in Constantinople at the time of the first crusade that Bohemond's true object in coming thither had been 'that by some means on his travels he might be able to seize the capital'. Later, in 1107, he led an expedition against Durazzo from Italy, which had been blessed as a crusade. Norman hostility to the Greeks did not die with Bohemond. In 1143 a group of Norman exiles staged a coup in Constantinople, and attempted to crown one of their own number emperor. In 1147 Roger of Sicily raided Greece and sacked Corinth. No wonder that the Greeks saw in the crusades a warning of the manner in which 'all powerful time might humble the high glory of New Rome'. Bohemond's naked ambition created a great rift, which widened steadily thereafter.

As long as the Moslem powers remained weak and disunited, this did not matter over-much. Though without Byzantine aid the first crusade would probably never have reached Syria, in the jubilation over subsequent victories this was forgotten. The need for support from Constantinople became apparent later, in face of a more vigorous and united Moslem opposition; but by then mutual distrust had struck too deep, and there was small prospect of obtaining it.

The crusading states needed reliable Christian allies in the east, because from the first they were weak internally. The crusaders who settled in the Levant formed, outside the cities, a numerically small aristocracy which ruled a subject population part Moslem and part Christian, whose way of life remained alien to theirs. In the towns they had only a modicum of control over the resident Italians, whose first allegiance was to their native cities. The Latin clergy, here as elsewhere, were largely independent of the secular authorities. So also, perhaps more seriously, were the military orders with their riches and their reserves of fighting men.

The monarchy was institutionally feeble. It had been born of the quarrels of the leaders of the first crusade, and those who, like

Raymond of Toulouse, were disappointed of the crown saw to it that they were as independent in their own new won lands as they could be. Antioch hardly formed part of the kingdom of Jerusalem at all. In the kingdom the land was divided into fiefs whose highly independent owners organized their resources with defence of their own tenures in mind. The castles which they built were masterpieces of military design, but their very architecture reflected strategic thought whose keynote was defensive. Their owners knew they could hold them, usually, till relieved: they were not anxious to risk their goods in perilous ventures into hostile territory, far from their fiefs. For such an enterprise, as for any major act of state or justice, the king could do little without the assent of his council of barons, the High Court of the kingdom. These barons distrusted one another: they had brought to the Holy Land the spirit of dynastic rivalry and feudal independence of their European forbears. In consequence, the kings of Jerusalem were not inclined to take risks, and preferred to remain at peace with as many of their Moslem neighbours as they could at a time. This policy did not accord easily with the militant spirit of the Templars, their most effective soldiers. It also shocked crusaders from Europe who, very naturally, expected the kings of Jerusalem to lead them forth in Holy War.

*

Internally weak and beset with diplomatic problems, the kingdom lasted just eighty years. Its prospects began to look steadily darker from 1130 on, when Zengi, *attabeg* of Mossoul, and his son Nur-ed-Din began to reunite the Syrian Moslems in holy war, the counter crusade against the Christian. In 1144 Edessa fell to them. The second crusade was launched to win it back, but though St Bernard preached for it and two kings, Louis of France and Conrad of Germany, took the cross, it achieved nothing. Under two strong rulers, Baldwin III (1143–63) and Amaury (1163–74), the kingdom of Jerusalem continued to thrive for a while, but all the time the Moslem opposition was increasing in strength. In 1164 Nur-ed-Din's Kurdish lieutenant, Saladin, was sent with his uncle to Egypt, and by 1170 he was in effective

THE CRUSADING STATES IN THE 12th. CENTURY

Shading shows land held by Franks before the fall of Edessa

control there. When Nur-ed-Din died, Saladin was able to take over his son's inheritance in Syria. His power now hemmed in the crusading states on all sides except from the sea.

In 1187 the kingdom of Jerusalem stood divided by the rivalry of factions: one led by Raymond of Tripoli, who had been a power in the land in the last days of the heroic leper-king, Baldwin IV, with most of the barons behind him; the other by the queen Sybilla, Baldwin's sister, together with her husband Guy de Lusignan and Rainald of Chatillon, Lord of Montreal. When Rainald broke truce with Saladin, Guy, anxious to prove himself, summoned all the kingdom's forces. Urged on by the Templars but against the advice of Raymond, he risked battle against Saladin at Hattin between Jerusalem and Tiberias. There on 4 July he and his entire army were overwhelmed. The whole military power of his realm was destroyed. In October Saladin entered Jerusalem 'attaining his desire, to set the mosque of Asha free, to which Allah led in the night his servant Mohamed.'

Hattin marks the end of an age in crusading history. This was not really apparent, however, until after the failure of the third crusade, which was launched to redress its consequences. The forces which were gathered show not so much that confidence had been shattered, but rather how deep a root the notion of the defence of Jerusalem had taken as the symbol of united Christian endeavour. They were the most impressive hosts that had ever left for Palestine. The emperor Barbarossa put himself at the head of a great army from Germany. The kings of England and France strained all the resources of their growing kingdoms to fit out their contingents. For all this, however, they did not achieve much. Barbarossa's death in Asia Minor virtually put paid to the German effort. Richard of England and Philip of France, uneasy comrades in arms, had fallen out long before they reached the east. After the prolonged siege which won back Acre, Philip felt he had done enough. Richard remained longest, to defeat Saladin in the field at Arsuf and to march his men to within sight of Jerusalem. But the risks of pressing further were too great. He made peace with his great opponent before leaving for Europe in 1192, but by this secured for Henry of Champagne, titular king of Jerusalem, no more than a strip of coastal land around Acre, and 'free access', for what that was worth, to the Holy City.

The disaster of Hattin demonstrated terribly the inadequacies of the crusader kingdom; that it had neither the institutional unity, nor the sense of common endeavour, nor even the sheer manpower to stand alone against a truly formidable enemy. The third crusade showed that a great demonstration in arms, led by the rulers of the west, was not a hopeful means to restore the situation. Kings like Philip and Richard were too great in their own lands to remain permanently away from them. However genuine the fervour actuating the rank and file of their hosts, they inevitably arrived too late and departed too soon. Their military resources could never be more than a temporary factor in the politics of the Levant. They could not contribute what the successful defence of Jerusalem demanded, a strong resident garrison or powerful Christian allies in the area.

The one real success of the third crusade seemed to be a step in the right direction; Richard's conquest of Cyprus from the Greeks, where Guy de Lusignan was made king. In fact, as a secure base for crusading enterprise Cyprus had its drawbacks. For to the hard pressed survivors of the old kingdom the island seemed to offer more inviting prospects than the mainland. Men began to drift away from Tyre and Acre, and the remaining barons of Jerusalem to think more of fiefs on Cyprus than of the defence of the Holy Sepulchre. In this, the conquest of Cyprus was symptomatic of a change which now began to colour new plans for crusading. Soon after the founding of this new Lusignan kingdom, Henry VI succeeded not only to his father's empire and crusading ambitions, but also to the kingdom of Sicily. With Henry ruling Sicily as well as Germany and Guy ruling Cyprus, the nature of western political involvement in the Mediterranean was altering palpably. Inevitably, western relations with Constantinople assumed new significance.

*

At one time during the reign of the great Byzantine emperor Manuel Comnenus (1143–80) it had looked as if the crusaders might find in the Greek empire the Christian ally they needed. He had married a western wife, affected western habits, and many Latins held honorific posts at his court. When in 1159 he arrived at Antioch with his army, many hoped he would soon lead a great Christian offensive. But past experience made him too distrustful of the Latins to disturb willingly the balance of powers in the Levant. When the new threat from Saladin became apparent, he was no longer in a position to help. His tremendous defeat at Myriocephalon in Anatolia (1176) at the hands of the Turks had destroyed his army and prestige. Worse still, it had brought into the open the latent hostility of his subjects to any pro-western policy.

After Manuel's death there were riots in the capital, and a terrible massacre of the Latins (1182), in which many Venetians perished (they had a settled quarter in the city). This tide of anti-Latin feeling carried to power his relative Andronicus: and when he too was deposed the same hostility to the west endured under his supplanter Isaac Angelus. So incensed was Barbarossa by the obstruction of Isaac and the Greeks during his march through the Balkans in 1190, that at one point he considered open war and the reduction of Constantinople. Many thought that Constantinople was the true destination of the great crusading fleet which Henry VI, his son, was assembling at Messina when he died in 1197.

This is the background against which the strange course of the fourth crusade must be set. It was the new pope, Innocent III, who sent out the appeal in 1198 for a fresh expedition, which began to gather slowly. One of its chief leaders was Count Boniface of Montferrat: his brother Renier had married Manuel Comnenus' sister, and been poisoned by Andronicus. Venice was to supply the transports to Palestine: her doge, Enrico Dandolo, had lost his sight in the anti-Latin riots in Constantinople in 1170. When the fleet was ready to sail for the Holy Land in 1202 there was not enough money to pay the transport: the crusaders agreed to compound for payment by capturing for the Venetians Zara on the Dalmatian coast *en route*. There Alexius, son of Isaac Angelus (who had now been deposed) and brother-in-law of Boniface's friend and overlord, Philip of Swabia, came to meet them. He proposed to them a plan whereby they should restore him and his father in return for a promise of Byzantine commitment in Palestine, and the submission of the Greek church to the papacy.

This was the crusade's turning point. To Boniface and other leaders the prospect of power and influence in the Greek empire was alluring; to the Venetians it opened possibilities of establishing a total monopoly of Byzantine trade to the west; to Dandolo, perhaps, the prospect of personal revenge appealed. Others, more naïve and more faithful to ideals, believed they would go on to the Holy Land with 'Greek knights' to reinforce them. The whole crusade went out of its course, and in the end twice besieged Constantinople. The first siege restored Isaac and Alexius. When the insurrection of the Greeks proved that the promises of the Angeli were beyond them to fulfil, the second captured the city for the Latins, and made Count Baldwin of Flanders the new emperor (1204).

'Never was so much booty taken in one city since the beginning of time,' wrote the crusadér Geoffrey Villehardouin, naïvely wondering at the spendid, spoiled riches of the proudest city of the east. The capture and sack of Constantinople, a Christian capital, was a tragic denouement to an expedition which had set out in a spirit of idealistic endeavour. The Latin empire which it founded was institutionally as weak or weaker than the kingdom of Jerusalem had been. The lion's share of the spoils, a quarter of Constantinople, the Ionian islands and much land on the Adriatic, went to the Venetians. The great fiefs, Boniface's kingdom of Thessaly, the de la Roche Duchy of Athens, Geoffrey Villehardouin's principality of Achaea, were almost independent of the emperor. Hated by most of their Greek subjects and above all by the native clergy, the Latins had no force to penetrate Asia Minor, where a new, hostile Greek empire rallied against them at Nicaea. To pursue the reconquest of Palestine was for them out of the question. Greece besides, in the next generation, seemed to offer more inviting prospects than the Holy Land for men seeking both adventure and a better patrimony than was theirs at home. More newcomers from the west were to be found at the court of the duke of Athens in the 1230s and 40s than at Acre.

The deviation of the fourth crusade and the foundation of the feeble Latin empire were thus among the reasons why European crusaders failed to seize the chances in Palestine, which arose for them when Saladin's empire fell into decline after his death. But one must be careful not to exaggerate the harm done to the impetus of crusading as such. The earlier crusades had won success as the result of the coincidence of the practical interests of traders and settlers with the spiritual ideals which inspired Urban II and the other evangelists of 1095. These practical interests were now finding different outlets. Greece offered finer opportunities than Palestine for those in quest of new lands. With Cyprus, Constantinople, and the Aegean all in western hands, support of the crusades as an element in commercial policy ceased to be important to the Italian cities. The torch of crusading idealism nevertheless still burned strong. No sooner was it clear that the fourth crusade would press no further, than Innocent III began to lay plans for another expedition to rescue Jerusalem. The crusades which St Louis and other princes undertook in the thirteenth century show that crusading still held its place as the highest expression of the chivalrous ideals of the aristocracy in the west. It held that place for two hundred years more at least.

During the thirteenth century, the crusade continued to appeal to material interests as well as to ideals, but they were not the same interests as before. At the political level the foundation of the Latin empire seemed to open up new possibilities. Had it not accomplished, in a different way, that union of eastern and western Christianity of which Urban II had dreamed? This was admittedly a very western way of looking at things, but to those who saw the affairs of the east at a distance only, also a very natural one. With a Latin emperor at Constantinople, a French duke at Athens, a Lusignan on the throne of Cyprus, and the kingdom of Sicily allied to the force of the western empire, the Latins' position in the Mediterranean looked very impressive. With so much in their hands it seemed impossible that another effort would not carry the crusaders from Acre on the coast to Jerusalem.

As the means to this end, the planners of crusading began to look to some Latin Mediterranean confederation, knit together through common Christian enterprise. Especially this concept caught the imagination of those rulers whose Mediterranean involvements enabled them to see the limitless political possibilities which might lie ahead for him who could make himself its leader. The emotional involvement in the crusade of the Church and a large section of the dominant class in the west would ensure him a pre-eminence not confined to the orient. Thus the practical future of the crusades came to depend more and more on the political and dynastic relations of the Latin powers of the Mediterranean. It also became associated with refurbished versions of the old ideal of a universal Christian empire.

10

Innocent III – the Papacy Triumphant

THE decades which followed the fourth crusade saw Latin
dominion extended to the furthest limits it ever achieved in the
Middle Ages. Within this period also, Latin Christendom appeared
united, as a single religious and political society, to a degree
which was never surpassed. This was very largely due to the
genius of Innocent III, one of the greatest rulers the medieval
church ever knew, who became pope in 1198.

Born of a noble Roman family, trained in the canon law of
Bologna and in the active work of the *Curia*, Innocent was
steeped in the tradition of papal supremacy which Gregory VII
and Alexander III had upheld before him. For him as for them,
the basis of this tradition was the concept of the church as a moral
and spiritual force working for peace, order, and salvation
throughout the Christian world. But he grasped more clearly
than any before him what was essential, if the church entrusted
to him was to achieve her ends both in this world and the next.
Papal plenitude of power could permit no ultimate division of
authority into separate spheres, spiritual and temporal.

> To princes power is given on earth, but to priests *also* in heaven . . .
> single rulers have single provinces, and single kings single kingdoms, but
> Peter, as in the plenitude so in the extent of his power, is pre-eminent
> over all, since he is the vicar of him whose is the earth and all that dwell
> therein.

Thus, though the pope might in large degree permit the independent exercise of their power by secular rulers, this did not mean
their power itself was independent.

> The pope is accustomed to exercise the office of secular power some-
> times and in some things through himself, and sometimes and in some
> things through others.

Innocent's claims for the papacy to political as well as, or rather as part of, spiritual authority, were clearly asserted and far-reaching.

His clarity of thought and expression were those of a lawyer. He saw where ultimate authority must lie, because in a truly Christian society all must be bent to one end. But he saw also the necessity to maintain different authorities in the free exercise of their appropriate jurisdictions. So his uncompromising assertion of papal supremacy was tempered by a wise understanding that the princes of this world had their own proper tasks to perform. He could not always restrain the interfering enthusiasm of servants who were inspired by the same ideals as he, but who comprehended the realities of political situations with less charity. Nevertheless, he always endeavoured to. His statesmanlike qualities were the key to his successes.

In 1198, when Innocent became pope, the affairs of the Roman Church were in a critical way. The question of the relations between papacy and empire was more pressing than ever. The power of Barbarossa's family, the Hohenstaufen, had grown. Henry VI, king of Sicily as well as of Germany and Lombardy, had been the most formidable emperor men could remember. He was dead, but if his dominions should remain intact, the pope in Italy would hardly be more than the creature of his successor. Of less urgent immediacy but of even more serious import, there were signs abroad that many were beginning not just to question the political authority of the Roman Church, but were turning away from it in spirit. Criticism of the lax morals and avarice of the clergy was general, and in many parts heretical sects had appeared: in southern France especially heresy was spreading rapidly. The local ecclesiastical authorities appeared unable to cope with the situation. Meanwhile, and never far from the foreground in Innocent's mind, the shame of the infidel possession of Jerusalem endured for all to see.

At the beginning of his pontificate the problem of the empire was the most urgent: it remained pressing almost to the end. When Henry VI died in 1197 his son Frederick was less than three years old. The one thing which Innocent's nonagenarian predecessor, Celestine III, had steadily refused to the all-powerful emperor was to recognize this child as emperor-elect. When Henry died unexpectedly, Frederick's succession, which it had seemed the obstinacy of an aged man could not seriously threaten, was at once called in question. All over Italy there were risings against Henry's late lieutenants. The lords of Germany in Henry's lifetime had sworn that they would have Frederick as their King, but this was no moment to stand on promises in favour of a three-year-old. The empire needed a ruler. One group, which included the majority of the great lords and bishops, met at Mainz and elected Henry's brother, Philip of Swabia. Another group elected Otto of Brunswick, son of the Welf prince Henry the Lion of Saxony, and managed to have him crowned at Aix. Both parties then appealed to Innocent for recognition of their candidate. Along with their claims he had to consider those of Frederick, who had been bequeathed to the care of the Holy See.

Three principles consistently guided Innocent in his handling of this situation and its drawn out and devious developments. Like Celestine before him, he saw the maintenance of the elective principle in the succession to the empire as essential, to safeguard the papacy against the power of a hereditary ruler of north Italy. Secondly, the union of Sicily with the empire, encircling Rome, must be broken at all costs. Both these principles militated against the two Hohenstaufen candidates. Thirdly, given the elective principle, the pope must have the right to scrutinize the 'fitness' of an elected candidate to rule the empire, and if need be reject him. As Innocent phrased it, this was a claim that the pope must take account of the personal character of the man whom, at the imperial coronation, he would consecrate as the protector and advocate of the church. But fitness for such an office could not be determined solely by moral qualities. No man would be a 'fit' protector and advocate for the church, in practice, unless he had the power and resource to engage the respect and obedience of his subjects.

As events worked out, these principles led Innocent to support in turn each of the three candidates. His original predilection, other things being equal, was for Otto, but he needed to be sure before he committed himself that Otto could make himself an

effective force in Germany. By 1204 Otto's cause was beginning
to fail, and the Pope's choice to veer in favour of Philip. In 1206
Innocent had virtually admitted his claims. The critical decision
seemed to have been taken; but Philip was murdered in 1208 by
a personal enemy, and Otto of Brunswick became the man of the
moment overnight. The Pope bent all his efforts to secure an
undisputed election. Otto was crowned a second time at Aix, and
recognized as emperor-elect.

This proved only the beginning of another chapter in the long
family feud of Welf and Hohenstaufen. As long as Frederick
remained alive, growing to manhood in Sicily, Otto knew that
any who opposed him could find a leader to whom to rally. He
could not afford, therefore, to be weak in central Italy, or to
ignore the appeals of those opposed to Frederick in Sicily, who
assured him that 'none but the wearer of the emperor's crown
may reign by right in Sicily'. In 1210 Otto marched his armies
into southern Italy. A union of Sicily and the empire under the
Welfs was from the papal point of view a prospect no less disastrous than union under the Hohenstaufen. Innocent had no
choice but to turn at last to Frederick. Elected at Nuremberg by
a group of princes who were Innocent's allies, he left Sicily.
Evading Otto's Milanese allies by a hairsbreadth in Lombardy,
he arrived to be welcomed rapturously in south Germany, where
loyalty to his house was strong. A grim civil war seemed to be
preparing. Frederick sought the alliance of Philip of France to
counter Otto's long standing alliance with John of England.
Before the rivals came to grips, Otto's army and his power were
destroyed at Bouvines by the cavalry of Philip Augustus.

At the great Lateran council which had been summoned from
all over Christendom, Innocent in 1215 heard the claims of the
rivals for the empire and pronounced in favour of Frederick. The
decision was foregone: the manner in which it was taken, ho-
ever, was a startling and public demonstration of the final
authority of the Pope over the empire. Furthermore, Frederick
did not gain his diadem without making important concessions.
Before leaving Sicily he had crowned his infant son king, thus
formally separating the island from the lands he was setting out to

win. At Eger in 1213 he swore to abstain from any interference in the elections of bishops and abbots in Germany. He swore also to aid the church against heretics, and at Aix in 1215 he vowed to go on crusade. These pledges were the evidence of his 'fitness' as a candidate for the empire. As such, however, they were pledges only, their proofs as yet unseen. They barely concealed dangers for the future. An emperor whose infant son was king of Sicily might become a very formidable figure for a pope to deal with, especially, perhaps, if he had made himself the leader of a victorious crusade.

*

One of Frederick's promises of 1213 had been to aid the church against heretics. By that time the effort to scotch this cancer had turned into a crusade within Christendom. This is a measure of how serious a threat the spread of heresy presented at the time, in the Church's eyes.

The actual crusade was directed against the heretics of southern France. Heresy and the root causes which encouraged its growth were, however, much more generally disseminated. The wealth and moral laxity of the clergy were provoking widespread anti-clerical feeling, and the boundary between protest and revulsion was crossed easily. Especially among the laity in the towns, religious sentiment often sought expression beyond what the formal rites of the church afforded. Such feelings sometimes found their outlet in mass movements, tinged with apocalyptic hysteria, such as the unhappy children's 'crusade' of 1212 (which the church discountenanced). They found it also in heresies such as that of Peter Waldo, a rich merchant of Lyons, who, moved by a minstrel's tale, gave his all to the poor, to follow an apostolic life of preaching and utter poverty. That his teaching might be surer, he had two clerics translate the New Testament for him into his native tongue. His denial of the powers of the priesthood brought inevitable condemnation on himself and his followers. Unfortunately this did not stop men reading and ruminating on his New Testament, nor his sect from multiplying.

The Cathar (or Albigensian) heresy was far further removed

from orthodox Christianity than that of Peter Waldo. Cathar doctrines were a form of the dualist religion, a blend of Christianity, Zoroastrianism, and other eastern creeds, which had been preached by Manes in the Roman empire in the second century A.D. The Cathars believed there were two co-equal universal powers: Jehovah, Lord of light, beneficent, the ruler of the realm of pure spirit; and Lucifer, author and Lord of the material world, of the vale of tears and darkness, who had imprisoned in the cloying bodies of men the souls of fallen angels. It was to redeem the souls of men, to show them the way back to the light, that Christ came. But for the Cathar, in contrast to Christian teaching, there was no true incarnation. Christ was pure spirit, his body a phantom body, bearing which the Virgin could have endured no travail. The way that Christ pointed to – his gospel – led not to the resurrection but to the total liberation of free spirit from the material world, born of flesh by bodily concupiscence.

From these beliefs stemmed the extreme asceticism of the Cathars. Their creed forbade them to take life of any sort, to eat any flesh, or even eggs, the product of bodily intercourse. It also forbade sexual union: marriage they saw as the ultimate compromise with the body, and the pregnant woman was their *pariah*. There were two classes in their sect, *Perfecti* and *credentes*: only the former sought to completely fulfil on earth these ascetic teachings. The *Perfecti*, who acted as the priests, were admitted to their status by a rite called the *consolamentum*. Without this rite none could enter the life of the spirit; the *credentes* took it, but usually only on their deathbed. In the meantime they enjoyed a wide latitude in their manner of life (especially, the Catholics averred, in the matter of sexuality).

The strength and appeal of the Cathar religion lay in the austere life of the *Perfecti*. Living and working among the people as they did, their purity of life contrasted glaringly with the laxity of many of the orthodox clergy. The spread of the heresy was facilitated by increasing commercial activity, and the western Cathars even managed to establish contact with dualist churches in the east. In Languedoc and in many towns in Italy, as Milan, Florence, and Viterbo, they flourished openly, in other places under cover. In southern France their heresy permeated the whole of society in its length and breadth.

There were many reasons for its fertility there (though in such a matter a complete explanation is of course impossible). The Catholic church in Languedoc was poor, provincial, and lax; its hierarchy worldly and dominated by the kinsmen of local aristocrats. Anticlericalism was a strong force, fanned by the worship of woman which the troubadours cultivated through a parody of religion, half serious, half literary bravado. The secular authorities were almost as weak as the ecclesiastical. The counts of Toulouse boasted vast domains, but only an ineffective authority over the rich bourgeois and the petty nobility, for whom heresy was often simply an excuse for refusing tithes and plundering church lands. The forces of order and authority which should have held heresy in check were here weak to an exceptional degree. Heresy flourished cheek by jowl with orthodoxy, among the high born and lettered as well as the common folk, in a way it could nowhere else.

'How can we expel the Perfect, for all the good reasons you have against them? We were brought up with them and we count our relatives among them – and we see that they live honourably.' These words, spoken by a southern knight to Bishop Fulk of Toulouse, explain admirably the special problem which the extirpation of heresy in Languedoc presented. Thirty years before Innocent III became pope, the heretics had been holding councils in public, and they could worst the native Catholic clergy in argument. By Innocent's time their religion was too well embedded for the ministrations of his Cistercian legates to make much impact. The scholars trained to out-argue the Cathars by Diego of Osma and Dominic (from whom the Dominican order took its origin) were too few to be effective. Force, and external force at that, seemed to offer the only solution.

Innocent had more or less determined on this course even before the murder of his legate, Peter of Castelnau, in Provence in 1208. His bull of 1209 gave an expedition against the Cathars the full legal and spiritual status of a crusade. The same remission of sins was promised to those who would serve in Languedoc for forty days as to those who went to Jerusalem. More important still, they were promised the lordship of the lands they should win from the heretics, in the same way as if these had been infidels.

This last concession was to give the crusade a bent which was not part of Innocent's original intention. To Simon de Montfort, the veteran of the Holy Land who gradually emerged as the crusaders' leader, and to the papal legates on the spot, it was clear that the southern lords would never eradicate on their own a heresy which permeated the whole society in which they had been brought up. Only their total replacement by the crusaders from northern France could achieve the end, and by means of a war which made no nice distinction between heretic and catholic among the southerners. The great victory of the crusaders at Muret in 1213 was not a victory of Catholic over Cathar, but of north over south. Its outcome was not the extirpation of heresy (that was only achieved later, by the inquisition, which was organized for this very purpose in 1233). It was the award of the greater part of the lands of the county of Toulouse to Simon de Montfort, at the Lateran council. His family in the end failed to hold them in face of the southerners' *revanche*: they passed to St Louis' brother, Alphonse of Poitiers, and when he died childless passed to the crown of France.

Nevertheless, the outcome of the crusade was a triumph for Innocent, though not quite the one he had wished for. The judgement in Simon's favour at the Lateran council was another visible sign, like the judgement between Frederick and Otto, that the authority of the Holy See was upheld in all lands and in all matters. Philip Augustus, the overlord in name of the lands Simon won, did not question the Pope's award of the property of one group of his subjects to another, and he accepted Simon's homage.

It was a triumph, however, which had drawbacks. A war which had been preached as a crusade had culminated in the disinheriting of many faithful and orthodox Catholics. This tarnished seriously the reputation of crusading. It also lent colour to the delusive belief that the tremendous forces which crusading had channelled could be profitably unleashed for purposes other than the defence of the Holy Sepulchre. Here there was danger for the moral prestige of the Roman church which directed the crusade, as the angry cry of one southern troubadour testifies: 'God will be revenged on those whose rapacity has cut the roads and closed the ports which lead to Acre and Syria.' As in the matter of the empire, so in that of the Cathars, Innocent sought a way and found one, but it was not the best way.

One sees something of the same sort in his handling of other affairs too. When the news of the storming of Constantinople by the Latins reached him he was aghast. For six years he had been negotiating with the Greek emperor for peaceful union of the churches. But he soon accepted the events which had forestalled him, and set hopefully about the hopeless task of reconciling the Greek clergy of the conquered lands to Latin supremacy. His long struggle to force King John of England to accept the archbishop of Canterbury he had nominated, Stephen Langton, was spectacularly successful, in that John not only gave way but made England a fief of the papacy. But the barons and churchmen who had looked to Innocent for support in their struggle with a tyrannous king had to be left high and dry. Up and down Christendom, Innocent interfered fearlessly and unhesitatingly in politics and private lives, and he hardly ever failed absolutely in his objectives. Unfortunately his success was often only partial, or gained at the cost of principles. There was too much truth in the remark of a Byzantine visitor to Rome: 'He is the successor not of Peter, but of Constantine.' He held in his hands all the threads of European policy: his handling of them was somewhat too deft for a priest's.

*

The best index of Innocent's overall achievement is the activity of the fourth Lateran council, which met at Rome in 1215, at the end of his pontificate. The chroniclers were awed by the size of the assembly and the distinction of its members. Every province of the western church was represented, and every religious order: as also the Latin patriarchs of Constantinople, Jerusalem, and Antioch, and the churches of Armenia and Bulgaria. The western emperor, the emperor of Constantinople, and the kings of France, England, Jerusalem, Hungary and Poland, all had proctors present to speak for them. Something like a representative parliament of all Christendom was brought together. In their presence the Pope presided, as the acknowledged director of the affairs, spiritual and temporal, of Christian society. He defined doctrine, upholding Peter Lombard's teaching on the Trinity against that of Abbot Joachim of Flora. He gave judgement between the rival candidates for the empire; concerning Simon de Montfort's rights in the county of Toulouse; between King John and his dissident barons. Here was the papal plenitude of power in visible action.

Even more impressive in the long run were the measures taken at the council for the reform of the Church. They show that Innocent had gauged correctly the most serious dangers confronting her, and taken their measure. The decrees condemning drunkenness among the clergy, against their feasting, hawking, and dancing, living in concubinage and advancing their children in the same cathedral chapter as themselves, give some impression of what he was up against. His solutions can be seen in decrees insisting on the duty of bishops to scrutinize the fitness of candidates for ordination, on the appointment in every cathedral church of a master trained in theology to educate the clergy, on the holding of regular synods in every metropolitan see. Regular procedures for the delation of heretics were laid down. The obligations of the laity, to confess, to pay tithes, to aid the ecclesiastical authorities, were clarified and defined. All the resources of method and education were combined with those of tradition and faith in a great, planned scheme to raise standards of Christian living and Christian ministry.

The final matter adumbrated before the council was the project for a new crusade to the Holy Land. At the end Innocent was still looking forward to the next endeavour. He did not live to see the fifth crusade founder in the marshes of the Nile delta. He died in 1216, leaving a record behind him of achievement which, whether one looks at it in terms of political or of spiritual striving, is immensely impressive. The fourth Lateran council, at which he addressed Christendom as its spiritual father and the acknowledged director of its affairs, was the high water mark of universal 'Romanism' in the Middle Ages.

Chance had played its part in his successes. In the empire the early death of Henry VI, and in England the stresses of internal politics played into his hands. In Greece and in Languedoc he made the most of the victories of men whose motives he did not approve. But there were also far deeper reasons for the triumphs of the Roman Church in his time. They rested, in the final analysis, on the unity of powerful religious faith in the west, Cathars notwithstanding, buttressed by the Church's near monopoly of learning. This was why the Church had been able to bend the questioning intellectual spirit of the schools and universities to her service; so that Innocent could take Peter Lombard as his guide to orthodoxy. This was also what had enabled the papacy to knit together the whole body of the clergy of the Roman obedience through the most effective administrative system that the Europe of Innocent's day knew. In consequence, the church he governed really did constitute, in Latin Christendom, a universal terrestrial power.

Within the empire, and in the kingdoms of France and England which were growing to new strength, papal government of the Church and churchmen was an active force. The increasing circulation of money which commerce was encouraging made it now possible for the papacy to tap the very considerable wealth of the Church in provinces far distant from Rome. The material resources needed to make papal lordship of the 'Patrimony of Peter' in central Italy effective were coming to hand. Security in this Italian homeland was essential to the papacy, the key to the maintenance of her political independence. Thus even money and mercenary arms were directed to the service of the Church's needs.

In Innocent III's day the Church proved herself able to contain the dynamic forces, material, spiritual, and intellectual, which were at work in the European society of Christendom, reshaping men's lives and outlook. Her great problem for the future was to contain them still, as they continued to develop of their own impetus.

SECTION THREE

c. 1216 – c. 1330

The Struggle of the Roman Church to
Maintain Her Universal Authority in a
Changing World.

11

The Universities and the Friars:
St Thomas, St Francis and Abbot Joachim*

THE century which followed the death of Innocent III (1216) saw
the Roman Church battling to maintain that leadership in western
Christendom which in his day she had achieved. At the political
level fresh and formidable dangers threatened her, and she was
drawn into new diplomatic entanglements. But what happened
in the end might have been less decisive, if deeper matters than
politics had not been involved too. The triumphs of the papacy
in Innocent's time had been made possible by the Church's ability
to contain and control new forces. As the thirteenth century progressed, these forces, nourished by inner dynamism, became
much less easy to contain or control. In the fields of intellectual
inquiry and of religious feeling this was particularly evident.

Here developments found tangible expression in two institutions new to Christendom, and whose vitality was closely interwoven with the life of the Church herself: the universities, and
the mendicant religious orders. The earliest universities emerged
as the result of the formalization of the structure of study in those
schools whose renown and continuous tradition of learning set
them apart, Paris and Oxford, Bologna and Salerno. Literally,
all the word 'university' implied originally was recognition of the
corporate existence of a group of scholars, capable of communal
action. The outward sign of such a body's existence was a school
in which instruction was offered to students, no matter where they
came from, and whose masters' licence to teach a subject (the
degree) would be accepted by any other school, anywhere in
Christendom. This last factor became in time the decisive one.

*I must acknowledge the influence on the views expressed in this chapter
of Emile Gebhardt's *Mystics & Heretics in Italy* (English translation, by
E. M. Hulme, Allen & Unwin, 1922).

Thus popes and kings came to found universities, by endowing their degrees by *fiat* with the same universal standing which the first universities had won by their fame alone.

These privileges made the great universities immensely powerful. Students came to them from near and far, because they knew that the degree they could obtain would be serviceable anywhere. The masters who taught in them, for the same reason, were not all locally recruited. They represented a cross section of the finest minds not just of one province or kingdom but of all Europe. Learned institutions organized on this international basis do not flourish without freedom of thought. This created a problem for the Roman Church, in its role of definitor of orthodoxy. As such, it could not afford to allow unlimited latitude of opinion in institutions which left the imprint of their teaching on every grade of the clerical body. On the other hand, to challenge the considered views of a body of scholars with the international reputation of, say, the Paris theologians, would be to imperil Rome's prestige among the whole educated priesthood.

The friars presented a different, but not wholly dissimilar problem. The two most important mendicant orders were the Dominicans and the Franciscans. The inspiration which fired Dominic to found his order was his wish to train a body of educated preachers, dedicated to holy living, who could combat the arguments and example of the Cathar *Perfecti*. This object demanded a standard of purity and abnegation in living which till Dominic's day was seldom found outside the monasteries, but combined with a freedom of movement denied to the cloistered monk. The origins of Francis's order were very different, and of that matter more will have to be said shortly. But as time passed the two orders drew steadily closer in their standards and aims, adapting the monks' vows of poverty, chastity and obedience to the vocation of the vagrant preacher.

Like the Cistercian monks before them, the mendicant orders were subject directly to the pope. The democratic framework of their general chapters was again similar to that of the Cistercian order. In these assemblies, to which each province in which their orders worked sent representatives, the ministers general (prime ministers as it were of each order) were elected, and all important questions concerning their organization, government, and activities were reviewed. At the local level, provincial chapters and provincial ministers reproduced the system in microcosm. The complete independence of the mendicants from the ordinary diocesan and metropolitan authorities was upheld by the papacy. Papal authority also gave friars studying in the universities special advantages. Their potential as an elite of educated preachers had not been missed.

In the war which the decrees of the Lateran council of 1215 had declared upon laxity of Christian living, the friars made themselves serviceable as the spearhead troops of reform. But their services were, nevertheless, potentially dangerous both to themselves and their papal masters. Because they were esteemed for their holiness, there were many who preferred to come to them rather than to the parish priest, to be shriven or married or to bury their kindred. This intrusion into the ordered pastoral relations of parish and diocesan life naturally roused the resentment of the 'secular' clergy (as the ordinary pastoral clergy were called), especially when thereby they lost fees paid, for example, for burials. In the universities, the special privileges of the friars were similarly resented by the 'secular' masters. The friars' privileges were the fruit of their orders' special and intimate relation with the Roman Church. For its governors, the problem was to prevent resentment of the friars' privileges leading to resentment against the authority which had granted them. They had to be careful, too, as to how they tried to circumvent this. The friars had good grounds for looking on themselves as an elite: the Roman Church must not appear to condone laxity.

Formal organization, on democratic lines, gave both the mendicants and the universities an independence which made them formidable. The currents of thought which flourished in the security of these *milieus* were more formidable still. To illustrate what is meant here I have chosen two examples: the history of the development of Aristotelian studies in the universities, and the development of the order of St Francis in the hundred years following his death. Both reflect developments of great importance in religious and cultural history.

*

In the twelfth century the work of Aristotle had been known in the west chiefly through Boethius' translations of his treatises on logic. Long before A.D. 1200 more regular contacts with the Greek and Islamic worlds, in Spain, Sicily and as a result of the crusades, were attracting attention to a much larger number of his works, especially those on natural history and philosophy. In the *Physics* and other treatises, Aristotle had sought to explain comprehensively the workings of the natural universe, by conclusions based ultimately on actual observation of what happened in it. The astonished west was thus brought face to face with an account of the workings of nature that was far more impressive than any it had previously heard of, and to whose soundness the evidence of the senses seemed to bear witness. It was, in addition, the construct of a pagan Greek philosopher, who had lived long before Christ's coming, and which had been worked out without any apparent reference to divine revelation.

The impact of this new knowledge on the scholarly world of the west was tremendous. Aristotle was to leave the mark of his pre-eminent authority on all philosophic and scientific inquiry for the rest of the Middle Ages. But there was a great deal in Aristotle which did not square easily with accepted Christian teaching: for instance, his claims for natural wisdom as the highest goal of human activity, his defence of the active as against the contemplative life. Indeed, his whole central conception of nature as an intrinsic force working towards its own more perfect self-expression could be seen as a challenge to Christian doctrines of the creation and of original sin. The commentaries on Aristotle of Arabic philosophers, such as Avicenna and Averroës, raised further disturbing issues. It was from Arabic translations that scholars in Sicily and Spain, and especially at Toledo, first made available to the west Latin versions of Aristotle's works on natural philosophy.

Aristotle's teachings were often as difficult to square with the

Koran as with the Bible. Averroës found his way round this problem by the doctrine of the 'double truth'. This asserted the absolute independence of truths established by natural reason, and those established by divine revelation. Being wholly independent, they might be wholly incompatible, and yet remain true, simultaneously, by their own incompatible standards. The dangers of such a doctrine were obvious. It gave the heterodox free licence to go about their lethal business of unhinging the faith of true believers, while preserving a nominal, non-rational orthodoxy. Even in the cultivated and tolerant court of the Spanish caliphs, Averroës found himself denounced by religious authority. The scholars of Paris who followed his teaching, such as Siger of Brabant and Boethius of Dacia, suffered likewise. But it was one thing to silence individual teachers, quite another to prevent others from drawing, from the same works of Aristotle and his commentators, the same dangerous conclusions. It was impossible to stop men reading Aristotle because his words had the ring of truth.

Between the years 1268 and 1272 the Dominican scholar, Thomas Aquinas, was debating fiercely in the Paris schools with Siger of Brabant. Thomas it was who succeeded ultimately in achieving a reconciliation of Aristotelian philosophy with the traditional Augustinian theology of the schools. His synthesis completely rejected the supposed incompatibility between reason and revelation: they pointed, he believed, in different ways to the same end. Aristotle's high opinion of natural wisdom and the social good which it prompts men to seek, so Thomas claimed, do not challenge Christian doctrines of original sin: 'Divine grace does not eradicate human nature, it perfects it.' The body is not the prison of the human soul, but the vehicle through which it achieves self-expression. Only through the self-awareness which it acquires through the body and through social contact can the soul reach out towards the higher goals that its creator has posited for it. The social well-being of men in this world and their salvation are not two separate ends, but different aspects of the same great purpose, for which the creator brought men into existence.

For Aquinas there was again no tension between the Christian idea of creation, and Aristotle's analysis of nature in terms of a chain of interacting, rational causes. Causation must have a beginning, for an infinite regress is unthinkable: ultimately it implies a first cause, an 'unmoved prime mover'. We may learn his ways either by contemplation of nature, or by listening to the inspired word of his prophets; his ways themselves, however, do not differ. Where he found reason and revelation in apparent contradition, St Thomas's answer was to look harder at the question, not to reject the one or the other. There was nothing cramping for Aquinas about orthodoxy.

This led St Thomas to some very striking and important conclusions. These are clearest in his social and political thinking, in which he drew largely on Aristotle's *Politics*. Taking as his starting point Aristotle's famous definition, 'man is a political animal', he made a clean break with the traditional view which regarded the purpose of secular political authority as restrictive, to curb the sinful tendencies of man's fallen nature. Government, whose end is the promotion of social well-being, he saw as something good of itself, whose valid purpose remained even where the rulers were infidels. This emphasis on man's social nature and social activity provided a basis of justification for the choice of the active life, of law, or politics, or simply of marriage and bringing up a family, in preference to the withdrawal of the cloister. In essence, St Thomas's was a liberal and optimistic teaching, a great triumph for breadth of outlook in Christianity. It permitted much more than a reconciliation of Aristotle's thought with traditional theology, a reconciliation of Christian living with an immensely varied series of priorities in the everyday life of the human world.

What Aquinas wrote was, in time, to modify profoundly the outlook of the Roman Church. Yet the immediate impact of his teaching spelt difficulties for it. Nothing that he taught subtracted from the all-embracing demands of Christian idealism, but these did appear less clear-cut in the light of his teaching. What, for instance, was the crusader to conclude from his statement that the government of infidel rulers has a lawful and justified purpose? For those contemporarily plunged into the problems of governing the Roman Church, which had committed itself to serious claims on men's political as well as their spiritual allegiance, the very breadth of such views as his could have inconvenient implications. Besides, Aquinas's reconcilation of faith with rational speculation, in making freedom of thought more respectable, made the latter harder to restrain. There were still plenty more dangerous and heterodox ideas which could be developed through the study of Aristotle.

Heterodoxy apart, the study of Aristotle's scientific writings encouraged interest in the natural world pursued for its own sake. Often, it is true, it was the spurious matter in Aristotle (and still more in the Arabic writers) which caught men's attention most. Thus Albertus Magnus, Aquinas's master, gave Aristotle as the authority for the extraordinary virtues he attributed to precious stones; to the agate which will drive away melancholy and phantoms; to the emerald which is a touchstone of chastity. But if their authorities sometimes overawed and sometimes misled the learned, they opened their eyes also to new dimensions of the world about them. The same motives, and the study of the same writers, promoted Roger Bacon's interest in mathematics and optics and Albertus's interest in the magical properties of gems. The study of Aristotle and the Arabic authors concentrated more attention on the problems of human and natural conditions, and so encouraged inquiry pursued independent of theological preoccupations. An assumed preoccupation with theology had been what in the past had often enabled the Church to channel and control speculation in the schools. Without it, control was becoming much harder to maintain.

*

Between the achievement of St Thomas and that of St Francis there is a curious parallelism. St Thomas, with a finer mind than Siger of Brabant and a surer insight into the bearing of Aristotle's writings, reconciled with faith views which from Siger's mouth sounded at once heretical and terribly convincing. Francis's message was not very different from that of another heretic, Peter Waldo, but his Christian humility was more orthodox, and he brought into the fold the same sort of spirits that Peter had led out of it.

Francis was born (*c.* 1181) of the same milieu as Peter Waldo, the merchant of Lyons: his father was a rich merchant of Assisi. As a gay young man who rode to the wars Francis told his friends that he would one day be a great baron: but an inner voice spoke to him of another vocation. By 1208 he had abandoned family and riches for a life of utter poverty, among the lepers and beggars. The full nature of his mission was revealed to him in the next year, as he prayed one day in the little church, the Portiuncula, at the gate of Assisi, and heard the words of Matthew's gospel:

> Everywhere on your road preach and say, the kingdom of God is at hand. . . . Carry neither gold nor silver, nor money in your girdle, nor two coats, nor sandals, nor staff: for the workman is worthy of his hire.

This was the basis for the simple rule of life which in 1210 Innocent III sanctioned for the little band of disciples which Francis had gathered about him. Twelve years later, their example of apostolic observance and simple Christian devotion had swelled this group into a great order. In 1223 Pope Honorius III approved a new, expanded rule, which the complexities of organizing such a large body of individuals made necessary. By this time the efforts and inspiration of the Franciscans were beginning to be felt all through Christian Europe.

The impact of Francis's message came largely from its optimism and its sheer simplicity. Uncomplicated by theology, his appeal was direct to the soul of the individual, to reach out towards its maker in hope and gratitude. He insisted that all of his order should bear a cheerful face to the world, 'rejoicing in the Lord' in all seasons and places. Excessive abstinence he condemned: 'Each man ought to take the nourishment that is necessary to him, in order that the body may render true and loyal service to the spirit.' Here Francis's teaching has the same direction as that of St Thomas: men must take note of the world around them, which is the expression not of the creator's will only, but of his munificence too. Here also is the authentic moral behind the stories of Francis preaching to the birds, and hearing in the voices of nature angelic music (stories which at face value have often the seeming of sentimental fiction). They express the joy of one who felt God's work in all around him, and was grateful for the simple privilege of living.

By establishing an organization of Tertiaries, persons following secular lives who had promised to keep in their hearts the principles of Francis's apostolic rule, the Franciscans kept direct contact with a great multitude of ordinary people who had been stirred by his message of hope and joy. For those in the order, however, there was another side to the rule, poverty. To this the founder attached first importance. Poverty, he believed, was the true bride of Christ. His own marriage to Lady Poverty, 'who had been despised since the death of her first bridegroom,' was immortalized by Giotto. 'O most poor Jesus,' Francis prayed,

grant me the treasure of sublime poverty: permit the distinctive sign of our order to be that it does not possess anything of its own beneath the sun, for the glory of your name, and that it have no other patrimony than begging.

The rule was in this matter very strict. The Franciscans might possess neither money nor goods, not even books. Their habits were coarse and simple, and sandals were forbidden them. The complete faith in God's bounty which these rules reflect was one reason why the first Franciscans impressed men so deeply. Their poverty stood out in glaring contrast to the wealth of the beneficed clergy, of whose lax morals so many complained. The belief that a life of devotion was inseparable from austerity was one deeply and generally held, as was inevitable in an age whose religious attitudes had been deeply influenced by monastic ideals. As the most perfect practitioners of the ungentle virtues, the Franciscans were for a time the wonder of the world. 'This order,' wrote Jacques de Vitry, summing up their early impact,

has revived religion in the eventide of a world whose sun is setting, and which is threatened by the coming of the son of perdition, that it may have new champions in the perilous days of Antichrist.

If their perfection in poverty was the key to their success, it raised problems, both for the Franciscans themselves and for the

Church they served. Their way of life was, in itself, an implied reproof of contemporary clerical standards, and others than Francis did not hesitate to make the reproof vocal. The fierce denunciations by his disciple, St Anthony of Padua, were inspired by the same revulsion at the corruptions of the Church militant which had driven many into heresy: 'Carmel is invaded by the desert, the clergy bear no fruit, only the lay are faithful.' He pictured the limbs of wicked prelates, 'fatted kine' hanging in the smoke of hell, 'the place of anathema, of misery, of pain ineffable.' Angry men of God had said this sort of thing before, but it naturally roused the hostility of those criticized. It threw into relief, moreover, the special position of the Franciscans, their separation from the ordinary clergy. Their organization and their wandering ways were making of them almost a rival priesthood.

Once they began to acquire institutional identity, new needs began to become apparent among the Franciscans themselves. As they grew in numbers, they began to build their own churches and convents, to house a host of preachers for whom casual hospitality could no longer be enough. Learned men were drawn into the order, who could not put their talents to full use without books at their disposal. In the new circumstances, to follow Francis's original injunctions to the letter ceased to be viable or appropriate. Above all, new conditions strained at the rule of absolute poverty, which for a religious order organized on the grand scale was impossible of obedience. The saving regulation, which permitted friars the use only, not the possession, of goods held in trust for them by friends, became more and more clearly a convenient fiction. But the rule of poverty was the driving force of Franciscan inspiration, the dominant theme of their growing mythology. Ugly tensions began to arise between those who saw the need to adjust to new conditions (the party in the order known as the 'conventuals'), and those committed to upholding the absolute purity of Francis's personal tradition (the 'spiritual' Franciscans).

The struggles of these two parties in the order, by the end of the thirteenth century, were beginning to involve the whole western Church. Because it was the popes' bulls that softened the

rigour of the rule, Rome was as often the target of the anger of
the 'spiritual' party as their weaker (and often wiser) brethren. In
the end it was the spirituals who lost out. In 1260 the Constitu-
tions of St Bonaventura, the great theologian who was then
minister general, overhauled the administrative framework of the
order, in order to adapt its energies to new conditions. From this
time on, the complaints of the spirituals became more querulous
as they found it steadily harder to give legitimate expression to
their ideals. In the end their fate was sealed by two bulls of John
XXII. The first, *Gloriosam Ecclesiam* (1317), condemned as
heretical the extremists who urged the literal observance of
Francis's earliest rule, without addition. The second, *Cum inter
nonullos* (1323), stamped as heresy the cherished Franciscan belief
that Christ and his disciples had held no possessions of any kind.
The first passed a sentence, which was bound sooner or later to
fall on those whose chief pride was in their patched habits and
fulmination against their brethren. The second, striking at a
deeply held tenet, very nearly precipitated the whole order into
schism. Before William of Ockham, the last of the Franciscan
leaders who then broke with Rome, was finally reconciled, great
damage had been done to the prestige and the unity of the Church.

*

The spiritual Franciscans might not have fared so ill if their party
had not become tainted with heterodoxy from a quarter of which
Francis knew nothing. Abbot Joachim of Flora (*c.* 1145–1202)
was a native of Calabria in southern Italy. Fate made him a·Cis-
tercian monk, but his nature was a hermit's: his fame was above
all as an inspired prophet. In long hours of retreat from the world,
spent ruminating on the writings of St John – the Revelations
and the fourth gospel – he believed he had penetrated to the secret
truths hidden under inspired writing. His discoveries led him
back to other books of the Bible, and to the teaching of the
Arabs: these confirmed that he had fathomed the mystery. The
Old Testament told the story of the first age of religion in this
world, the age of the Father: the New Testament of the beginning
of its second age, that of the Son: John foretold the third age, of

the Holy Ghost. Joachim believed this third age was close at hand. Moslem and Christian authority alike pointed to the dawn of a new era, beginning in the year 1260. There would be signs to herald the new order, tribulations and the reign of an Antichrist. The Church of the third age would be a new Church of 'monks', freed from the cares of the world, 'living by the spirit occupied in prayer and psalmody'. In their lives, the Kingdom of God on earth would be realized.

Joachim was too natural a mystic to be very precise in his description of things to come. For many in the early days of the Franciscans, however, it was all too easy to understand what this new church of 'monks' must mean. Gerard of Borgo's *Introduction to the Everlasting Gospel* (c. 1253) seems to have found in the contemporary scene almost every sign for which Joachim had bid men watch. His book and others like it gave Joachim a tremendous vogue. The safe passing of the year 1260 discredited only the more precise and extravagant of his would-be followers. With many of the spiritual Franciscans and a great number of ordinary people also, prophecies of very strange things in the near future had by then fastened themselves as firm beliefs. Among the spirituals a kind of sub-mythology began to grow picturing Francis's ministry as a sort of second advent, its detail distorted by current rancours. Thus in the works of the spirituals' leader, Angelo Clareno, Francis's vigil in the cave at Rieti becomes a version of the transfiguration of Scripture, in which his three disciples wake to hear him talking with Christ himself, and the thunder of the divine voice resounding with the words 'obey the rule to the letter, without amendment.' The extravagance of imagination, which stories such as this reflect, served as leaven to the spread of more important ideas, prevalent among the spiritual Franciscans, and coming to be accepted by others too.

The new kingdom of the Holy Ghost which Joachim foresaw was not to be a kingdom of this world, as men had known it hitherto. Joachim's prophecies turned men's eyes away from the terrestrial church over which the popes presided. So, in ways more subtle and serious, did St Thomas's justification of the active life for the true Christian, and Francis's call for spiritual revival at the individual level. There was more in these messages than the church of Innocent III could contain. A gap was beginning to appear between the organized institution which historians call the Church, and what contemporaries thought of as the life of the spirit. Such a gap was no doubt bound to become apparent in time. The exaggerated and sometimes hysterical beliefs prevalent in the period brought it out into the open and made it immediately obvious. This is one of the reasons why the Joachites and the spirituals were so important.

The strange events of 5 July 1294 show how strong an impact such currents of thought had made. On that day the cardinals, who had since April been debating who should succeed Nicholas IV, elected as pope Peter Murrone, an aged and unlettered hermit, who now took the name and title of Pope Celestine V. The moment was one when the Church's affairs seemed to be mounting towards crisis: Italy and the papal patrimony had been wasted by long wars: Acre, the last crusading stronghold in Syria, had fallen three years before: schism seemed to be impending in the order of St Francis. The cardinals were hard-headed men whose family rivalries had long held up any new papal election. Their choice was of course catastrophic: no man of Peter's antecedents could have hoped to guide the great administrative institution which Innocent III and his predecessors had created. In less than six months he had laid aside the tiara, a disappointment to himself and everyone else. But it is a measure of the impact of the visionary, apocalyptic spirit of which Joachism was an extreme manifestation that the cardinals should have hoped, by turning to a rude, unlettered and unwordly hermit – publicly renouncing the spirit if not the trappings of papal monarchy – to solve the problems of their Church. It is also a sign of the growing force of new ideas as to what that Church ought to be.

12

The Struggle of the Popes and the
Hohenstaufen

IN Frederick II of Hohenstaufen, the emperor whom Innocent
III had raised and recognized at his Lateran council, the medieval
papacy faced the most formidable political adversary it ever
encountered. In terms of sheer territorial authority he was the
most powerful emperor the west had seen since the days of
antiquity. Besides Germany, Lombardy, and the Arelate* (the
three traditional imperial kingdoms), the Norman kingdom of
Sicily was his by inheritance. He had, it is true, promised to
relinquish this last inheritance to his son on becoming emperor,
but in 1220 he persuaded Pope Honorius III to assent to his continuing to rule the kingdom for his lifetime. His second marriage
(1225) to Yolande of Brienne brought him the title of king of
Jerusalem. Though there was no moment when his rule was
unchallenged through all these dominions, all at one time or
another felt the weight of his authority. Contemporaries, who
had heard strange things foretold for the near future, were
awestruck by the unprecedented extent of his empire. For the
chroniclers who recorded his deeds Frederick loomed larger than
life: he was *Stupor mundi*, the wonder of the world.

On a strict legal interpretation, Sicily was no part of the empire:
the two were quite separate. Frederick himself recognized this
formally in the agreement with Honorius for the continuance of
his rule there. But in his mind, and hence in the pattern of his
policies, Sicily, the land 'whose inheritance is more glorious in
our eyes than all our other possessions,' was the very heart of his
empire. Sicily was richer as well as more glorious. The taxes of
Sicily and the profits of royal monopolies, as of silk and corn,

*The old kingdom of Burgundy in the Rhone valley, the 'last vestige' of
the Carolingian Middle Kingdom, which became united to the German
empire in 1033.

paid for Frederick's endless wars: Moslem mercenaries from the south were the most trusted imperial soldiers. After the death in 1218 of his rival Otto, in Germany, and his own coronation in 1220, it was to Sicily that Frederick turned. He knew that the first step toward putting his empire on a sound basis must be the restoration there of the strong, authoritarian tradition of the Norman kings, which the revolts of German barons and Moslem emirs after his father's death had jeopardized. It took five years of hard fighting to reduce them. But from then on the Sicilian kingdom was the basis of all his dominion, for as long as he lived.

This was what marked off Frederick's empire from that of his predecessors. Under him, the emphasis shifted away from Germany, the traditional heart of the medieval empire, to Italy, its antique seat. Conscious exploitation also gave antique traditions a new vitality. Rome herself and the name 'Roman' acquired a significance they had not possessed in the days when Barbarossa wrote 'my army is the Roman army, my council its senate.' Frederick II's words have a different ring: 'We cannot bring honour to the empire, unless we honour too that city, whence we know the empire itself drew its origin.' When in 1237 he overthrew the Milanese at Cortenuova, and captured their *caroccio* (the emblematic war chariot round which the city's levies rallied) he sent this spoil to Rome, to prepare the Romans to accord him a triumph 'in the manner which the senate and people decreed for the Caesars of old for their victories.' It was as the successor of Julius and Augustus, the first and greatest of the Caesars, that court encomiasts hailed him. He himself prayed that his day 'should see the honour of the blood of Romulus revive,' with the restoration of the imperial peace which had made Rome famous in the days of Augustus.

Frederick's Sicilian upbringing gave a further dimension to this cult of antiquity. Until its conquest by the Arabs, Sicily had been part of the Greek empire, and the traditions of late Roman state administration had never been entirely forgotten there. The famous assizes of King Roger in the twelfth century were based on the Code of Justinian. An effective royal bureaucracy had under the Normans tightly controlled all the fiscal and judicial

aspects of government. The omnicompetence of royal administration in Sicily constituted a system of government radically
different from the feudal overlordship which was what Germany
and Lombardy understood by monarchical rule. There feudal
lords and communes exercised, on condition of loyalty and
service, most of what we would call public authority. The Germans and Lombards thought of the 'restoration' of empire in
terms of a power which could effectively guarantee the secure and
peaceful exercise of their rights of local autonomy. Frederick
thought of it in terms of the maintenance of peace and justice
through the direct activity of an imperial government modelled
on that of Sicily. This conception of empire, closer to the ideas
of antiquity than anything his predecessors had imagined, was
part of his inheritance from the Normans. Its spirit was sym-
bolized in Caesar's image on the famous gold coins Frederick
struck, the Augustales. The design was copied from the coin of
Augustus, the coin on which Christ himself gazed when he bid
men render unto Caesar the things that are Caesar's. This was
Frederick's answer to the Petrine commission of the popes.

To doctrines of the omnicompetence of secular sovereign
authority, certain further heritages to Frederick from Norman
Sicily lent a sinister tinge. Sicily was the meeting place where
three civilizations mingled, the western, the Greek, and the Arab:
and the courts of the Norman kings had been the centre of a truly
cosmopolitan culture. In Frederick court-culture found a new
patron of individual genius, who gathered about him men of real
distinction. Roffred of Benevento, whom he brought from
Bologna to teach law in the new university he founded at Naples,
was one of the most famous jurists of his day. Leonard Fibonacci
was probably the first westerner to fathom the mystery of the
alcataym – algebra. Michael Scot translated for Frederick
Averroës' *Treatise on the Soul* and Avicenna's *History of Animals*.
Modelling their style on that of the Provençal lyrists, the poets
of his court produced the first vernacular love poetry in Italian:
Piero della Vigna is said to have invented the sonnet form. The
chief interests of the artists of the court were thus secular, of the
scholars scientific. Frederick's own book, on the *Art of hunting*

with Hawks, shows he was himself a keen observer of nature, describing different species of bird accurately, noting their nesting habits and their migrations. But his strongest personal predilections were for the learning which the Arabs had made their own, the subjects on the fringe of science, metaphysics and astrology. These interests of his seemed to many to have carried him to the brink of scepticism, perhaps even to infidelity.

'Tell us,' Frederick told Michael Scot,

How many abysses there are and the names of the spirits that dwell therein . . . and whether one soul knows another in the next world, and whether one can return to this life and speak and show oneself.

In his 'Sicilian questions', he circularized the most famous scholars of the Arabic world with a series of dangerous queries: 'What are the proofs of the immortality of the soul?'; and 'How are the words of Mohammed explained: "the heart of the believer is between the two fingers of God"?' This prying after knowledge seemed unhealthy. The sceptical tone alarmed men, and Frederick's confidence in the wisdom of the Arabs suggested his heart was closer to the infidel than to Christ. His private life and conduct served to confirm their worst suspicions. When he travelled, Frederick took with him his menagerie of strange beasts (many of them presents from Arab potentates), and his harem of Saracen women. To astounded observers they revealed tastes for exotic knowledge and sinful delights. Such sights lent credence to stories of his maltreatment of successive Christian wives (which were probably true): and of horrific experiments he had undertaken – as of his having sealed a man to die in a barrel, and set men to watch and see if his soul would be perceived emerging when he died (these stories were certainly exaggerated). In a man of such strange ways, flagrantly carnal and a probable freethinker, it was not hard to see the lineaments of an enemy of Christ. *Stupor mundi* was a fitting name for Frederick: he struck men with awe and wonder, but he frightened them too much to acquiesce in his rule with equanimity.

*

Nevertheless, his reign commenced with fair auguries, and for a period continued well enough. In Germany in particular Frederick was successful to begin with. Sheer distance from his Sicilian headquarters and the difficulties of communication here dictated a policy of remote control. Frederick's two main concerns were to maintain internal peace, necessary if German affairs were not to distract him from more important matters, and to safeguard the succession in his own house. The best means to secure both these ends he saw as lying in alliance with the great territorial princes – the men whose discontents were more dangerous than those of any others, and whose control over imperial elections was growing into an established constitutional right. In return for their support he was prepared to be very generous. In 1220, as the price of their agreement to elect his son Henry king of the Romans and emperor designate, he conceded to the ecclesiastical princes (the archbishops of Mainz, Trier, and Cologne were the most important of them) virtually sovereign rights in the lands they held from the empire. Many of the lay princes won valuable concessions in 1227 for supporting Frederick's crusade: in 1232 they were granted virtually the same privileges as their ecclesiastical peers. Frederick was even prepared to sacrifice his own son, when in 1234 Henry's support of the Rhenish towns, which wished to be free of princely control, threatened the *entente* of empire and princes. For deposing one of his own sons, Frederick gained the election of another, Conrad, to succeed Henry. He thus preserved the *entente*, and the office of king in his house. But the weakness of his policy was revealed not very long after. He had given away so much to the princes that there was little left for them to gain by loyalty to him. But even then it needed the encouragement of Frederick's enemies elsewhere to persuade them to abandon him.

*

The issues of Frederick's reign were decided not in Germany but in Italy. Because he had determined to make Sicily the keystone in the arch of his empire, the establishment of imperial control in central Italy and Lombardy necessarily preceded any attempt to retrench the power of the German monarchy. In this Italian task, Frederick had to consider the attitudes of the Lombard city communes, and of the papacy. It was clear at the outset he would be likely to encounter troubles with both.

Memories of their struggles with Barbarossa had left the Lombard communes instinctively suspicious of imperial intervention in north Italy. Many of them had taken the opportunity which the struggles for the empire in Innocent III's time afforded to extend communal authority to the territory around their cities. Any reassertion of imperial rights was likely to threaten gains of this kind. The interregnum in the empire had seen also the revival of the old bitter enmities of town and town, as of Milan and Cremona. Those towns which had sided with Otto IV in 1212, like Milan, feared reasonably that Frederick would allow himself to be used as the instrument of rivals' revenge. Such towns were not likely to bow before Frederick without a struggle. Their prospects of success in resistance, however, must inevitably depend on whether the pope would again prove their ally, as he had in Barbarossa's day.

Frederick, indeed, could not even reach Lombardy, except by sea, without crossing lands in central Italy, in the March of Ancona and the duchy of Spoleto, which were part of the pope's patrimony. To permit him free passage through these territories would go clear against traditional policy and was not in the papal interest. If Frederick were to establish effective imperial rule in Lombardy, as he succeeded in doing in Sicily, the political independence of the Roman see, hemmed in between the northern and southern centres of imperial authority, would be a dead letter. This political independence seemed vital to the papacy, not just for the sake of traditional claims to lordship over the lands of the patrimony, but for the safe continuance of all the high endeavours in which it had been labouring for nearly two hundred years. The Bishops of Rome realized well enough that, reduced to the status of creatures of an Italian emperor, their commands would never be heeded outside Italy by churchmen or laymen in the way they had been in the past. From Frederick's point of view, any pope was almost certain to be intractable, since in their political relations with him rights to passage across or of lordship over land in Italy could not be separated from much larger issues.

Alone, neither the papacy nor the Lombards looked much of a match for Frederick, in a war fought on Italian soil: together they might be formidable, even to a Sicilian king. His object had to be to keep them apart; and if possible to manoeuvre the Pope into a position where it was hard for him to support the Lombards. His best chance of doing this was by making the causes which the papacy proclaimed as its own appear to be his also. Men had always recognized that, though in practice they were often at loggerheads, the relation between empire and papacy, as the two Roman, oecumenical powers in Christendom, ought to be one of recriprocal cooperation. One such cause paramount in many men's minds was the crusade. If Frederick could make that clearly his, it might become very hard for the Pope to oppose any step which he took ostensibly for its furtherance. If he could win back Jerusalem from the infidel by his arms, it might become very hard to oppose any step he took at all, especially against the Lombards. The Lombard cities were notorious centres of the Cathar and Waldensian heresies. If Frederick sought to achieve there what Innocent III had preached a crusade to achieve in Languedoc, how could Innocent's successor complain?

To pursue this line of policy, without letting its disingenuity show too openly, certainly demanded great diplomatic skill, but this Frederick possessed in a high degree. He had taken the cross formally in 1215: for ten years he managed to win the Pope's consent to postponing fulfilment of his crusader's vow until he had restored order, first in Germany, then in Sicily. In 1225, at last, he agreed that he would leave without fail for the Holy Land, if he were given two years to prepare the venture. It was in this year that his marriage to Yolande took place, which made him titular king of Jerusalem as her consort. Preparation for his expedition was the avowed object of the imperial diet summoned to Cremona in 1226. Its agenda neatly balanced the interests of church and empire: discussion of measures for the crusade; for the extirpation of heresy; for the restoration of imperial rights in Italy. It looks as if the first and second were really excuses for the third, and the plan to bring Lombardy into control under colour of putting the imperial dominions in order before the emperor's departure for Palestine.

The diet proved abortive, for Frederick had here over-reached himself. The summons of armed imperial vassals to Cremona in Lombardy, to a diet which would consider imperial rights in Italy, was a threat too clear for the Lombard cities. With Milan again at its head, the old Lombard league was renewed; and the cities closed the Alpine passes to Germans coming to the diet. Frederick's harsh treatment of churchmen in the recent process of restoring order in Sicily at the same time gave Pope Honorius just sufficient excuse to refuse to excommunicate the Lombards for obstructing a crusade until he was satisfied on other matters. In consequence, on the day in 1227 when Frederick should have left on crusade he was not ready. Honorius was dead, and his successor, Gregory IX, had made a clearer appreciation than he of the emperor's manoeuvres. He excommunicated Frederick for failing his solemn vow. The tables were thus turned: from now on the emperor's first duty as a Christian was to reconcile himself with the church. This must come before all else, extirpation of heresy or any crusade.

Frederick took the only course which offered any possibilities in the circumstances. On 28 June 1228, he left Brindisi for the Holy Land, the sentence of excommunication notwithstanding. After calling at Cyprus, he landed at Acre on 7 September. His crusade in the event saw no fighting. Frederick was counting on the difficulties of the Ayoubite sultan of Egypt, Al-Kamil, who controlled Jerusalem and was afraid of the power of the Khwarismian allies of his nephew An-Nasr, sultan of Damascus. The emperor was able to obtain from him, by negotiation and without a blow, a ten years truce for the Christians, and the return to them of Jerusalem with a corridor to the sea at Jaffa (but with free access for the Moslems to their holy places, the Dome of the Rock and the mosque of Asha). The emperor thus won back for the Christians their Holy City, for the last time. In its way this was a signal success, but the circumstances in which it was gained reduced its significance drastically in Christian eyes. The patriarch

of Jerusalem and the crusading orders would have nothing to do
with the excommunicate emperor's treaty, and the barons of Out-
remer made their final ratification of it conditional on the pope's.
It was accepted for no more than it really was, a successful
manoeuvre of imperial diplomacy, not a Christian triumph.

Frederick could not remain in the east to make more of his
venture. In his absence Apulia had been invaded by the forces of
the pope and other enemies, led by John of Brienne, Yolande's
father, whom he had forced to renounce his title of king of Jerusalem when he married her. The emperor's return soon saw these
enemies in disarray, and Gregory anxious for terms. The Pope
agreed now to ratify the treaty with Al-Kamil, and to lift the ban
of excommunication. But this was really only a breathing space.
Having lost the key moves in the diplomatic struggle in 1226–7,
Frederick had restored the *status quo ante*, or something like it.
He had won a success in the east, but one not sufficiently untar-
nished to shame the Pope into acquiescence in his objectives. He
was no longer excommunicate, but he had no longer a crusader's
vow, whose fulfilment could be made conditional on a free hand
to deal with the Lombards. Lombard promises of support for
his son Henry against his friends the princes in Germany were
soon to show that the problem of Lombardy could not be ignored.

*

At the diet of Mainz in 1235, the last he ever held in Germany,
Frederick made it clear he now intended to deal with this matter
once and for all. 'Pilgrims and beggars pass there freely, only I,
the emperor, may not cross my own dominions.' Thus he complained to the princes whom he summoned to follow him and
'restore the heritage of the empire' in Lombardy. His judgement
that Barbarossa's Treaty of Constance, the Magna Carta of the
Lombard towns, was null in view of their obstinate rebellions,
amounted to formal declaration of war. It was a war that was to
last longer than his lifetime. The Pope, unable to deflect him to
another crusade, had no alternative but to join his enemies. Into
the struggle the parties involved poured all their strength. Papal
and imperial propaganda lent it a hysteric quality of finality. The

Pope's encyclicals equated Frederick with the beast of the Apocalypse. Imperial proclamations portrayed him as the saviour emperor, destined to restore peace to Rome and Italy, and played on old prophecies that Antichrist would one day sit in Peter's chair. A populace in Italy which had been over-excited by the preaching of men inspired by the visions of such persons as Abbot Joachim, gave eager attention to such matter.

On paper the empire's resources were materially the greater. After his decisive victory over the Milanese in 1237 at Cortenuova, it looked indeed as if Frederick might achieve his ends swiftly by sheer force. But in 1239 he failed to take Brescia by siege, and, as so often happens, one reverse served to put heart into a crumbling resistance. Time was against the emperor. A long war was more than Frederick's Sicilian resources could take without strain, and after the Mongols' appearance on Germany's eastern border in 1241 he could look for no more help from that quarter. Lombardy remained a battle-ground, but he was forced more and more to rely on uncertain allies; the Cremonese, old enemies of Milan: Eccelino da Romano who pursued under cover of the emperor's war his family's struggle with the Estes: a whole 'Ghibelline' party whose resources were committed not for the sake of the empire but for their own private ends. Their support for Frederick committed their enemies the more firmly to the Pope's cause. The ruthless efficiency of Frederick's 'vicars-general' in Tuscany and the parts of Lombardy he controlled demonstrated that what Frederick called 'the restoration of the rule of Justice' was indeed what the Lombards called Sicilian tyranny. North Italy could see now what his idea of secular sovereignty meant in action, and it confirmed that the cities were fighting for their whole traditional manner of life.

At the head of the Ghibelline party, and appearing (when he did) surrounded by Moslem troops and with his harem and his menagerie, Frederick cut a strange figure of the Messiah emperor that he claimed to be, who called on men to 'take the bars from your doors, that the Caesar may come, at whose approach the evil spirits shall be silent, who have so long oppressed you.' By the time of his great defeat before Parma in 1248 he had taught men to fear this Caesar well enough, but not to love him. By then even his own intimates had sought to practise against his life, as did Piero della Vigna, and his personal physician who had sought to poison him. Time, fear and exhaustion with the struggle had told, to the point where his dreams for empire stood revealed for what they were, a Sicilian chimaera.

Because the popes had much less in the way of material resources, they had to commit themselves in the struggle even more desperately than the emperor. Where they and their allies could not face him in the field, they could labour almost everywhere for his ruin and could cut off his supporters from Christianity itself. In 1239 Gregory excommunicated Frederick anew: in 1240 he gave the war against him the status of a crusade. Both in Sicily and in Germany he, and Innocent IV who succeeded him, sought to stir up revolt. In Sicily they had not much success, but in Germany they were more fortunate. The Pope, with his power to uphold episcopal authority against troublesome clerics and to dispense laymen from obstacles to fruitful dynastic marriage, had more to offer the princes than Frederick, who had already given them nearly all he could give. In 1245, Innocent IV was ready for the final and drastic step. He had escaped from Italy to Lyons, and had summoned a council which could meet safely there, far from Frederick's armies. He had built up a sufficient party among the princes in Germany to be sure of the election of a papal anti-king. In the presence of the council and of Frederick's own envoy, the imperial chancellor Thaddeus of Suessa, he solemnly pronounced the emperor deposed. Shortly after, Henry Raspe of Thuringia was elected in his place by the Pope's party in Germany. Thus the war was extended through the whole of the imperial dominions. Three years after this, as has been told, Frederick's army was routed in Lombardy outside Parma. Two years after that Frederick died, at Fiorentino in central Italy, still fighting to the last.

The emperor's death did not end the war. In Germany there were still two kings; Conrad, his son, the elect of 1237, to whom he bequeathed all his empire; and William of Holland, who had been elected by Conrad's enemies when Henry Raspe died in 1247.

In Italy the Ghibellines of Lombardy and Tuscany had no cause to lay down their arms, for their enemies remained such as they had always been. In Sicily, once Frederick's bastard son Manfred had established himself as Conrad's lieutenant, a Hohenstaufen was still in control. After the experiences of the last generation's whole lifetime, the popes could not rest while this remained so. As long as the Hohenstaufen family had sons, they might claim Frederick's whole inheritance and even one day restore it. So even Conrad's death in 1254 could not put the Pope at ease, for Manfred made himself king of Sicily, and Conrad left a son in Germany, Conradin. Conradin was too young indeed for the electors to consider now for the empire, but he was of 'the race of vipers', and could one day aspire to his grandfather's heritage. (For family tree, see Appendix, p. 326.)

*

Once Conrad and William of Holland were both dead, Germany was left to sort out for herself the rivalry of William's two elected successors, Richard of Cornwall and Alfonso of Castile. In Italy everything came to depend on the popes' finding foreign aid in order to eliminate Manfred, who, with his father's Ghibelline supporters, was too powerful for them to cope with on their own. Alexander IV hoped for much from the English king, Henry III, who was attracted by the prospect of a Sicilian crown for his younger son Edmund. The revolt of the English barons in 1258 brought this scheme to nothing. The quest had to continue, while Manfred was securing himself still more firmly. At last Urban IV found in Charles, count of Anjou and brother of King Louis of France, an instrument more determined than Henry of England, if less wealthy.

In the final effort to bring its crusade against the Hohenstaufen to a victorious close, the papacy committed all its resources of material wealth and spiritual authority. By the threat to relieve the creditors of the Tuscan banks from their oaths of obligation, the Pope swung the greatest financial interest in Italy behind Charles. The commercial world at large was warned that support for Manfred would be to invite the ruin of any private fortune.

Such frantic efforts secured Charles troops and money, and a safe passage. He reached Rome in 1265 and was made senator. At Beneventum in 1266 he won a great victory over Manfred, who died in the rout of his own forces. Two years later the ill-starred attempt of Conradin, with a band of German followers, to revive the Hohenstaufen cause in Italy, was crushed at Tagliacozzo. Conradin, just sixteen years old, was taken and executed. This was the end at last of the popes' war against Frederick's family, and the beginning of the career of a new foreign dynasty in Sicily, the Angevins.

Tagliacozzo marked the end of an epoch: the slim chances for a restoration of Frederick's empire died with Conradin. Never again, in the Middle Ages, had the Church of Rome to face a rival in Christendom, whose oecumenical claims and political authority were comparable to Frederick's. Together with its allies, the papacy had won a great victory, but the results of the victory were not all to the papacy's interest. Short of resources, it had been forced to throw so much into gaining the immediate end as inevitably to sacrifice control of the ultimate outcome. The actual consequences at the end of the struggle can best be seen by an examination of what was left in Frederick's various dominions when the authority of the Hohenstaufen was gone.

In Germany the name of the empire remained, but not as a basis on which strong monarchy could be rebuilt. The successive bids of Frederick and the popes for princely favour had transferred the real authority to the electors. Frederick had hoped to make the princes' electoral power the buttress of hereditary succession by ensuring that an heir of the royal blood be always elected in his father's lifetime. But Innocent IV taught the princes that their interest did not lie in perpetuating the authority of a single family, which must undoubtedly one day seek to undermine the privileges that it had given away to gain their support. The consequence was that the thread of continuity in monarchical government, which only hereditary succession could guarantee, was lost. What was left was the continuity of princely government in the princes' respective territories, and of princely dynastic rivalries. The German kingship dwindled to the status of a prize, sought after by noble families who saw in it a means to a temporary advantage over competitors. The electoral empire, really a *congeries* of half independent principalities, had no real unity to make it a force in European politics. The history of Germany becomes henceforward a story of internal struggles, over matters inevitably divorced in most instances from the currents of external affairs.

In Sicily, after his victories over Manfred and Conradin, Charles of Anjou ruled over the same lands that the Norman kings had held long before him. But his kingdom was impoverished by the tremendous strains to which the great emperor's wars had exposed its resources, and retained only the shadow of its former prosperity. The ambitions of Frederick and the alliances of Manfred in central and northern Italy had, moreover, shifted the focus of government away from the island to the mainland provinces, and Naples had eclipsed Palermo as the centre of royal administration. The island's grievances had passed unheeded under two Hohenstaufen rulers: Charles's ambitions were almost as great as his predecessors', and his demands no less exacting. Thus were sown the seeds of the revolution which broke out in the 'Vespers' rising of 1282, when the barons and townsmen of the island took arms to shake off Angevin dominion, and called a prince of Aragon to rule them instead (see chapter 13, page 188). For many years afterwards the two kingdoms of Sicily, the Angevin and the Aragonese, were at war. Thus, as in Germany, in Sicily the papal–imperial struggle ended with the authorities of what had once been a unified realm engrossed in conflict with one another.

In northern and central Italy the end results were substantially similar. But because the authorities and interests involved here were much more numerous at the time when Frederick's troubles with the pope began, the confusion in the end was much greater. Before the outset, old quarrels already divided town and town, and one feudal family from another. There were quarrels too within the cities, both in Lombardy and Tuscany. Family rivalries divided the ruling oligarchies; the commercial aristocracy of the trade guilds feuded against the older nobility; rival factions among the powerful, the clergy, and demagogues, all alike bid for the support of the discontented people. All sought to draw such advantage as they could from supporting one side or the other once the great conflict of the church and the empire began. In the confusion of the situation changes of allegiance were kaleidoscopic, and had little to do with the issues at stake between the nominal principals in the war. The labels Guelf (for the church) and Ghibelline (for the empire)* came to denote the allegiance of certain families, guilds, and individuals in certain towns, and little more.

These labels nevertheless became very important. In the absence of any external authority (such as the empire might have been) to restrain them, disorders became endemic and local feuds ingrained. Groups of rivals, too evenly balanced to succeed individually, sought to strengthen themselves by communal organization. Because the family was the basic social unit recognized in the customary law of most cities, these groups became hereditary and self perpetuating. Their struggles conduced for a time to a condition of chronic instability. Those who lost for the moment and had to leave their cities, being no less organized than their enemies, took with them into exile, in the institutions of their 'party', the cadre of rival governments. Revolution in the Italian cities did not, in consequence, have to face the problem of forging new institutions; party organization put these ready to hand. In the long run the parties formed during Frederick's wars and their aftermath dictated the shape of future conditions in Italy. The families who were long to control the affairs of Florence and Genoa owed their power to commanding influence in the Guelf and Ghibelline parties respectively. In Lombardy the Pallavicini and the da Romanos, allying with the Ghibellines of the towns of their localities, began to build their authority as one-time imperial vicars-general into princely rule. They were the first forerunners of the Italian despots of the Renaissance.

*These are the Italian forms of the German 'Welf' and 'Waiblingen', said to have been used as battle cries by the forces of the rival Welfs of Saxony and the Hohenstaufen (Waiblingen was an important Hohenstaufen castle: the Welfs, both in Germany and Tuscany, were allies of the popes).

These parties in fact became so important that no influential Italian family could afford to stand apart from them. The popes themselves were usually Italian noblemen, and so were their cardinals. Inevitably party struggles permeated to the Curia itself. Thus the Colonna cardinals, in the late thirteenth century, represented the Ghibelline interest in the college, and became the leaders of a ready-made opposition within the governing body of the Roman Church itself. Not only, in fact, had the popes broken the authority of the empire in Italy: they had broken the only power which might restrain local Italian quarrels from threatening their own authority.

Throughout the empire that Frederick II had ruled, the result of the pope's struggles with him were the same; the fragmentation of unitary political authority. For the papacy, this was a very high cost of victory. The channelling of both interest and effort in a large part of Christendom into internecine strife attacked the roots out of which the popes' own claims to leadership in the Christian world had grown. Notional as it was, the emperor's pre-eminence among Christian rulers had been a valuable symbol of the union of Christendom in common interest and endeavour in this world. Now that the empire's claim to oecumenical authority was revealed as completely hollow, the oecumenical authority of the church looked less impressive.

There was still, it is true, the crusade. Though the purpose for which it had lately been preached had much tarnished its reputation, the crusade still represented a common Christian political ideal. It was to discuss the launching of a new crusade to Palestine that, six years after Tagliacozzo, Gregory X summoned a general council of the church to Lyons. As earlier to the disingenuous Frederick, so also to this sincere and upright churchman, the crusade seemed the best means to weld together the divided spirits of Christendom.

13

The Crusade in the Thirteenth Century

THE history of the thirteenth century crusades is very different
from those of the twelfth. The Frankish kingdom of Jerusalem and
its fortunes are no longer the focus of interest, because as a political unity that kingdom had ceased to function effectively. Instead,
the ambitions and adventures of the great powers and princes of
Europe command the scene. The Emperor Frederick II, King
Louis IX (St Louis) of France, Richard the brother, and Edward
the son of Henry III of England, all led expeditions to the east.
Charles of Anjou nursed projects greater, perhaps, than any of
theirs, though he failed in the end to implement his schemes. The
interests in the crusade of all these parties were varied, and were
so entangled with the internal politics of Europe that they are
often hard to follow. But their ideas were always conditioned by
political circumstances in the Latin east and among its Greek and
Moslem neighbours, and the story may be clearer if we begin by
discussing these.

All through the first half of the century the Franks still controlled most of the towns of the Syrian coast, from Ascalon to
Beirut. Acre was the capital of their kingdom, now that Jerusalem
was lost. For most of the period their kings were either minors or
absentees: their duties were discharged by regents, appointed by
the High Court of barons and strictly controlled by it. It was not
easy, in this body, to obtain unanimous consent to consistent
policies. Another source of weakness to the kingdom was the
rivalry of the two great crusading orders, the Templars and Hospitallers, who were the richest landholders in the realm and controlled most of the inland castles. Much more serious still was the
bitter commercial rivalry of the Venetians and the Genoese,
whose merchants formed the most powerful and prosperous
element in the coastal cities. Their local hostilities ran too deep

178

for their native cities or the barons to control, and there were long periods when they were at war with one another. This was not a trouble in the Syrian cities only, but throughout the whole eastern Mediterranean.

The real strength of the Latins in the east was not in Syria, but in Cyprus and Greece. Cyprus under the Lusignan kings was flourishing and prosperous, and Famagusta was becoming an important commercial centre. Most of the barons of Syria held fiefs in Cyprus, and some, as the Ibelins, were very powerful there. The institutions of the kingdom of Cyprus and the crusading zeal of its aristocracy showed that it was the true heir to the traditions of the old kingdom of Jerusalem. Throughout the century it served as an advance post, where crusading armies assembled and laid their final plans. The king of Cyprus and his knights took a part in the fifth crusade (1218), and fought beside Louis IX and his Frenchmen in 1249–50. The control of Cyprus was of great value for the crusade: the only trouble was that the Franks of the island were not strong enough to embark on unsupported ventures of their own.

The Latin emperors of Constantinople were never sufficiently strong to make any contribution at all to crusades elsewhere. From 1235 onwards, once the Greeks of Nicaea had re-established a footing on the European shore of the Bosphorus, Constantinople was in constant danger of recapture. The last Latin emperor, Baldwin II de Courtenay, spent much of his long reign in the west, seeking for military aid: he had little success, for the Venetians were the only people who had much to gain by supporting him. Without their fleet, indeed, the Latins would have lost Constantinople much sooner than they did. In 1259 the combined land forces of the Latin empire were defeated heavily at Pelagonia. Two years later, while the fleet and the emperor were away from the capital, the soldiers of Michael Palaeologus entered it, almost without a blow. The Latins were entirely unable to stage any come-back. Once again, a Greek emperor ruled thenceforward at Constantinople.

The real centre of Latin power in the lands of the old Byzantine empire was in the Peloponnese, far from Constantinople. Geoffrey

I and II and William de Villehardouin were able and successful rulers in the great principality of Achaea; so were their vassals, the dukes of Athens of the house of La Roche. The court of the Villehardouin princes was renowned, not in Greece only but in the west too, as a school of chivalry, and many knights from Burgundy anᴅ Champagne came there to acquire an apprenticeship in arms and honour. Like the barons of Cyprus, the Franks of Greece treasured their crusading tradition, and many of them joined St Louis in his first, ill-starred, expedition. They were also, unfortunately, the most reliable vassals on whom the Latin emperors could call for military service. William of Achaea was taken prisoner at Pelagonia in 1259, and was only released after the Greek recapture of Constantinople, and on condition of surrendering to the Greeks a number of his castles, including the great fortress of Mistra. From then on, he and his successors were on the defensive.

Read from a modern map, the resources of Latin lordship in the eastern Mediterranean look impressive. This appearance is deceptive: partly because in many places Latin lordship represented a very flimsy control over lands ruled in name only, but most of all because the Latins were disunited. Acre and Cyprus acknowledged different kings. The princes of Achaea were vassals in name of the emperors of Constantinople, but so distant from him as to be virtually independent. A still deeper cleavage, of background and outlook, separated these aristocrats from the merchants and pirates of Venice and Genoa, who managed most of the trade of Syria and fought each other for control of the Greek archipelago. If the resources of the Latin east were to be used to the profit of the crusading enterprise (in whose name most of the *congeries* of lordships which composed it had been conquered), some unifying force had to be found to weld them into common effort.

The dream of uniting the Latin east in a great Mediterranean empire is a recurrent theme in the history of the crusades in the thirteenth century. Frederick II saw its potential, as one might expect, for his marriage had made him king consort of Jerusalem, and Cyprus was nominally supposed to be a vassal kingdom of the empire. He was not able to spend long enough in the east to make anything of his rights, however. Louis IX remained there longer. He was far more successful in winning the personal allegiance of the Frankish aristocracy than Frederick had been, but he did not aspire to dominion for himself in the east. Charles of Anjou, Louis's brother and Frederick's supplanter in Sicily, did aspire to such dominion, and schemes to establish it dominated his policies for fifteen years. In the end, the fortunes of the crusade had come largely to depend on his success. They also, of course, depended on the conditions among the neighbours of the Latins in the east, always a key factor in crusading history. Among them, there were some very important changes between the time of Frederick and the time of Charles.

*

In a tent by the river Onon in eastern Siberia, a boy was born in 1162 who was to be known to the world as Genghis Khan. By 1206 this boy had made himself emperor of all the Mongols, the most powerful group of nomad tribes on the steppes of Asia. By the time he died, in 1227, his conquests had so extended his empire that it stretched from the Dnieper to the China Sea. His son Ogotai extended it even further. One of his armies, under his lieutenant Batu Khan, overran Russia, and in 1241, after defeating the king of Hungary, appeared on the frontiers of Germany. Next year it was the turn of the Seljucid Turks of Anatolia, whose sultan's forces were overthrown at the battle of Kosë Dagh, between Trebizond and Sebastia. By this time the rulers of Syria had felt the repercussions of the Mongol conquests: they were being harried by bands of Khwarismian soldiers, who had fled west when the Khwarismian empire, beyond the Oxus in Khorasan, was overrun by Genghis. The Mongol menace was to come much closer in the reign of Mangu, who became khan of the Mongols in 1251. In 1256 his lieutenant Hulagu invaded Persia, and in 1258 Baghdad was taken and sacked. The last of the caliphs, the orthodox rulers of Islam who were of the Prophet's own family, was put to the sword. In 1260, when Mangu died,

Damascus and Aleppo had fallen, and Syria seemed destined to become a Mongol province.

In fact, the Mongol invasions had by this time reached their furthest limits west and south. The Mongols never occupied Hungary: after Ogotai's death (1241) their troops withdrew into Russia, whose princes for the next two hundred years acknowledged the *ilkhans* (subordinates of the great khan) of the Golden Horde as their overlords. The Seljucids of Anatolia, like the Russians, became vassals of the Mongols, but not for so long a period. Amid the ruins of the Seljucid sultanate, Osman, founder of the Ottoman Turkish dynasty, had made himself an independent prince by 1300. In Syria Mongol control was even more short-lived. The Mongols were driven back into Mesopotamia, after their decisive defeat at the hands of the Egyptian mameluke, Sultan Baibars, at Ain Jelat in 1260.

The Mongol invasions brought about a revolution in the pattern of power in the near east. Driven back from Syria, they still remained very much a power to be reckoned with. By neutralizing the Seljucids of Anatolia, they had contributed greatly to the resurgence of the Greeks, whose emperors of Nicaea gained thus the free hand they needed for operations in Europe, to retake Constantinople. More important, their invasions destroyed the Ayoubid sultanate of Damascus, whose rulers' quarrels with their fellow Ayoubids (the line of Saladin) in Egypt the crusaders had exploited for their own ends. This more or less coincided with the palace revolution in Egypt, organized by the Sultan's Mameluke bodyguard, which led to the deposition of the last Ayoubid and his replacement by one of the Mamelukes themselves. The Mameluke sultans were able and efficient rulers, and Moslem fanaticism was in their early days one of the chief props of their authority. The massacre of countless faithful Moslems in the cities which the Mongols had sacked in Persia and the Khorasan had struck terror into the whole Mohammedan world. It was to Egypt that the faithful looked for aid; and it was in Cairo that the caliphate was resurrected, in the person of al-Hakim, a descendant of the caliph's house who had escaped from Baghdad. The Mamelukes were thus not very comfortable neighbours for the Christians of Acre: the more so since effective control of Syria was essential to them as sultans of Egypt, if they were to contain the Mongols at the Euphrates rather than the Nile.

The pattern of power in the near east, which emerged in consequence of the Mongol invasions, dictated the choice of alliances on which a crusading diplomacy could be developed. The resurgence of the Greeks suggested that something might be hoped for from alliance with them, and led to the revival of negotiations for a reunion of the Greek and Latin Churches. The Greek emperors were ready to listen to proposals, which seemed to offer a degree of security against future attack from the west. Innocent IV, before he died in 1254, had made soundings with the emperor John Vatatzes; twenty years later, at Gregory X's Council of Lyons, the envoys of Michael Palaeologus made their formal adherence to the Latin communion. The reunion was, on the Greek side, purely a diplomatic move; even in name it lasted only six years. There were also moments when some sort of understanding with the Mamelukes seemed feasible policy. The sultans of Egypt had no real interest, of course, in the maintenance of the weak Latin kingdom as a third force in Syria. As long, however, as the arrival at Acre of great hosts from the west remained a possiblity, they could not afford to ignore overtures. A Mongol–Christian alliance might be a very dangerous enemy for them.

This was the alliance which raised the highest hopes in the west. The Mongols were pagans, whose religious beliefs were believed to be vague and tenuous. The sack and slaughter they had wrought in Bokhara and Samarkand and Baghdad suggested they must be relentless enemies of Islam. Many of their subjects were known to be Christians, and prospects of their conversion were long thought to be good. The Mongol rulers did in fact toy with Christianity; it was not clear until the end of the century that Islam would triumph among them. The envoys of the great khan were present at the Council of Lyons, and heard Gregory X appeal there to the princes of Europe to join a new crusade. In truth, however, the Mongols and the crusaders of the west were too remote, in distance and culture, to understand one another. The Mongols entertained the missionary envoys St Louis sent them royally, but the message which they sent back to him revealed that their real interest was in conquest, not Christianity: 'We advise you to send us a sufficient sum of money in yearly contributions for us to remain your friends. Otherwise we will destroy you, as we have destroyed other kings.' The journey across the steppe to the Mongol khan's capital at Karakorum in any case took so long, that effective cooperation with them in military enterprise was not feasible.

*

The time when the crusaders had a real chance of re-establishing themselves in Syria was before the coming of the Mongols, when the Ayoubid empire that Saladin had founded was being undermined by internal quarrels. The fifth crusade (1218–21) came very near success. It was an experiment with a new crusading strategy. The failure in Palestine of the third crusade had convinced its organizers that a direct attack on Egypt, the headquarters of Ayoubid authority, was likely to yield more profitable results. This reasoning was sound. Damietta, on the Nile delta, was taken, and the sultan of Egypt was ready to give back Jerusalem in return for it. But the crusaders turned down his offer, and later he got them at his mercy, cut off from their bases by the rising of the flooded Nile. They had to surrender Damietta, and returned empty-handed. Frederick II, in 1229, preferred negotiation to fighting, and proved its worth: Al Kamil of Egypt was glad enough to buy a free hand in his relations with Damascus by a ten year truce and the return of the Holy City to the Christians. It was with the Christians that Frederick failed. His high-handed treatment of the barons of Syria and his contempt for the High Court led to a civil war between the Frankish aristocracy led by the Ibelins of Beirut, and the imperial legates whom he left to represent him when he returned to Europe. When the ten year truce that he had arranged expired it was not renewed. On 17 October 1244, the Egyptians defeated the crusaders and their allies from Damascus overwhelmingly at Gaza. Just a fortnight before, the Khwarismian mercenaries of the Egyptian sultan had taken and sacked Jerusalem.

This was the situation which Louis IX hoped to restore when he sailed from Aigues Mortes in August 1248. He had been four years preparing his crusade: vast sums had been raised in France to equip the expedition, and it was a large and well organized host that assembled in the autumn in Cyprus. Next spring this host sailed out, bound for Egypt, and with plans in view similar to those of the fifth crusade. Damietta was taken in the summer. In February 1250 the king's forces had begun their advance up the Nile. They were cut off among the channels of the delta in the presence of an Egyptian army. In the attempt to fight their way out, the crusaders were overwhelmed: Louis and all those who were not killed were taken prisoner. His Queen Margaret heroically rallied the panicking garrison of Damietta, and the determined show of resistance which she made there persuaded the Egyptians to agree to her husband's ransom and that of his men. More than half of them by then were dead. His crusade as a military venture was at an end.

Louis remained in the east until 1254. He made efforts to effect an alliance of the Christians with the Mongols; his envoy William of Rubroek reached Karakorum, and there took part in a great debate before the khan between the Mohammedans, the Buddhists, and the Nestorians. His embassy, however, had no practical results. Louis also did his best to instil some sort of unity among the Franks of the east: in this he was more successful, for his efforts gained respect as those of a disinterested and chivalrous leader. But when the cares of his kingdom called him home, nothing remained to keep alive a spirit of cooperation which only his personal influence had achieved. His departure was followed by a long period, during which neither the papacy nor any of the princes of Europe could spare much attention to the affairs of the east. Too much effort was being concentrated in the great struggle of the Church against the Hohenstaufen. This interval saw very important developments in the east: the rise of Baibars the Mameluke to be sultan of Egypt: the Mongol invasion of Syria: the Greek reconquest of Constantinople. In the eastern Mediterranean the scene had changed greatly by the time that Charles of Anjou emerged from the struggles in Italy as the triumphant champion of the church.

*

As such, and as the most powerful Latin prince of southern Europe, it was natural that the popes should look to Charles as the potential leader of further crusading endeavour. He was ready enough to take up the role, but, unfortunately, not quite as the disinterested crusader that his brother Louis had been. What stirred him was not the fate of the Holy Places of Jerusalem, but the same dream that had captivated Frederick II in the past, of founding in his own house a great Latin empire in the Mediterranean. Time had lost Charles some advantages. The kingdom of Acre was weaker than it had been in Frederick's day, and there was no longer a Latin ruler at Constantinople. Besides, Charles had made many enemies in Europe. To be champion of the church meant in his case much less than it might have done earlier. It meant simply that he was the most important secular lord among the Guelfs, the military leader of a party which had defeated its Italian enemies, but not yet destroyed all of them. Charles's dynastic ambitions, and the hostility towards him of the Ghibellines of Italy, meant that he could never be quite the kind of crusading captain St Louis was.

He set about to secure his ends with far-sighted skill and determination nevertheless. As soon as he had triumphed over Manfred and secured Sicily he began working to concentrate in his own family all the remaining rights of overlordship of the Latins in the east. In 1267 he arranged the marriages of his daughter Beatrice to Philip de Courtenay, the heir of Baldwin, titular emperor of Constantinople, and of his own son Philip to Isabella, heiress of William of Achaea. If either marriage were to prove barren, the claims and inheritances involved were to revert to Charles himself, and his heirs. Ten years later, in 1277, he bought outright the hereditary claim of Maria of Antioch to the kingdom of Jerusalem, and was accepted as king by the High Court. The registers of Pope Martin IV record that he aspired to suzerainty over Cyprus also, though the Pope refused to sanction this. With this one exception, his rights by 1281 extended over all the Frankish territories of the east Mediterranean. (See family tree, Appendix, page 325.)

Of the claims Charles had acquired, that to Constantinople represented the most glittering prize, because it could give his family an imperial title. Hence, as the city was in Greek hands, Charles focused on its recapture as his first objective. He planned an expedition (with papal blessing) as early as 1268. Three matters, however, successively forced him to postpone the scheme. The first was Conradin's invasion of Italy. The second was the last crusade of his brother Louis IX to Tunis in 1269, where the great crusading king of France died of fever. The third was the pontificate of Gregory X. This pope rightly distrusted Charles as a man who was actuated by political ambition rather than crusading zeal. He saw the best hope for Christendom in the east as lying in a reunion with the Greeks, and at his Council of Lyons in 1274 their church was formally brought into the Latin communion. The conditions of the union, recognizing the Greek rite and avoiding, as far as possible, disputed theological issues, are testimony to Gregory's breadth of mind and vision. Unfortunately his tolerance was unrepresentative as a contemporary attitude, in either east or west.

The Pope's call, at this same council, to the princes of Europe to take the cross, stood unanswered, largely because the thwarted Charles and his nephew, Philip III of France, were not prepared to respond. The reunion proved to be a paper triumph: it was bitterly resented by the Greek clergy, and it was with difficulty that the emperor Michael persuaded sufficient of them that it was needful to go through the motions of adherence for diplomatic ends. The insincerity of the Greeks showed soon, but it was not till 1281, when a Frenchman wedded to Charles's interest, Simon of Brie, became pope as Martin IV, that the union was broken off formally. It thus took thirteen years for Charles to reachieve the position of 1268, and in the meantime, with the election in Germany of a new emperor, Rudolf of Habsburg, Ghibelline hopes had begun to revive in Italy. Nevertheless Charles now pressed ahead with his old plans.

In the spring of 1282 a great expedition was assembling at Messina. Its aim, sanctioned by Pope Martin, was 'the restoration of the Roman empire usurped by Palaeologus'. The long years which had elapsed since the threat of 1268 had given the emperor Michael the chance to make his preparations. He was in touch with all Charles's enemies, with the Ghibellines of Lombardy and Tuscany, with the discontented barons of the island of Sicily, and, most important of all, with the exiled servants of Manfred and Conradin at the court of Aragon, whose king Peter was married to Manfred's daughter, Constance of Hohenstaufen. Sicily, a potential storm centre in the middle of Charles's own dominions, formed the key to the plans which Michael and John of Procida, Manfred's one-time chancellor and leader of the Ghibelline conspirators in Aragon, were hatching. In 1282 at Easter the citizens of Palermo rose and massacred the French, the first act in a carefully planned rising which spread swiftly through the whole island. Michael had been so skilled, that he did not have to fight to aid the Sicilians whom he had paid to rebel. It was to King Peter of Aragon that the islanders offered the crown. On 30 August, five months after the bells for vespers had sounded the signal for revolt in Palermo, Peter's Aragonese host landed at Trapani.

So in the end it was not against Constantinople but against Aragon that Martin IV blessed a crusade. The church had become too wedded to Charles's cause to desert it, even in the moment of a disaster whose origins were purely political. While Charles grappled with the Sicilians, Philip III of France crossed the Pyrenees to execute the Pope's sentence on King Peter and to depose him, an expedition which failed miserably. Thus Charles's ambitions, instead of establishing a Latin empire in the east among the crusading states, ended by extending the struggle of Guelf and Ghibelline from Italy through the whole western Mediterranean. 'O Lord, since thou hast determined to ruin me, at least grant that I may go down by small steps': thus Charles is said to have prayed when he heard the news from Palermo.

The sides were sufficiently evenly matched for his prayer to be granted.

While Charles and Philip of France fought the crusade against Sicily and Aragon, to which they had committed themselves and the papal interest, the soldiers of the Sultan of Egypt closed in on the remaining Frankish forts of Syria. Acre fell on 18 May 1291; and the kingdom of Jerusalem became, thenceforward, a title to which no territories attached. As a military enterprise, to defend and secure the Holy Places of Christendom, the story of the crusade was at an end.

It was not the fall of the last strongholds in Syria that closed the account for crusading, but the Vespers of Sicily. Acre was doomed from the moment it became clear that no relieving force from western Europe was likely to intervene. It was also clear, with Charles occupied in the Aragonese war, that no further western attempt against Constantinople was to be expected. This meant that, on the Greek side, there was not likely to be much further interest in reunion of the churches. The Franks of Achaea, being now the vassals of Charles's son, were drawn into his struggles: so were the Venetians and Genoese, as the Guelf–Ghibelline war revived all over Italy. No one paid much attention to the embassy from the Mongols who came to find the Pope in 1289, in the hope of discussing alliance against the Egyptians. The defence of Syria, let alone the recovery of Jerusalem, had become politically impracticable.

*

The fall of Acre had a psychological impact, as the fall of a last stronghold always will. But it was not only the collapse in Syria, or the extension of the Guelf–Ghibelline struggle, which at the end of the thirteenth century set the seal on the future of the crusading venture. The events in the east which had marked the passing years also had had effects on the minds and attitudes of men in Europe. They had made it hard for them to view the traditional objectives of the crusade in the same manner as their forbears had done.

When the great Majorcan scholar, Ramon Lull, heard of the

fall of Acre, he was not sure that it mattered. 'If the Nestorians can be brought into the fold, and the Tartars converted, all the Saracens can easily be destroyed,' he wrote. The conquests of the Mongols, and their strict protection of the caravan routes of central Asia, had opened the eyes of Europeans to a new dimension of the world, in which the Levant, where Islam and Christendom struggled, appeared geographically comparatively insignificant. It was not only Franciscan missionaries who traversed Asia overland by the route the Mongols had opened. In 1275 the Polos arrived at the court of Kublai Khan at Shangtu in China. Cathay was to be a land familiar enough in the reckonings of Italian merchants in the next century. As it became clear that there dwelt, beyond the frontiers of Islam as they had been known, a countless multitude of pagans and unbelievers, war against Islam to secure the Holy Places of Jerusalem inevitably lost some of its religious significance.

The revelation to Europe, in consequence of the Mongol invasions, of the vast Asian hinterland was of comparable impact, in terms of pure geography, to the later discovery of the Americas. The results of the discovery are not, however, easily defined. A lasting European interest in geography itself was certainly engendered. Probably fictions, inspired by travellers' tales (such as the invented marvels Sir John Mandeville saw on his imaginary journeys) reached a wider audience than the sober truth of, say, Marco Polo's story. It is worth remembering, however, that Columbus was to study Marco's book with close attention. In religious and learned circles, this interest in geography was mirrored in a desire to learn more about non-Christian creeds, a sign of a dawning realization that missionary endeavour might prove a more effective weapon against unbelief than military enterprise.

For a long time hopes for the conversion of the Mongols were entertained. The Franciscan and Dominican missionaries had some considerable success in the early days. In 1307, John of Monte Corvino, who had worked among the Mongols for many years, was consecrated as the Catholic Archbishop of Peking. Only three of the seven friar-bishops who had been sent to perform the office of consecration finished their journey, however: and his career had no sequel, his see no successor. There were others who, shocked by the barbarism of the Mongols, reacted very differently to these heroic friars. To such, the Mongol invasions brought home how close the traditions of Islam and Christianity were. Roger Bacon and Ramon Lull both urged in their writings the study of Islam and her institutions, with the hope in mind that Christendom might make common cause yet with a Mohammedan world, converted to the way of truth by learned missionaries. Their hopes were even more vain than those for the crusade in the past. What they wrote is nevertheless testimony to the way in which new knowledge of the world was beginning to effect a radical alteration in the traditional attitudes of Christian Europe.

Bacon and Lull were men of the schools, members of a small, learned elite. It would take a long time for reflections like theirs to percolate through to the castles and halls of France and England, where the families lived who had sent sons to follow leaders like St Louis to the Holy Land. The crusade was to remain long a cherished ideal among the military aristocracy of the west. But in the long run queries were certain to be raised, including some very serious ones. Their asking would reflect not only on the standing of the crusade, but also on that of the Roman Church which had preached and organized it.

In the context of the new geography, the word Roman was bound to lose some of its universal connotations. The kind of political authority which the Roman Church claimed was also very hard to fit into the new perspectives of distance overland. John of Monte Corvino, writing home in 1305, declared that it was twelve years since he had heard any news from Europe. The whole framework of universal, Christian, politico-religious idealism, which had inspired the crusades, began to be meaningless in the context of such remoteness.

14

France and England: The Growth
of National Communities

THE great struggle of the papacy and the empire in the thirteenth
century was fought out in Italy and Germany. But the popes did
not have allies in these countries strong enough to outface the
hereditary power of the Hohenstaufen: they had therefore to call
in champions from outside. The crown of Sicily was offered first
to Edmund, an English prince, then to Charles of Anjou, a
French one. Another English prince, Richard of Cornwall, was a
claimant for the German crown from 1257 until his death in 1272.
When, in 1283, a crusade was blessed against Aragon, because her
king Peter had aided the Sicilians against Charles of Anjou,
Peter's crown was promised to another Frenchman of royal
blood, Charles of Valois. The provenance of these champions is
significant. They remind us of the growing influence in Christian
Europe of the northern kingdoms, where important developments were taking place at this time.

Magna Carta, the great charter which the barons in 1215 forced
King John to seal, played a dominant role in English history in
the thirteenth century. It defined, in formal legal language,
specific limits to the king's rights over his subjects and their lands
in England. It was confirmed, after John's death, by his son
Henry III. As a record of right which the king had accepted as
valid, it provided a definite basis, round which those who were
suspicious of royal government could take their stand. Henry
III's government was unfortunately such as to make the great
territorial barons of his realm very suspicious. While the activities
of his officials seemed to be undermining their privileges at
home, the king chose to favour men of foreign extraction more
highly than them, and spent money freely in unsuccessful ventures abroad. In these last, his barons were determined to refuse
him any more assistance than he was entitled to. Centred round

their chartered rights, the stand of the great men of the kingdom fostered among them a tradition of communal action.

Henry's Sicilian involvement brought about in 1258 the show-down which had been looming for nearly thirty years. He had bound himself to Pope Alexander IV to pay more than his purse would allow, unless his barons would help by agreeing to extra-ordinary taxation (a 'gracious aid'). When the baronial leaders began to discuss the conditions on which they would grant this assistance, it soon became clear that the confirmation of the Great Charter could no longer be nearly enough. Since 1215 the scope of royal government, directed by an efficient bureaucracy, had been quietly but vastly extended, and issues on which the Charter was silent had become newly significant. A committee of great men was therefore set up to look into matters which called for reformation. They were at work for over a year, and in the end produced a series of demands to the king, which are very revealing.

They demanded that the names of the king's councillors should be known, that the names should be of men whom they approved, and that the king should genuinely govern by the advice of these named councillors. They demanded that three times a year the king and his council should meet with twelve great men chosen to represent 'the community of the land'. They named Hugh Bigod, one of themselves, to be chief justiciar, and set him to make a great judicial tour of the land, to inquire into abuses committed by officials against any free man whatever. Perhaps most striking of all, they demanded that the king's courts should protect his barons not only against officials, but also against the subterfuges which their own tenants might adopt in order to avoid or lighten their tenurial obligations. The baronial reformers were honest enough to admit the corollary too, that the king's courts should give redress against barons to their tenants, if the barons themselves sought to press their rights beyond what was due.

These demands for reform were the rallying cry of those who followed Simon de Montfort in the confused civil war which ended only with his death at Evesham in 1265. Their moral is much clearer than the motives which led individuals to join the king or Earl Simon in the actual fighting. They make it plain that the rights of the king over his tenants, and their rights over theirs in turn, were no longer regarded in England as matters which could be treated separately. We must remember here that, in a largely agricultural country where virtually all men of any account were propertied, terms of tenure were much more than legal issues: they were predominant social factors. By demanding in effect that all questions of free tenure should be settled by the same law, and normally in the same courts (by the common law and in the king's courts), the baronial leaders were recognizing that the kingdom should be regarded as a single community, with a single directive government. As the *Song of Lewes* (written to celebrate Simon de Montfort's victory in 1264) put it: 'The governance of the realm is the safety or ruin of all. . . . When any member is injured, the whole body is made of less strength.' The dawning awareness, which these words reflect, of common interest binding together the kingdom as a community was not lost when Simon de Montfort died. It had made its mark on many others besides him, including King Henry III's son, who was soon to be king.

Edward I, in contrast to his father, was shrewd in his ambitions and a great warrior. He conquered Wales, and very nearly conquered Scotland, and he fought a long war in Gascony against the king of France. He had also witnessed his father's troubles with his subjects and drawn his conclusion therefrom. He saw that if, in the service of his ambitions, he was to make the most of the authority and rights he had inherited, he would need to enlist the support of the community at large for the way in which he used them.

It is not clear that Edward was really much more anxious for his subjects' welfare than his father was, but he certainly went through the motions of being so. He and his councillors devised statutes to protect landlords from the dodges of their tenants: to ensure that, in the disposal of property, the intentions of those who left or gave it were safeguarded: to secure rapid redress against defaulting debtors for merchants, who could not linger when the fairs and markets that they attended were over. Above all, Edward sought to give publicity to the reasons which dictated the turns of his policy. This cast a consultative atmosphere over the whole business of government.

It had been customary in England in the past to call on representatives of local communities to appear before the king and his council when matters affecting them were being adjudicated. Edward extended this practice, by summoning from time to time representatives from every shire in his realm (and sometimes from a number of important boroughs too) to come before his council, together with all his barons. These representatives were bidden to come 'with full power for themselves and for all the community of the shire to counsel and consent to those things . . . which shall be agreed upon.' Edward often took the opportunities which such great assemblies offered to explain to his subjects why it was that, in the general interest, it would be necessary for him to obtain taxes from them. Precedent had already established that for taxation to be lawful the assent of all the baronage was necessary: Edward's practice associated with their assent the presence of a much larger gathering of his subjects.

These meetings, which brought together barons and commons, were called parliaments: they were the germ from which the British parliament grew. The men who came to them were, from the boroughs, burgesses, members of a city's governing class: from the shires, knights, local landlords chosen by their fellow squires in the county court, under the eye of its president, the king's sheriff. It was to the sheriff that the king's writ came, ordering him to assemble the court and choose the representatives. The words 'counsel and consent' in the writ did not mean, quite, all they said. The king was summoning these people at his pleasure, because he thought it might be convenient for him to let them know what he was doing. His practice, however, helped to create an impression that he would consult his subjects, indeed ought to, when matters of grave and general concern were under review, especially if they might lead to a demand for taxation. In 1297, when, owing to the wars with France and Scotland, the burden of taxation had been heavy for three years, Edward for the first time found himself in serious difficulties with his subjects. He was forced to promise concessions in return for their aid, among them the undertaking that neither he nor his heirs would ever seek to raise extraordinary revenue without the formal assent of the 'commonalty of the realm'. The principle, that to commit the whole community's resources, the consent of a body representing it was needed, was henceforward clear.

What was not clear in 1297 was precisely who had to be present to constitute such a representative body. But as time went by the representatives of shires and boroughs were called to parliaments ever more frequently. The bids for popular support of rival baronial groups seeking to govern in the name of Edward's son, the inept Edward II, strengthened the growing parliamentary institution. The significance of its representative character was by then coming to be comprehended much more clearly, particularly with regard to grants of taxation. According to the treatise on *The Method of holding Parliaments*, written almost certainly during Edward II's reign, the voices that should really count in this respect were those 'of the knights of the shire, the citizens and burgesses ... who represent the whole community of England.' This was not yet formal constitutional doctrine: but the Statute of York of 1322 came near to making it so, when it laid down that matters affecting 'the whole estate of the realm' must be considered in parliament, by the 'archbishops, bishops, earls, barons, and the commonalty of the realm'.

England was a rich kingdom, whose farmers were the chief suppliers of raw wool to the European market (woollen cloths being probably Europe's most important export). Edward I, in his wars, had proved that it was possible to raise among the local communities of the realm substantial hosts of knights and archers, who would do effective service in the field for long periods if the king could equip and pay them. The 'whole community of England' could provide her king with the wherewithal to do great things. The fact that he might have to bargain with the 'community' in order to tap its full resources was in one sense a limit on the potential of his position. It made him the more formidable, however, when he could gain its cooperation.

*

The internal history of France has strong similarities with that of England in this period. But there is one great difference, which at first sight seems to make their development almost antithetic. Where in England we see limits being established on royal absolutism, in France we see the growth of absolutism itself. Three principal reasons for this different course of developments in France may be given. In the first place, in France in the early thirteenth century, there was no tradition of communal resistance to the king's administration, such as the struggle for the Great Charter created in England. In the second place, France was, as she still is, a country of far greater area, with a great diffusity of local customs and traditions. The third reason is of a quite different order; it is the extraordinary personality of the king who ruled France from 1226 until 1270, St Louis.

The first of these reasons is virtually self-explanatory, but there is one point connected with it which deserves to be noticed briefly. The royal demesne of the French kings represented a private patrimony far richer than that which any English monarch inherited. Philip Augustus seems to have been able to carry almost the whole financial burden of his wars in Normandy with the resources of his royal demesne. In the same wars John of England had to strain the resources not only of his private estates but of his whole kingdom so severely that his vassals felt their rights to be in jeopardy. Louis IX might never have won the respect that he did from his subjects, if the wealth of the demesne had not made him independent of their aid to an extent that his English contemporary Henry III never could be of his. It will be well to bear in mind the advantage which this wealth of their demesne gave to the French kings, while we are discussing the more complicated questions of the diffusity of provincial life in France, and of the significance of the career of St Louis, which require closer attention.

The great provinces, as Brittany, Flanders, Burgundy, Normandy and Languedoc, which together formed the kingdom of France, were historically as well as geographically distinct. Semi-independence under their own dukes and counts had given separate individuality to their cultural traditions, social structure and customary law. Even when, as was the case with both Normandy and much of Languedoc, these provinces lost their old ruling houses and came directly under royal administration, they retained their separate character. Hence there could be no conflict, as in England there sometimes was, between the king and the 'whole community of France'. The things which bound together the English community, a common law, common social institutions and tradition, did not exist for the whole of France, only for the provinces individually.

In those provinces which were still ruled by powerful feudal princes, themselves the king's vassals, these noblemen were often at odds with their subjects and tenants: these in their turn looked to the king for protection and justice. This created opportunities for royal authority, backed by an efficient and expanding bureaucracy, to make its influence directly felt. The best example of this was the case of Flanders. The resentment of the artisans of the great Flemish industrial towns against the ruling oligarchies of the municipalities had led to outbreaks of violence, which gave Count Guy in the 1280s his chance to enforce measures, curtailing the privileges of the ruling merchant communes. Against him, the city patricians invoked the royal authority, and gained the king's protection. So they became known in the social struggles of Flanders as the *leliaerts*, the party of the lilies of France. Because their insecurity made their need for protection constant, the interventions of the king's courts in the internal affairs of the county became constant too. A similar process was going on at the same time in other provinces, as Burgundy, and Gascony (of which the king of England was duke); the difficulties of subjects with the ducal rulers led to the constant invocation of royal authority, and this in turn made royal authority effective by habituating men to its activity.

Intervention naturally roused resentment, and before the end of the century King Philip IV found himself at war with both the

Count of Flanders and the Duke of Gascony. There would have been trouble much earlier but for the immense respect for royal authority which the rule of St Louis had created. His success as a ruler was one of the most remarkable achievements of his time, and essentially a personal one.

Louis IX was not a genius in the ordinary sense of the word. In many ways indeed he was a very conventional man of his age. The saintly acts which men remembered of him, as washing the feet of the poor on Maundy Thursday, and associating with lepers in efforts to ease the horror of their living, were the expressions of a kind of active piety familiar to all periods, but especially popular in his, which was also that of St Francis. Similarly, the autocratic temper of Louis's mind and his consciousness of the need for a ruler to live generously and magnificently, were nothing out of the ordinary. But the combination is remarkable: it is only a very unusual spirit which has the internal resources to make a practice of ideals of rigorous and humble abnegation in the midst of a life of display, without signs of strain showing. It did not make him, it should be added, a particularly humane or attractive personality. He had his full share of conventional bigotry: he supported the efforts of the Dominican inquisitors to root out heresy in Languedoc with the same zeal that he showed in pious self-denial after the Franciscan mode, and to more effect. What made him impressive to his contemporaries was his continuous effort to live up to all that was considered highest in very diverse, but thoroughly conventional ideals.

This was what won him veneration from men in very varied walks of life: from churchmen for his piety and alms-giving: from knights for his chivalrous courage and his zeal for the crusade: from subjects for the impartiality of his justice. This last is the key to the mark he made on the subsequent history of his own kingdom. Here again, a personal factor was the crucial one, Louis's deep conviction that to see justice done among his subjects was a duty laid on him directly by God, a personal religious responsibility. In its discharge he was continually active. 'In summer, after hearing mass,' wrote his biographer, the seneschal de Joinville, the king went often to the wood of Vincennes, where he would sit with his back against an oak; ... those who had any suit to present could come to speak to him without hindrance from any man.

Of course, even in the district around Paris, Louis could not see to everything himself: delegation was essential. It was, however, often direct and personal, and the system that he built was coloured by the king's anxiety to ensure that his servants observed the same high standard of impartiality as he.

This was the object of the commissions of inquiry – *enquêteurs* – whom Louis sent into the provinces in 1247

to examine the grievances which may be brought against us, as also the allegations of injustices and exactions of which our officers, bailiffs, foresters and their subordinates may have done without our witting.

Many of these first *enquêteurs* were friars, a reminder that for Louis, to do justice was fundamentally a religious duty: the reports of their busy activity show how his 'love of fair and open dealing' reached out to the great mass of people, to win their respect and gratitude. But they also show something else: how easily abuse could creep into a system, which depended for its working on the efforts of officials with wide and ill defined powers. They are full of tales of petty tyranny which show that, unprotected, the small man's instinctive reaction to the powerful official was to seek to buy his favour, not to resist or to complain. Louis's efforts to ensure that justice was done inevitably meant making the network of official supervision more ubiquitous, and so more professional. The oak of Vincennes is only one side of the story of Louis's quest for justice: the other is a great extension of the numbers and activities of royal administrators. Without his hand to guide and direct, there was much room for the system to become oppressive.

*

This becomes apparent if one compares the administration of St Louis with that of his grandson, Philip IV (1285–1314). The first thing one notices is the growth in professionalism. The king's judicial council has become a body of professional judges, the *Parlement*, the formal record of whose judgements goes back, significantly, to Louis's own reign. The framework of a central department for royal finance, the *Chambre des Comptes*, with a professional staff, has also been organized. Locally, in every district governed by a *bailli*, one will find a king's proctor, a professional advocate holding a watching brief for the royal interest in all local litigation. But the dominance of the professionals is clearest at the very centre of all, in the king's council. The key men, as Pierre Flote, Guillaume de Nogaret, Guillaume de Plaisians, Enguerrand de Marigny, are all administrators of experience, who owe their influence to their education, their proved ability, and their close personal association with their monarch.

The government, which these men and their master directed, struck a different note from that of St Louis. Most of the administrators who were now so prominent were men trained in the Roman civil law, in the schools of Orleans and Montpellier: this education encouraged a more secular outlook than that of the friars and clerks whom Louis had trusted. The impact of this training appears from a comparison of the activities of the commissions, headed by men like Nogaret and de Plaisians, which toured the provinces under Philip, with those of 1247. The priorities of Louis's men have simply been reversed: the business of asserting and protecting royal rights now takes pride of place over the protection of the individual from injury. The practical result of this was a tremendous multiplication of the number of cases which were drawn into the royal courts. Royal intervention could be justified on a host of grounds: because the king's officials claimed that the matter in issue was one which only the king could judge; or because there was an alleged royal interest involved; or because one of the parties had letters of safeguard giving him the king's special protection. In this process of continuous interference, those who had most privileges, in particular the clergy and the provincial nobility, inevitably suffered. Long before Philip's reign ended, complaints were beginning to be very widespread.

The very system which Louis had devised to remedy injustice

now made its remedy difficult. The king could promise to control his officials and respect antique privileges (as he did in his 'reforming ordinance' of 1303): in practice it had become impossible to check in detail the activities of a great army of officials, except through more officials. In any case Philip could not afford to restrain them much, because he needed to make the most of every right he possessed. His projects were ambitious. He quarrelled with the papacy: he had designs in the empire: he had to fight one war with the king of England from 1294 to 1303, and from 1297 until the end of his reign another war with the Count of Flanders. Like the king of England he found that his ordinary resources were not enough, even when swelled by such expedients as devaluation of the coinage, and the confiscation of the debts of Jews and Lombards. He had therefore to tax his subjects, though they were already complaining that they were often being asked to give him more than was due.

In the quest for readier cooperation from the subject, the French king sought to improve relations with him by the same means as Edward I did in England, by consultation and by giving more publicity to his policies. Thus in France in Philip IV's time there appeared an institution very reminiscent of the English parliament, the Estates General. This assembly brought together, in response to the royal summons, the representatives of the French clergy, of the nobility of the provinces over which royal rule was direct, and of the great cities (the third estate). To them at the crises of Philip's reign the king's ministers explained his policies: in 1302, his reasons for taking a stand against Pope Boniface; in 1308 those which had led him to take action against the Templars: in 1314, the danger of the situation in Flanders.

There were three very notable differences between these Estates General and the English parliament. Firstly, the nobility of the provinces and the third estate were kept apart, unlike the knights of the shire and the burgesses in England. There was thus never the same chance for a solid union of aristocratic and commercial interest to establish itself. Secondly, the stage management of the assemblies and the propaganda for royal policy were more skilfully arranged by the French. The representatives of the estates were not just told what the king was doing; they heard the king's ministers explain the situation to the king and ask him to take action, and were swayed to endorse their request. The king's policy therefore appeared not merely to enjoy popular support, but to be formed in response to popular demand. Thirdly, and most important of all, the Estates General did not fix grants of taxation, as the English parliament did. In 1302 and 1308 the king did not ask them for money, and in 1314 only to agree in principle that there should be taxation. They were left no room to bargain for specific concessions in return for specific contributions. This was why the Estates General met much more rarely than the English parliaments: its function in furthering royal policy was not essential, but, as a forum for giving publicity to the royal intentions in crisis, only useful.

There was consultation over taxation in France, but it was managed in another way. The king decreed that his subjects should pay him taxes: he then sent his officials into the various provinces to meet their assembled notables and discuss with them how the money was to be raised. He gave these officials wide discretionary powers to agree, in his name, to points which the provincial estates might take this opportunity to raise. Thus, though demands for taxation did produce promises of redress for grievances, they produced no theoretical limits to royal right, because the contributors did not bargain with the king directly. As time passed, the practice of France, therefore, confirmed the king's right to demand taxes, not, as in England, the subject's right of assent. Through the Estates General and the provincial assemblies, a sense of common interest, communal obligation and communal effort was fostered by careful propaganda. Thus far, developments in France and England were similar. But in France a sense of national interest developed in pace with the growth of royal absolutism, instead of setting limits thereto, as it did in England.

At the very end of Philip's reign there was concerted resistance to royal government. It was concerted, however, not nationally, but in the provinces. Philip's successors were able to cope with the 'leagues' of provincial nobles, which were formed in the last year of his reign; firstly because the interests of the provinces kept the leagues apart (each province obtained a separate charter, guaranteeing local privileges), and also because, within the provinces, the privileges which noblemen wished to guarantee were very often those which others, citizens and free men, wished to see abolished. The divisions of class and class, as those of district and district, were wider in France than in England. Until the provinces acquired a greater degree of internal institutional unity than they possessed in the early fourteenth century, the royal authority had no effective rivals.

*

If one compares the works, such as the *Song of Lewes* and the *Method of holding Parliaments*, written to defend limited monarchy in England, with the apologetic of French absolutism, a world of difference seems to separate them. Yet in a way the ideas they are seeking to express are not so far apart. There is a phrase which recurs frequently in the writings of the French: 'The king is emperor in his realm.' Jean de Blanot, writing in St Louis's time (*c.* 1255) uses it; so does William Durandus of Mende, some forty years later; so does Philip IV's especial apologist, John of Paris. It is a lawyer's technical phrase, meaning that the king in his kingdom exercises the same rights of sovereignty which are ascribed to the emperor in Roman Law. He can make laws which are universally binding, and repeal them: he, and he alone, can legitimate base-born children and ennoble common men: above all, there is no appeal from his sentence, because 'in temporal matters he has no superior but God.' According to the teaching of the Roman lawyers, the emperor had these powers, because he embodied personally the whole public authority of his empire and its people. The laws of the emperor always overrode the regulations of subordinate authorities, because these catered only for the needs of particular groups and interests, his for the well-being of the empire as a whole. The claim of the French lawyers was that France was in itself an empire. Thus it was as the representative of the whole community that they claimed for their king that 'what pleased him was law for all'. This claim therefore reflects basically the same idea as that of the English author, who claimed for the shire knights and burgesses the predominant voice in parliament, because 'they represent the whole community of England.' Both views are rooted in the same idea, of an authority which represents the whole national community.

In these two kingdoms in this period, the same notion can be seen gaining ground. It is the notion that the realm constitutes a community which is legally and socially whole and self-sufficing, in temporal matters at least. It was not only in France and England, moreover, that this idea was taking hold: similar developments attest its growing significance elsewhere. In the Spanish kingdoms, in Aragon and in Castile, representative bodies not unlike the English parliament, called the *Cortes*, had come to claim, as it did, to embody the whole authority of their communities. These kingdoms, like England and France, significantly began to play a more important part in European affairs at the same time: Aragon's king came to the aid of the Sicilians in 1282, and Alfonso of Castile became Richard of Cornwall's rival for the kingship of the 'Romans' in Germany. In Scotland, when in 1290 the death of the Maid of Norway left the succession in dispute between three collaterals, it was asserted that because Scotland was a kingdom, a community whole and entire, its inheritance could not be divided among them. Five years later the formation of the 'auld alliance', of Scotland and France against England, showed this northern kingdom, too, entering on the stage of European politics. These various developments, in different countries, tell again the same story which the history of France and England told. The legal status and claims of kingdoms, as sovereign entities, were in all these territories becoming distinct from the network of limited and specific rights of individual lords over lands and men which historians have called feudalism.

What we see here beginning to take shape is the doctrine of secular national sovereignty. In the early fourteenth century, admittedly, few can have been even dimly aware of the future implications of contemporary ideas. To many ordinary freemen, in France and England and elsewhere, the authority of a locally powerful lord was still more immediately relevant than that of a distant king. The lawyer and the landlord still had to feel their way through a maze of tangled and overlapping hereditary rights. But the impact of new ideas and institutional development was nevertheless apparent, even in their everyday world. This is clear in adjustments to the scale of value attached to the web of allegiances of lords and men, which constituted the contemporary social system. Allegiance to a king, or to a sovereign ruler, was beginning to be seen as an allegiance of a different order to any other secular bond.

There are many signs of this difference which could be re-marked: the clearest examples come from the France of Philip IV's reign. Here, during the king's wars, all private feuding between noblemen was forbidden by royal ordinance, since in such time all effort should be concentrated in the common need. In such time, the king's apologists explained further, no man can of right refuse to contribute from his property towards the ruler's necessities, for his needs really represent the needs of all. No vassal, explained Jacques de Revigny, the *doyen* of the Orleans lawyers, is bound to aid his lord against the king; though he is bound to aid him against all other men. To fight a king is a higher treason than to fail a lord, because the king's public authority is greater than that of any private individual.

These statements acknowledge the rights of the secular ruler, who acts in the name of the community, to be so very sweeping as to leave scant room for other allegiances. In such countries as England and France, institutional and administrative develop-ment gave practical force to the ideas about government which they express. This put great power into the hands of their kings. The authority which they were coming to wield, with the assent, tacit or express, of their subjects, was indeed so considerable, that it was hard to see how it could fit into the framework of a united Christendom, with a single directive authority. The growth of secular public authority in Europe's western and northern kingdoms thus presented a new challenge to the universal political authority of the papacy, less obvious than that of the emperors had been, but in its way even more dangerous.

15

Boniface VIII and the Onset of Crisis in the Church

IN the early 1290s, the governors of the Roman Church found themselves facing a series of urgent and dangerous problems. Though peace had been patched up between France and Aragon, the island of Sicily was still in the hands of an Aragonese prince, Frederic, and Charles the Lame of Naples, the son of Charles of Anjou, was struggling to recover it, with formal papal backing but with little prospect of success. All up and down Italy the wars of nobles and cities and the civil strife of parties, in which the princes of the church themselves were involved, were ravaging land and people. At the same time, the quarrels of spirituals and conventuals were threatening the Franciscan order with schism: both parties were armed with conflicting papal bulls, and looking to the pope and his councillors to support them against their rivals. Acre had just fallen, and it was to the papacy men were looking for some plan to restore the Christian cause in the east. A combination of crises had arisen, in which general confidence in the leadership of the Roman Church in Christendom was patently coming under strain.

The election in 1294 of the hermit, Peter Murrone, as Pope Celestine V was an indication of the bewilderment and desperation of the cardinals. The six months' pontificate of a man without letters served only to complicate the situation by introducing total confusion into the church's administration, and the abdication which ended it rendered his successor's position insecure. There was no precedent for a pope's laying aside the tiara, and some doubt as to whether one could do so lawfully. In the circumstances, the choice of Cardinal Benedetto Caetani as his successor may not have been a wise one. He became pope as Boniface VIII. Able he certainly was, but he was also arrogant, old and inflexible, and deeply ambitious, not for himself only but for his family too.

He was in addition a canonist, steeped in the literature of theoretical papal claims to sovereignty in Christendom. He could brook no questioning of the established texts of St Bernard and Hugh of St Victor, and the decretals of Innocent III and IV, which for him put out of doubt the papal right to wield the two swords, of spiritual and temporal power. Faced with a series of intractable political problems, his rigid, juridical attitude in this matter rendered harder a task that was already sisyphean.

The most serious of the dangers that lay ahead were not really clear when Boniface became pope. The papacy had emerged triumphant from its struggle with the Hohenstaufen a quarter of a century before. Concentration on events in Italy and the Mediterranean area, then and since, had partly concealed how crucial, in that struggle, had been the money and arms which France and England had provided in the church's cause. In the 1290s it began to be apparent at last what the price paid by the papacy for their assistance had been. Much more had in fact been bartered than promises of the crowns of Sicily and Aragon to English and French princes. Boniface was to be made very sharply aware of this.

Part of the price had been paid in hard cash.. Gregory IX had begun the practice of taxing the whole clerical body throughout Europe for the purposes of the crusade, charging a proportion of their annual 'spiritual' revenues (income from tithes, that is, and from property held in 'free alms', i.e. by the service of prayer for the community and for the donor). The wars against the Hohenstaufen and the Aragonese had rated as crusades, and for them the clergy had been taxed in the same way as for the Holy Land. When the papacy called secular champions from France and England to its aid, the problem of defraying their expenses thus had a simple solution: they were allowed to collect and keep the crusading tenths of the clergy's spiritual revenue. Henry III of England would have faced financial crisis long before 1258, had it not been for the contributions which the English clergy had made to his treasury, nominally for the conquest of Sicily. The French had done even better out of clerical taxation. The Aragonese crusade alone had brought to Philip III in 1284 a grant, from Martin IV, of a tenth of all clerical revenues in France for four years, and to Philip IV a similar grant from Nicholas IV in 1289 for three years. The very natural result of all this, though not on the papal side an intended one, was that the kings of France and England had come to regard financial assistance from the clergy of their realms as rightly due to them, whenever their diplomatic and military commitments made it necessary for them to demand aids from their subjects.

Taxation helped to habituate the clergy to cooperating more closely in royal secular policy than they had done in the past. Other factors also served to draw the kings of France and England and their native clergy closer together. In the thirteenth century the papacy, in order to defray costs of administration and to reward its Italian servants and allies and their families, greatly extended the practice of 'providing' Italians to benefices outside Italy (especially to stalls in cathedral and collegiate churches), and of reserving the presentation of benefices to itself in advance for this purpose. The 'provisors' nominated drew the revenues of the benefices which they obtained, and paid others (often inadequately) to discharge their duties in their absence. That native clergymen should have bitterly resented this system was natural. They resented also the demands made of them by papal legates when these were in their country, and the expenses to which litigation in the courts of Rome often put them. They looked to their own kings to protect their interests against foreigners from the *curia*. Their kings had more to offer them besides protection, for their political influence enabled them to ensure preferment for their own servants and favourites. There tended, in consequence, to be a preponderance of kings' men among the leaders of the French and English clergy. Both their own interests, and the extension of royal authority, associated the ecclesiastical communities in these kingdoms more and more closely in the national life. Thus the papacy had to pay for the support of the kings of France and England by sharing with them not only the revenues of their clergy, but also, more important, their allegiance.

It was among the secular clergy that this gradual alienation from Rome was most marked. The regular clergy, the monastic orders such as the Cluniacs and the Cistercians, and all the friars, had been from their foundation more accustomed than the seculars to direction from Rome; and because the internal organization of their orders was international, preferment at royal hands was less likely to come their way. They included, unfortunately, the very richest sections of the whole clerical world. They were usually louder in their complaints at the new burdens which kings were imposing on them, than in protest at the demands of the papacy. As long as the kings of France and England remained the popes' faithful allies the divided allegiance of their clergy, and the different attitudes of regulars and seculars towards their situation, did not matter very greatly. In 1294 the outbreak of war between France and England brought the problems that it created suddenly into the open, to hurry on a crisis for Pope Boniface.

The war which broke out in that year between Philip IV and Edward I was sparked off by a clash between French and English sailors off the Breton coast. The background to it was the growing friction between their respective officials in the duchy of Gascony, which Edward held as a fief from Philip. Its origins had nothing to do with papal policy at all. Both kings, however, had become accustomed to planning their campaigns on a scale which could only be paid for if the entire communities they ruled, laymen and clergy alike, contributed to their expenses. Edward in 1294 immediately took power to seize stocks of wool, which much alarmed the English Cistercian monasteries. Philip instructed all the metropolitans of France to assemble their clergy and obtain their agreement to pay him a subsidy. In England there were bitter complaints from the Cistercians: in a number of provinces in France they flatly refused to pay anything, and the king instructed his officials to seize their goods. Boniface had no option but to intervene. In 1296 he issued his bull *Clericis Laicos*, which forbade all clergy to contribute in any way to taxes imposed by the secular authority, except when these were sanctioned by the Pope.

The issue which *Clericis Laicos* regulated was very important.

What right had a secular ruler to ask clerics, who were undoubtedly his subjects and undoubtedly rich, to contribute towards his needs from properties held within his realm? Boniface's answer was clear. The church's properties had been given her for spiritual ends, whose direction was the province of the Holy See. To apply clerical wealth to ends which it had not approved was to trespass on papal sovereignty, and 'a horrid abuse of secular power'. In law and precedent his case was strong: in common sense and contemporary conditions it was much less so. The riposte of the French and English kings showed quickly where its weakness lay. Boniface could state the law as he chose, but he had no power to enforce his ruling. Indeed, placed as he was at the time, he could not even afford the attempt to do so.

For the crisis had come on him at an unfortunate moment. Boniface's chosen method to bring order to the patrimony of St Peter around Rome was through the advancement of members of his own family, by building up, for his nephews, a great Caetani heritage in the papal lands of central Italy. Their preferment had entangled them and the Pope with the Colonna, one of the most formidable noble families of Rome, with two cardinals among its members. In March of 1297 the quarrel between the two families broke into open war in the Papal State. To Boniface's sentence of excommunication and deposition from all their offices, the Colonna replied with the denial of his authority: 'We do not believe that you are lawful pope.' By making themselves out to be the champions of Celestine V, the Colonna bid for the alliance of the spiritual Franciscans, for whom Celestine was a hero and martyr (he had died in confinement in 1296). These visionaries could prove very dangerous adversaries for the spiritual father of Christendom. Men like Friar Jacopone da Todi had a mastery of apocalyptic denunciation, which was the more effective for being wholly uncoloured by politics.

Edward in England was meanwhile bringing his clergy to heel, by the simple method of withdrawing from them the protection of his common law. To avoid the consequences of this, most of them were glad to buy back the king's peace, and to petition the Pope to moderate his bull. What Philip of France had done was even more effective. He prohibited the export of specie in any form out of his kingdom. The pope could not hope to fight the Colonna without aid from the revenues of the French clergy, and without transporting bullion from anywhere else through France. The situation of Frederick II's day, when the papacy's wars in Italy had been paid for with the coin of France and England, was completely reversed, and Boniface had no option but to compromise. He did not withdraw *Clericis Laicos*, but he glossed it in two other bulls. *Ineffabilis Amor* permitted clerics to pay taxes to a secular ruler, if a situation of genuine national emergency justified his demand for them. *Etsi de Statu* (July 1297) made it clear that it was lawful for the king to decide himself whether such an emergency had arisen.

This outcome was a considerable victory for Edward and Philip, particularly for the latter. Whatever reserves Boniface might make in principle, their right to tax their clergy, along with their other subjects, was conceded, which was the practical point which had been at stake for them. There, for Edward and England, matters rested: he was to have further difficulties later with Boniface, but there was never another open rupture. Philip's case was different. He was used to acting in a more high-handed manner than Edward, and had made for himself a position of greater strength. He had made contact with Boniface's other recent enemies: the Colonna had been in touch with the French court since 1296, before their quarrel with the Pope became open. Philip's councillors had seen the Colonna's ferocious manifestos, denouncing Boniface's 'entry by fraud into the papacy', bidding him to withdraw and calling for his suspension, until a general council should have considered the validity of his election, and their demand was backed by a number of the spiritual Franciscans. The king's advisers therefore knew that if a new confrontation were to occur, they could count on support from outside France, and they believed that they could safely counsel their master to make no concessions to the Pope. They probably did not expect any confrontation to occur in the circumstances at all.

*

212

What was disturbing the king's councillors far more than relations with Boniface about the year 1300 was the situation in Languedoc. The great inheritance of the counts of Toulouse had been directly administered by royal officials only since 1271: and it was one of the areas where, in 1295 and 1296, clerical resistance to royal taxation had been most obstinate. The activities of the inquisition, firmly supported by the royal authorities in the suppression of the Cathar heresy, were known to have excited bitterness. The lords of Languedoc had traditional connexions with the English Duke of Gascony, with whom the king of France was now at war. Suspicions both of anti-French and pro-Cathar leanings seem to have drawn the attention of the king's officials in 1301 to the activities of Bishop Bernard Saisset of Pamiers, who had obtained his see through papal favour. He was arrested on charges of sedition and heresy. The latter accusation meant that he would be tried, almost certainly, before the inquisition, which permitted the accused no right to speak in his own defence. Probably it was thought it would be useful in the province to make an example of him, and that Boniface, after his recent setback, would not risk intervention on his behalf. Bernard, seeing his life in jeopardy, however, appealed to the Pope. By taking up his cause, and demanding for him as a cleric a fair trial in the courts of the church, Boniface brought on a second and far more serious confrontation between himself and Philip.

His action was courageous; he must, after what had passed, have known that he was taking risks. But he knew his law, and the position it bound him to maintain: perhaps he knew it too well. For the issues raised in Bernard Saisset's case were more serious and far-reaching even than the matter of taxation. The charges against him included treason. For Boniface to claim to judge the matter as of right was, therefore, in effect to claim that he, and not Philip, was the proper arbiter as to what was or was not treason committed by a subject against the king of France. This meant that the affair must bring into the open questions about the precise nature of the sovereignty which the Pope claimed to exercise in the Christian community, and how far it gave him the right to intervene in the temporal affairs of a Christian kingdom.

The stand Boniface took was so clear as to constitute a direct challenge to Philip. It was based on the broadest and most general principles. His bull *Ausculta Filii*, addressed to Philip personally, opened with the text of Jeremiah:

I have this day set thee over the nations and the kingdoms, to root out and to pull down ... to build and to plant.

While thus reminding the king of the nature of papal sovereignty, Boniface summoned the clergy of France to Rome to meet him in council in November 1302,

that we may have your advice, as to what may best be done to preserve the liberties of Holy Church, and for the reform of your king and kingdom, and for the good rule thereof.

The last words were the key ones. They make it clear that the clergy were to sit in judgement on the king's actions, and that it was the Pope's right to amend them if he saw fit.

It was in this council (which was, needless to say, ill attended) that the bull *Unam Sanctam* was promulgated in December 1302. It was the clearest and probably the most logical statement concerning the temporal sovereignty of the popes that was ever made. 'There is but one Holy Church, outside which there is neither salvation nor remission of sins.' These were the opening words: since the church is one body, it continued, it can have only one head, 'that is Christ and Christ's vicar, Peter and Peter's successors.' Hence all powers necessary to salvation are in the hands of that vicar: hence, 'if the secular power strays from the way, it shall be judged by the spiritual.' There was little new in these statements: even the precise wording was largely borrowed from well known texts. It was the clarity of the statement that made it impressive, leaving no room for doubt or casuistry: and the fact that, without even mentioning him, it publicly condemned the conduct of the most powerful king in Europe.

Before December 1302 Philip had already made it clear that he was going to take up the pope's challenge. His response to *Ausculta Filii* was to summon the Estates General. A doctored version of the bull, which turned it from a call to repentance into a declaration that all who denied the pope's control of presentation to all benefices in France were heretics, was read to the assembly. This was followed up with a long catalogue of Boniface's alleged offences, avarice, nepotism, irregularities in presenting to benefices, and much more, delivered by Pierre Flote, Philip's chancellor. The propaganda was skilfully prepared and presented and had its desired effect. It brought the representatives of the clergy into line with the king's wishes, and elicited a prayer from the nobles and the third estate that he act to defend the rights of the kingdom and of the French church.

This was what Philip needed. His intention was to arraign Boniface before a council, which should depose this pope who had dared to intervene between him and his subjects. To lay before this council, the king now had ready to hand the piteous complaints against Roman tyranny of the three estates of his realm. His councillor Nogaret was ready with a further series of charges against Boniface, accusing him of being no pope, and a heretic. The difficulty, that the king of France had no authority to summon a general church council (the only body competent in canon law to judge an accused pope), had been provided for. Nogaret was in contact with the Colonna, and had made a rendezvous with them in Italy. His mission was, with their aid, to seize the Pope, to bring him into France, and there force him to summon a council for his own undoing.

If the council had ever met, it might very probably have condemned Boniface. Nogaret had a method of securing convictions, effective if repugnant. The evidence which he collected afterwards shows how he would have proceeded. There were to be charges raising genuine issues, allegations of simony, and of the taint of heresy in the wording of the Pope's bulls; and the question of the validity of his election was to be brought up. But the real force of Nogaret's indictment was to consist in repugnant and obscene personal slanders on Boniface, culled from the tittle-tattle of the streets in Italy. This was calculated to achieve its effect by sheer weight of denigration. There were stories that Boniface was an unbeliever; a Sodomite; a dealer in magic. Repulsive little tales about the procuring of women and advances made to bootboys would have left little shred of dignity about Boniface, if he had lived to hear them alleged against him in a public trial. He would probably not even have been able to answer them: Nogaret certainly planned to demand the procedure of the inquisition, which allowed the accused no right to speak for himself. Certainly the plans of Philip and his adviser for the ruin of his adversary were very skilfully laid.

In fact Nogaret's scheme miscarried and his council never met. He reached Italy safely enough and joined forces with Sciarra Colonna. On 7 September 1303 Boniface, lying sick at Anagni, was surprised and seized by them and their men. But before any steps could be taken to move the proud old man, the citizens had risen and delivered him. Nogaret had to flee back to France. Boniface had just strength left to struggle back to Rome, where he died on 12 October.

There was no need for a council after that. What had happened had rendered *Unam Sanctam* a dead letter. The laws which Boniface had quoted in it might be sound in theory: they were demonstrably out of step with political facts, for practical purposes empty words. It was no good seeking to discipline or depose a king of France by papal authority. His people, laymen and clergy alike, were too solidly loyal to the line of St Louis, as was proved publicly by the reaction of the Estates General and the acquiescence of the French bishops in royal policy throughout the crisis. *Unam Sanctam* remained unrepealed, but no pope ever sought again to give effect to the papal superiority over kings in secular matters, which it alleged. The universal secular authority of the papacy, which had successfully challenged that of the empire, broke against the sovereignty of the king of France. This is testimony to a profound change since the days of Innocent III in the political structure of Europe. No pope could lord it any longer over kings and princes in the way he had done.

*

Boniface's disaster was to have a sequel, however, which showed that this was not the whole story. In 1303 Philip seemed to have won on every essential point, and to cap his success, in 1305 a Frenchman became pope. The papacy seemed to have become his instrument, for Clement V never left France: his pontificate began a long exile from Italy for the popes. Nevertheless, Philip found he could not have his way with him entirely.

In 1307, hard pressed for money as a result of his wars in Flanders, Philip sought to turn Clement's subservience to his own ends. He arrested all the Templars in France, and seized their immense wealth. An indictment, on the same repulsive lines as that to be made against Boniface, had been prepared by Nogaret, accusing the whole order of the Temple of cloaking under oaths of secrecy a system of organized vice and communal sacrilege. The order, from its foundation, had been directly subject to the Pope. To force Clement's hand, Philip coupled his demand for action against it with an open threat to reopen the case against Boniface, and to subject the Holy See to the appalling indignity of the posthumous trial of a pope. In spite of this, Philip's attempted *coup* fell short of the mark. The Templars were never formally condemned. At the council of Vienne in 1312 Clement simply dissolved the order, exonerating Philip at the same time from all blame in this matter and that of Boniface. The goods of the Templars outside France, which Philip had coveted, were transferred to the Order of the Hospital. All this was done by Clement, not by judicial sentence, but by a simple act of sovereignty in his capacity as head of the church – by that same universal 'plenitude of power' which Boniface had defined in *Unam Sanctam*.

Philip's partial failure in the matter of the Templars is not hard to explain. Horrid charges, concocted by Nogaret and backed up with 'confessions' wrung from individual Templars under torture, were enough to satisfy the Estates of France that their king's action was proper. But the Templars were an international order: elsewhere there was no Nogaret, and no torture, and frank scepticism about the charges against them. The Pope was able to act this time in 'the plenitude of his power', because only Philip and the French wished him to act in another way, and it was not merely their affair. Philip's attempt to force the Pope's hand for a

third time thus only succeeded in demonstrating that papal
authority was still far more strongly entrenched than it had
seemed in the aftermath of Boniface's misfortune. By the mere
fact of its existence, as a universal power in a Europe, many of
whose ecclesiastical institutions were international (as the mendicant and monastic orders, and the learned communities in the
universities), the papacy continued to be immensely powerful.

There is a very important moral in this. The key to the outcome of this affair of the Templars proves to be the fact that it
was not just an issue between France and the papacy. This
suggests that the earlier quarrel of King Philip and Pope Boniface also needs to be looked at in a broader context than that of
Franco–papal relations, if its true significance is to be appreciated.

Philip himself did not think of the affair as one affecting France
only. His plan to bring Boniface to trial before a council makes it
clear that he considered it as one in which the whole of Christendom ought to be involved. It is important to remember here that
Philip, though not a very attractive character, was a pious man
in a conventional way: his dearest dream was of leading a great
European crusade after the example of his grandfather St Louis.
He would not have acted as he did if he had not thought his
actions could be squared with the general well-being of Christendom. He had justification, moreover, for permitting himself to
think they could be so squared. The idea of proceeding against
Boniface through a council was not a French one; it came
originally from the Colonna manifesto of 1297. It was not the
French, but the Colonna and the spiritual Franciscans who first
raised doubts about the validity of Boniface's election. Outcry
against the pontiff came not from France alone, but from all
over Christian Europe. If this had not been so, Philip's chal-
lenges to Boniface would not have been so successful, and would
in fact probably never have been made.

The whole story of their confrontation is really symptomatic
of much more besides the growing power of national sovereigns.
It reveals a change that had taken place in the attitudes of men,
not in France only but all over Europe, towards the established
Roman church and the claims of her pontiff. Boniface's intran-

sigence brought this change out into the open, but it was not the cause of it. It was the product of the whole history of papal activities over the last fifty years and more: of the papacy's failure to supply adequate leadership in the crusades in the east: of her inability to find room for the holy fervour and the high ideals of the spiritual Franciscans within the fold of the church: of her entanglement in the Guelf–Ghibelline struggles in Italy: of her incessant quest for money, which was spent for ends which appeared to be entirely political. The attitudes of the Estates General and the leaders of the French clergy during Philip's quarrel with Boniface are indications of the way in which these things had affected men who were, for the most part, perfectly sincere and adequate Christians. A still clearer and much more vivid impression of their effect and repercussions is to be found in the writings of a contemporary of Boniface who lived not in France but in Italy, in the treatment of the popes in the *Divine Comedy* of Dante Alighieri.

In Dante's poem, Boniface VIII, with Nicholas III who came before and Clement V who came after, are all to be found together in the *inferno*, in the pit of the simoniacs. This is what Dante has to say to them:

> Tell me, how much treasure Our Lord required of Peter, when he put the keys into his keeping? Surely he demanded nought but 'Follow me' ... Shepherds are ye, such as the evangelist perceived, when she that sitteth upon the water was seen by him committing fornication with the kings.... You have made a god of gold and silver for yourselves: wherein do you differ from the idolator?

These angry words show what Dante thought about the pope's power to bind and loose on earth, and about their entanglement in contemporary politics, and about the revenues which were gathered in to Rome from the churches all over Europe. Papal politics and cupidity seemed to him to be what had plunged all of Italy into strife, and much of Europe too. The temporal power of the popes seemed the chief obstacle in the contemporary world to terrestrial peace and concord, which among men is a necessary condition if the life of the spirit is to flourish. The activities of the papacy had ceased for him to have anything to do with the message which Christ brought, 'goodwill towards men'. Yet Dante was as sincere and upright and orthodox a Christian as any man of his day.

What Dante wrote shows the degree to which events had undermined, for him and his contemporaries, all confidence in the ability of the papacy to provide leadership in the Christian community. It had become so deeply entangled in politics, and the ecclesiastical hierarchy through which it ruled was so ridden with vested interests, that they were no longer able to promote the Christian life. Nevertheless, to Dante the unity of Christian peoples in this world appeared as a religious necessity, a condition vital to the church's fulfilment of her true mission. He, and the many who thought like him, were at one with Pope Boniface that the church was a single body, and that it required direction towards one end. Only they had ceased to believe that the popes were giving proper directions, and had therefore to look for them elsewhere.

Dante's own hopes were centred on a revival of the empire, which he believed for a time might be close at hand, when Henry of Luxemburg marched into Italy in 1310. But in this he was old-fashioned, misled by his studies in classical history: Henry's failure was a foregone conclusion. The day of universal empire had passed definitely with the death of Frederick II. Dante's French contemporary, Pierre Dubois, had other ideas: his hopes reposed in a grand European confederation, to be led by the princes of France in a new crusade. But there was not much in his schemes either: the day of the crusades had passed too, and few in Germany and Italy were enthusiastic for the rule of the French princes he wished to see set over them. There remained, however, a third alternative, in which others than Dante and Dubois thought they could discern some hope, and which was to be very important in the future.

Boniface VIII's troubles had drawn attention to the authority which a general council of the church might, in an emergency, have to exercise. It was the only authority which could canonically judge a pope who was accused of heresy. Contemporary institutional developments suggested further possibilities in such an assembly. Through some system which gave representation to all sections of the Christian community, a council might offer a prospect of bringing together people and authorities in Europe, whose interests and outlook seemed to be drawing them further and further apart. It might also, by the same means, constitute an authority so broadly based as to rise above the trammels of local vested interest, and so be able to tackle the ingrained abuses in the ecclesiastical system. Ideas such as these were much in the minds of two scholars, Marsiglio of Padua and William of Ockham, who in the 1320s found refuge from papal censures at the court of the Emperor Lewis of Bavaria, whose support for the Ghibelline enemies of the papacy in north Italy had led to his excommunication.

In their works and those of Dante the true moral of the unhappy career of Pope Boniface VIII stands out clearly. It is not that the ideal of Christian universalism, which was at the root of the thought behind the bull *Unam Sanctum*, was dead. It is not that the authority of national kings had become all powerful, great though it was. It is that by the fourteenth century men no longer believed that the traditional authorities in the Roman church were capable of upholding or furthering its traditional ideals, secular or spiritual. The old confidence of European Christendom was shaken: men were ceasing to ask how they should build a greater unity, and beginning to wonder how they could maintain what there was.

SECTION FOUR

c. 1330 – c. 1460

The Decline of the Ideal of the
Unity of Christendom, and the Triumph
of New Forces.

16

Economic and Social Development
in the Later Middle Ages

THE close of the thirteenth century, which saw the collapse of the crusader states and the rise in France and England of embryonic national communities, was a time also when important changes in the tempo of economic and social life in Europe began to exercise an influence. An age of expansion was drawing to a close; a new period of stabilization and in some respects of recession, was commencing. Such developments are of a nature which makes it impossible to pin them down to any precise set of dates, and it is very difficult to generalize about their effects accurately. But if a generalization is attempted, one might say that the most striking effect, broadly, was what might be described as an invasion of government into economic and social relations. If it is asked why this 'invasion' took place, one might answer, again speaking very broadly, that this was due to the fact that, while expansion of European commerce and population had reached their limits, the development of commercial and productive techniques had not. Thus pressures were created which could not be contained at the local and individual level, but only by better organization in business, increased social solidarity, and, in the long run, direction by government in the economic and social fields.

Certain widespread symptoms of this changing aspect of things are very clear. The earlier age of expansion had given wide opportunities for individual effort and achievement. This was reflected in the immense profits realized by merchants from, for instance, Venice and Genoa in the early twelfth century, in ventures organized by partnerships of two or three men. It was reflected also in the great achievements of small groups of nameless and forgotten peasants in the clearance and settlement of waste land. It stands out most clearly of all in the history of how individual and enterprising noblemen won inheritances for themselves far from home in the period of the crusade. Their adventures gave birth to a whole literature of knight errantry, whose most amazing feature is its limitless geographic background: there is no knowing whither a story will carry the hero who leaves a poor hearth and heritage in France or England at its opening. In the fourteenth century such stories still captivated, but they had lost much of their realism. It was an age of combination rather than individual effort: of conquests won not by individuals, but by bands of mercenary soldiers (as the Catalan company, which overran Frankish Greece in 1311); of leagues of towns and guilds of workmen, organized for self-protection; of leagues of landed noblemen, formed to maintain their class privileges; of peasant revolts. This fashion for combination is a clear indication that circumstances had become in this period harder than in the past.

In considering economic and social developments in this last period of the Middle Ages, which often seems to be an age of stagnation and decline, it is well to remember that they were the prelude which made possible the achievements of a later period of expansion. If one compares the European expansion in the sixteenth century with the earlier expansion, from the eleventh to the thirteenth century, one will notice that in the later period governments played a much larger part, individuals a less crucial role. This is a consequence of processes which took place in between times, and which I have called an 'invasion of government into economic and social relations'. It is also a sign that the period in between, and which we have under review, was not just one of stagnation, but of formation too.

In this process of formation, three factors seem to have been particularly important. The first of them has been already mentioned: the fact that European commercial expansion had for the time being reached its limit, and in some areas was suffering a recession. The second was the combined effect on economic life of endemic war, and the series of great plagues, the first of which was called the Black Death (1347–9). The third was an immense advance in techniques both of production and of commercial exchange. In the rest of this chapter we shall look at the effects of each of these three factors in turn.

*

The commercial expansion of the earlier Middle Ages produced a pattern of exchange, in which Europe's most important single export was finished cloth, and her most important imports were the silks and spices, which came from the Orient through Italy, and the furs, wax and honey which came from the Baltic. It also produced urban concentrations in the chief areas of exchange and production. Ghent, Bruges and Ypres in Flanders, and Florence in Tuscany were centres of the cloth industry. Venice, Pisa and Genoa in Italy, and Lübeck and Danzig in east Germany were great centres of import; the towns of the Rhine and Bruges close to its mouth flourished on the traffic which flowed along the river north and south. In all these towns, the need to control and regulate their own economic affairs had prompted demands for a measure of internal self-government, which most of them won in the twelfth century. The leaders in their struggle for liberty, and their descendants, became their governors, an hereditary urban patriciate.

Thus a framework was established within which the stabilization of commerce (and hence of demand for finished goods) inevitably produced tensions. For those cities whose prosperity was primarily mercantile, the danger was the competition of rivals in the markets where their merchants bought. In the case of Venice and Genoa this led to cut-throat competition to corner markets in the east by means of advantageous agreements with the local authorities there, and it led also to a series of long commercial wars between them, fought out in the Levant and the Aegean, which lasted all through the fourteenth century. By the time Venice finally emerged triumphant in the fifteenth century there was no room for a rival; the wars of the Tartar emperor Tamburlaine (1358–1405) and of the Ottoman Turks had upset the flow into the markets of the Levant of the commodities which the merchants of Italy sought there. The German towns which flourished on the Baltic trade had to face the same problem of competition in the same period. They, however, found a less destructive and violent means for overcoming their difficulties, by leaguing with one another to exclude all outside rivals.

The most important and striking example of this was the Hanseatic league, whose members virtually monopolized the trade of the Baltic and the North Sea. The merchants of Lübeck, the most important of the Hanse towns, had, as early as the twelfth century, obtained privileges for themselves in the markets to which they travelled, London, Novgorod and Bruges. By admitting other towns to a share in their privileges, on condition that they cooperate to exclude any outside rivals, a powerful league was slowly built up. Its key centres were at Lübeck and Danzig, which controlled the Baltic trade; Hamburg and Bremen, which controlled the North Sea; and Cologne on the Rhine. In the 1360s, when the power of the Hanse was at its height, there were over seventy cities in the league, and it had set up a Diet, in which their representatives all met to discuss decisions on common policy. They were sufficiently strong and united to embark on a major war with Denmark, which ended in 1370 with a peace that rounded off their control of the Baltic trade. It also gave the Hanse from now on more or less complete control of the very important herring fisheries of the Baltic Sound. Salt herring was a staple element in the diet of Catholic Europe, and the Hanse control of the fisheries was one of the chief sources of their power and prosperity. The migration of herring shoals away from the Sound in the early fifteenth century was to be one of the reasons for their decline later.

The Hanseatic league was not a sovereign state, but a federal union of independent towns. Their united resources gave the league the naval and military resources to undertake wars against the Scandinavian kingdoms and England, in order to keep their merchants out of its markets. Other city leagues in Germany used the same means to solve different problems. The main object of the leagues of the Rhenish towns was to protect river traffic from depredation in the course of the feudal squabbles of the nobility, and from the tolls which princes and nobles imposed in their territories. The most famous of these was the Swabian league, formed in 1376, which at one point counted over eighty member-cities, and was powerful enough to challenge the forces of the dukes of Bavaria and Austria. It was almost certainly its success which inspired the attempt of the emperor Wenceslas, at the Imperial diet at Eger in 1389, to restore order in his dominions by the creation of eight peace leagues, with considerable internal autonomy and covering the whole territory of the empire. The experiment quickly broke down, owing to the opposition of the nobility. It is nevertheless an impressive demonstration of the potential for improved government latent in the leagues for a ruler who could harness their loyalty and resources to his own ends.

The object of the Hanse and the Rhenish leagues was to protect and promote exchange. In the great productive centres, association made its influence felt in a rather different way, in the internal organization of city life rather than in external policy. The object of the craft guilds was, nevertheless, essentially the same as that of the town leagues, to exclude competition. A craft guild was an association in a given town of the masters of a trade, of the cutlers, say, or the haberdashers or the clothmen, who combined to control prices, wages, and the standards and conditions of sale of their products, and to monopolize their manufacture. The guild was an independent corporation, with its own hierarchy of officials, its scheme of training and apprenticeship, and common funds. These last met the costs of administration, of the upkeep of the hall where the guild members met, and could help to pay also for such civic amenities as hospitals and churches, to protect the health both spiritual and physical of all engaged in the trade. In many cities the guilds became so rich and powerful that membership became the essential qualification for taking part in the communal government.

Guild monopolism promoted and protected patrician government. The guild worked through the family: a member's children had the right of entry, others could only enter if they could find a master to apprentice them, and the outsider's chance was poor against members' cousins and collaterals. For the labourer it was nearly impossible to rise into this aristocracy, which, being formed partly to protect its members by regulation of wages against competition in the labour market, inevitably excluded him. These circumstances lent themselves to oppression of the artisan, especially when prices were high, as was often the case in the aftermath of plague or famine, when these employers' organizations could help to prevent wages rising in response to the scarcity of labour. To better themselves, labourers therefore copied their masters, and formed associations to maintain high wages and improve their conditions. This was a threat to guild control which the members were determined not to permit; and they used their control of urban government habitually to outlaw all associations of workmen. But distress usually led to the re-formation of such associations, often under cover of religious purposes. When the artisans were thwarted too often, their frustration erupted in ferocious social revolt.

Of the many examples of this pattern of pressure, the history of Florence provides an excellent instance. Florence was the greatest city of all Italy, and the centre where the finest cloths and woollens of Europe were manufactured. Her artisan population was by contemporary standards enormous: Giovanni Villani, writing in 1350, believed that the clothmakers' guild (*Arte della Lana*) alone employed thirty thousand workers. There were twenty-one guilds (or arts) in the city, whose members controlled its republican government. By the fourteenth century the eight 'greater arts' had emerged dominant after struggles with both the Ghibelline nobility and the lesser guilds. No sooner did their authority begin to become established than the signs of proletarian discontent began to look threatening.

In 1324 and 1334 the authorities of the city found it necessary to make statutes forbidding associations of workmen: in 1338 the wool guild even forbade assemblies of artisans for religious purposes. The year 1345 saw the first artisan revolt, led by the wool-comber Ciuto Brandini, which was successfully put down. Twenty-three years later in 1378 revolt broke out again on a wider and much more terrible scale. The *Ciompi*, the very poorest labourers, were this time wholly beyond control. They captured the Palazzo of the commune and virtually held the authorities to ransom. The latter were forced to recognize the *Ciompi* themselves as a guild, and their leader, Michele Lando, as Gonfalonier of Justice, the highest office in the city. Like most artisan revolts of the period, this one, having achieved a degree of success, found its force spent. Within four years the old patrician guilds were able to destroy all open traces of its triumph. From then on, however, the patricians and their children lived in the constant fear of another proletarian rising. It was this fear that made possible, in the fifteenth century, the veiled despotism of the Medici, who, though patricians, had been implicated in the revolt of the *Ciompi*. Under the guidance of this great merchant family which, while aristocratic by connexions, was yet loved by the people, Florence was slowly transformed from a disorderly republic into a princely state by the time of Lorenzo the Magnificent (1469–92).

The history of the towns of Flanders provides a parallel to that of Florence in the same period, with some interesting contrasts. Here, at the end of the thirteenth century, the rising tide of unrest among the artisans of the great cloth towns gave Count Guy of Dampierre his first chance to bring the patrician governments of the cities under his control. The patricians looked to the king of France for protection; and it was against King Philip IV that the craftsmen of Bruges, who had risen and killed their royal governor and his patrician aides, fought and won the great victory of Courtrai in 1302. For twenty-six years afterwards Flanders was continuously disturbed by social revolts, which spread from the cities into the countryside. The king and the count made their peace and both joined forces with the patricians against the craftsmen; in the end Courtrai was revenged by a victory at Cassel in 1328. The massacre following this battle did not end the social struggle but embittered it. It continued to rumble all through the fourteenth century, erupting from time to time into open civil war, and staining the history of Flanders with memories of riot, murder and massacre. It was the same story as that of Florence, only more violent and grim, for it became a struggle of patrician and artisan not in one town only, but in three, Ghent, Bruges, and Ypres. The craftsmen of Bruges showed no more mercy to the patricians of Ghent, when they could lay hands on them, than to their own masters, and vice versa.

What ended the internal and internecine struggles of the Flemish towns was the rule in their county of the Valois dukes of Burgundy, who were counts of Flanders also from 1384 until 1477. Under them, at last, the towns enjoyed a paternal government, which laboured for the prosperity of all classes, not one or another. The Valois dukes, as a result of their shrewd dynastic policies, came in course of time to control not only Flanders, but nearly all the small territories of the Low Countries as well, as Brabant, Hainault, Holland, and Guelders. Thus the Flemish towns enjoyed under them a greater freedom of commerce with their neighbours than they had ever known before. The dukes encouraged the migration of artisans out of the towns into the country districts, and cloth weaving began to become a rural industry. The patricians of the cities found meanwhile that peace and order could assure their prosperity as well or better than restrictive regulation of labour. Thus in Flanders, as in Florence, the social stresses caused by the exclusiveness of the guilds were alleviated by the intervention of a paternal government which saw that the prosperity of its subjects could be a mainstay of its own power. But there was this difference. Florence became a princely state herself: the Flemish towns were integrated into the economic life of the combined dominions of the Valois dukes of Burgundy.

It was in consequence not only Flanders that benefited by the ducal government. Its protection secured the future of the growing market of Antwerp, which would otherwise certainly have had to fight for survival against Bruges, and of Dutch shipping, which might otherwise have been driven from the seas by the Hanse. The sort of successful commercial policy which the dukes initiated was pursued by other rulers, elsewhere, in the face of similar problems. Louis XI in France (1461–83) took the markets of Rouen and Bordeaux under his protection, and helped to encourage silk manufacture at Lyons. He fostered close association between the monarchy and the ruling families of the great towns of his kingdom. These are signs that we are beginning to move into an age of associations on a much more powerful scale than those of city leagues, employers' guilds, and artisans' confraternities. The producer, the merchant, and even to some extent the labourer were beginning to find a more effective protection than they had known previously, under the wing of monarchy, which had the resources of the whole national community to support it.

*

The pattern of pressures generated by the great plagues and the endless wars of the fourteenth and fifteenth centuries was not so very different from the one we have just been examining. Perhaps the chief difference was that it was in the countryside that effects of plague and war showed most clearly, for the country had much less capacity for recovery after plague or devastation than a town did.

The Black Death was one of a series of factors whose cumulative effect was to bring about a general decline in agrarian prosperity, in some parts amounting to real impoverishment of the country. In France and Italy devastation caused by continuous wars played a part in this process perhaps greater than that of the plague; the great European famines of 1316 and 1317 had lasting effect too. Even before that there are signs that the increase in the rural population had in many parts reached its limit and begun to decline. But the impact of the Black Death was much more dramatic than any of this. It was a bubonic plague, carried by rats, but accompanied by pneumonic outbreaks which were still more fatal. It seems to have started in China, about 1333; in 1346 it was raging in Sicily, and by 1348 it had reached France, Spain, England and Germany. Its impact was devastating. In Paris, it was said, over eight hundred people died of it by the day. At Montpellier the population was so decimated that the burgesses were soon inviting repopulation from as far afield as Italy. In some parts whole villages were virtually wiped out by plague, in others many of their inhabitants fled before it.

It is clear that most contemporary accounts of the plague are exaggerated. The economic effects were certainly severe in the areas where it hit hardest: they included scarcity of labour, high prices, and the falling off of rents due to lack of tenants ready to take up vacant holdings. We need not doubt that genuine observation lay behind remarks such as that of the English chronicler Henry Knighton: 'There was such a scarcity of labourers that women and even small children could be seen at the plough and leading the waggons.' But settlements which were entirely deserted as a result of the plague are hard to find, and stories of one man in ten or twelve left alive are clearly out of proportion. Probably there were few areas where the death rate was more than one in three in the first epidemic (for the plague proved to be recurrent: outbreaks continued at intervals well beyond the medieval period). Its impact also varied considerably in intensity from place to place.

With all these reservations about its fatality there can be no doubt about the bewilderment and terror that the plague caused. 'A father did not visit his son,' wrote Guy de Chauliac, the Pope's physician at Avignon, 'nor a son the father. Charity was dead. Even the doctors did not dare visit the sick for fear of infection.' Many ascribed the disease to more or less supernatural causes, as to the influence of the comet which had appeared in 1345. The hysteria of the ill-informed manifested itself in movements such as that of the Flagellants of the Rhineland, who came through towns dancing, lashing themselves, and calling on men to repent, and in massacres of the Jews.

Because the plague was universal and shocking and very frightening, people reacted strongly to its immediate effects, probably more strongly than they warranted. Both in France and England this led directly to royal ordinances concerning labour, prices and wages. The object was, as far as possible, to pin prices and wages, which had soared, at their pre-plague level, and to prevent men leaving their occupations in search of better pay. Needless to say the measures were not successful, but the issues involved, once raised, could not be put aside. Petitions to the king to enforce by statute low wages for labourers were urged again and again by the burgesses and knights of the shire in the English Parliaments of the later fourteenth century. This very soon became the cause of social unrest. In several English counties there were riots at the sessions of the justices appointed to enforce the statute of labourers of 1351. Both France and

England, not long after the first appearance of the plague, were to have their first taste of peasant revolts, in the rising in 1358 in France of the peasants of Champagne, Picardy, and the Beauvasis (the *Jacquerie*), and of the artisans of London and the peasantry of the southern and eastern counties of England in 1381. Neither the Black Death nor labour legislation were direct causes of either of these two revolts. They were, however, contributory causes, and one cannot help wondering whether the revolts would ever have taken place if it had not been for the shock of the plague and the sudden gulf revealed after it between the interests of lord and labourer in the countryside.

This growing gulf between the men who tilled the soil and their masters was perhaps the most marked development of agrarian history in the later Middle Ages, and the intervention of government into their relations brings it into the foreground. It was the natural result of a process which began long before the plagues: the commutation into rents of the old labour services which peasants had used to do on the lords' farm in return for the tenure of their holdings. The spread of commutation was partly due to the surer return rents gave in a period when agricultural prosperity was unstable. It owed something, too, to the example of the past, for the settlers in waste land, so much of which was cleared in the thirteenth century, nearly always paid rents. A third factor was the growing sophistication of the life of the landowner, to whom the expansion of commerce had offered a wider range of finished goods and luxuries for purchase. As he became habituated to a higher standard of living, a regular, calculable income, of the kind rent seemed to assure most effectively, became more necessary to cover its recurrent expenses. The overall effect was the break-up of what survived of the tight, local association of master and man in exploitation of the soil, and their division into broad social classes.

The landowner, in effect, was acquiring a greater freedom from the land itself. This freedom made landowners as a class (the 'nobility' in France and Germany, the 'gentry' in England) more socially self-conscious, more aware of their existence as a specific way of life. This made them more attentive to the privileges, interests, and pastimes which marked off their class from others. Thus in Germany in the time of the town leagues we also come across leagues of nobles, with curious chivalric titles such as the Fellowship of the Lion or the Order of St William, which were founded to defend the rights of the nobility against the city burgesses. Where royal government was more effective than it was in Germany, the landowning class combined to exert pressure on it. In England knights of the shire in Parliament presented together 'common petitions' to the king, demanding that he páy attention to their interests by regulating wages and repressing the extravagances of their social inferiors. Communal activity such as this encouraged the individual landowner to be aware of himself not just as a member of his own class but as a member of that class within his own national or territorial community. The success with which the government of this community managed its affairs came therefore to matter more to him.

It would be pointless to search too hard for signs of the growth of a sense of social solidarity in the peasant class, corresponding to that of the nobility. Such movements as the *Jacquerie* and the English peasants' revolt afford glimpses of something of the kind; but on the whole, peasant life, bound to the soil, allowed little room for class solidarity to develop. What the growing gulf between landowner and peasant did promote, however, was a growing awareness on the part of the former of the collective existence of the latter as a social order with interests different from his own. This did not necessarily tend to humanize the attitude of the nobility towards social inferiors. In Germany and Bohemia (the one country where, in the Hussite communities of Tabor and Horeb, peasants did achieve a degree of independent social organization), many who were once free were reduced to serfdom, with the legislative connivance of local assemblies of the estates of the nobility and clergy. But there were places where a more humane attitude was apparent. 'The human creature is made in God's image, and generally by natural law he has the right to freedom.' These are the opening words of the charter by which Charles of Valois, in the first years of the fourteenth century, freed the serfs of his demesne. The serfs of the French royal demesnes in Languedoc were freed about the same time. This did not, of course, free the peasant from economic exploitation: it did, however, mean that the terms of his customary tenure were protected at law. In England also, but somewhat later (towards the end of the fifteenth century) the king's common law courts began to give protection to manorial tenures. These are small beginnings, but of something very important: the intervention of government to protect the socially and economically helpless.

*

So far throughout this chapter, we have been looking at changes in the situation of the people with whom governments had to deal. When we come to look at the great technical advances of the late Middle Ages, it is the changes in the situation of the governments which had to deal with people that are most strikingly apparent. The most important advances which are here involved are the development of banking, the beginning of large-scale capitalist finance, and the advance in the techniques of war. These are matters not without connexion.

Banking began to be developed into a system by the great merchant companies of Tuscany in the thirteenth century. These merchant companies, associations of merchants pooling their capital, had developed far-flung interests, in particular in the trade in woollens and cloths, which were the basis of Tuscan prosperity. This made it useful for them to appoint their own representatives (factors or agents) to act on their behalf in centres where cloths and wools were bought and sold, in London and Bruges, for instance. Transport of specie, to pay for the agent's purchases, was risky and expensive. It was much easier if he could obtain money locally from an independent party (say a cleric who was travelling from London to Rome), and pay with that, giving the cleric a letter of credit, entitling him to draw in local currency in Rome from the company's agent there the same sum which he had handed over in London. The company made a small charge for transferring the credit from one currency to another: meanwhile the agent in London had money available for purchases, on which also the company reckoned to make a profit.

So useful and simple was this system that the companies soon found very large sums deposited with them for transfer by credit. The papacy in particular made use of them, depositing the local proceeds of, say, crusading taxation in England with a company's agent in London, and drawing the money in Rome or elsewhere (or indeed making it payable to a creditor). As the facilities which the merchants offered were more and more extensively used, their system of accepting deposits, affording credit and exchanging from one currency to another developed into a business in its own right, the business of banking. As the potential of this business became clear, companies which went in for it began to appoint agents in centres where they had not maintained them before, as Paris, Avignon, and Lübeck, and to multiply their commercial interests. Their agencies began to attract large long-term deposits, and they often paid the depositor a small sum for the use of his money while it was in their keeping. They were thus able also to make advances, charging for the loss of 'their' money's use or for risk. Such transactions caused some mild discomfort of conscience, smacking of usury, which the Church condemned, but too many people found them useful for this to make much difference. Long before the end of the Middle Ages payment of interest had become a general feature of all large scale capitalist finance. The Church's disapproval had ceased to signify: she connived at the system herself.

The very large sums which banking companies and their agents had at their disposal made it possible for them to advance ready cash on a major scale to princes and governments in need. This enabled the latter to raise money at short notice for immediate and pressing expenses, on the security of revenues which it would otherwise take a long time to collect. For the banker this operation was risky: nearly all governments in the long run borrowed more than they could afford to repay, at least at the terms agreed. Thus the Bardi and Peruzzi of Florence in the 1340s were bankrupted by the default of the English king, Edward III: and the Medici prosperity was severely damaged by the unwise advances of their Bruges agent to Charles the Bold of Burgundy in the 1470s. Nevertheless, companies went on advancing money to rulers: it gained the companies useful protection, diplomatic influence (very important, for example, to the Medici), and some of course drew their profit before disaster struck. Besides, their whole fortunes were never dependent on this dangerous business. The Italians were never bankers only: they were general merchants who ran their banking business in harness with all sorts of other commercial enterprises.

The main purpose for which rulers wanted to raise large sums in ready cash was to meet the costs of war. Always steep, these were becoming steadily more so, with technical advance in the military arts and increased military professionalism. Plate armour, with hinged joints, and the weight carefully distributed for easy carriage, was driving out chain mail in all parts of a knight's equipment. It was far more costly to manufacture than a coat of chain mail. Expert armourers, such as those of Nuremburg, flourished on their skill in design and production. The design of fortresses too was becoming more complicated, and they were more expensive both to build and to reduce. Shipbuilding also was improving. In Charles V's time (1364–80) in France the royal naval arsenal at Rouen employed a small army of shipbuilders and workers, and the admiral became an important royal officer.

Far and away the most important development in the art of war, however, was the use of gunpowder. No one knows who invented it. Roger Bacon, in the thirteenth century, seems to have known of its incendiary quality, but not its potential to propel a missile. This however was known not so long after. In 1324 they were casting brass cannon in Florence, and there were cannon and powder in the Tower of London in 1338. Development from this point was slow: the earliest firearms were not very efficient, and for a long time made little impact on the manner in which war was waged. But by the fifteenth century heavy artillery was beginning to revolutionize siege warfare. Mohamed, sultan of Turkey, brought sixty-two great guns to the siege of Constantinople in 1453, which in six weeks pounded gaping breaches in the great walls of the imperial city. Hand-guns were never, in this period, as useful as the English long-bow; but the Hussite general John Zizka made cannon terrible in the field, mounting them on huge farm wagons. In the last campaigns of the Hundred Years War, French superiority over the English in artillery was becoming a decisive factor. 'He had a greater train of artillery, of great guns, bombards, serpentines, ribaudequins, and so on,' wrote Berry, Herald of Charles VII, in 1450, 'than men could remember any Christian king to have possessed before him.' They won him the crucial battle of Formigny that year, and of Chastillon in 1453.

The bigger guns needed for siege warfare, and adequate supplies of powder for them, cost more than any but the richest could afford. The guns needed experts to handle them; they were heavy, clumsy, and difficult to transport, and powder posed a problem of supply. Their effect told nevertheless. The little stronghold of the petty *seigneur* ceased to be a safe retreat from princely power. No town or fortress was secure, unless a fortune could be spent on its defensive works and walls. Shipbuilding also was revolutionized by the need to mount cannon on board ship: ships required for this a deeper draught and greater sail power. The Portuguese *caravel*, designed to meet these needs, with three masts and weighing some 230 tons when fully laden, was the ship which enabled the sailors of Henry the Navigator to reach Madeira (1419) and the Azores (1431), and to begin to sail along the coast of Africa towards the equator. In all these ways a new dimension was added to the expense of military and naval enterprise. Only princes could really afford the outlay which serious fighting was beginning to involve, and even they could not afford it on their ordinary revenues.

To raise money in military emergencies princes looked to advances from complaisant bankers. They often needed more than complaisance, however, for they would probably have to raise more money shortly, from the same source for the same purpose. They needed to be in a position to offer security for loans, which would enable repayment to keep up with repeated borrowing. Their only ways to make available such security were by constant recourse to the taxation of their subjects, and through the better exploitation of the natural resources of their territories. Long before the invention of gunpowder the rising costs of war had led to new and important fiscal experiments. Of this much has been said in earlier chapters, which need not be repeated. One development must however be noted, the taxation of products as well as people. In England this took the form of customs, duties levied at the port on all wool and hides exported. The customs were first levied in Edward I's time (1275), and significantly we soon find him raising loans from Italian bankers on the security of their revenue. In France the *gabelle* became one of the most lucrative of all royal taxes. It was a tax on salt, a commodity in universal demand, which as from 1341 all producers had to bring for sale to the royal *greniers de sel* in their province; the king there took a cut on the profit. The long-term result of experiments such as these was a gradual realization that, since rulers drew wealth from the produce of their subjects, it was to their interest to protect those subjects in the economic enterprises on which their prosperity depended.

This point is underlined by Nicholas of Oresme, the councillor of Charles V of France, in his treatise *On Money* (c. 1370). When the king calls in the coinage and tries to draw a profit by weakening the alloy, he cheats not only his subjects but also himself, says Nicholas, for on good coin the prosperity of the whole realm depends. It was the belief that Nicholas was right, and that the point he was making held good not just for the coinage but for the whole commerce of a realm, that, more than anything else, prompted rulers to take a more active interest in the economic and social life of their subjects. It was not just a sense of duty which led men like Philip the Good of Burgundy to take the trade and industry of their territories under their care. It was the knowledge that this was the key to securing for themselves larger revenues, greater authority, and more influence.

Jacques Coeur (1395–1456), master of the mint and superintendent of all royal expenditure in the time of Charles VII, was a new kind of councillor for a king of France. He was a merchant on the grand scale, with a fleet of ships of his own, houses of business in most of the principal cities of the kingdom, and commercial interests all over the Mediterranean. He negotiated advantageous concessions from the sultan of Egypt for French merchants in the Levant, and advanced enormous sums to the king for his wars. In the end he became so powerful that jealousy led to his disgrace and ruin. But his example, and that of the many great merchants with whom kings had dealings, was not lost. A little later we find Louis XI in 1471 organizing an exhibition of French produce at Tours to encourage buyers from abroad, and Edward IV (1461-83) in England sharing with his subjects in the risks and costs of commercial ventures. This is royal economic policy in a new form, geared not just to the possibility of exaction, but to the potential profits of commerce.

It is important to remember here that not all wares for sale were made in towns. The wool and cloths which were the staple commodities of England's trade, for example, were produced in the country. Urban life in this period in any case depended on the produce of the countryside for survival. We are not dealing with a development which affected sections of the community only. Certainly we are dealing with a framework of economic life in which towns set the tempo, but this is a sign of its increasing complexity and sophistication, not of the dominance, pure and simple, of the towns themselves. They were the points at which commerce, production and industry came into contact, where the farmer sold his produce, where the gentleman purchased his tapestries and his books and his armour, and where the burgess lived, the meeting place of people of different class and different culture. They were nodal centres in the life of the whole community, not, as they had once been, centres of an existence largely independent of that of the surrounding world, and sharply differentiated from it.

The overall significance of this, and of all the developments we have been examining in this chapter, was to involve individuals, whether they lived in town or country, more closely in the life of wider communities. Guilds and confraternities and social classes are examples of such wider communities: but the most important of all was a man's country, in whose life these other communities were associated. This necessary involvement of people in local and national affairs left individuals less room than they had had in the past to respond to the calls of a wider community still, the universal Christian society, in whose name such enterprises as the crusade were launched. Moreover, though the new conditions did not make men any less Christian, they made them less attentive to those calls of Christian activity and obedience which could not find expression within the already complex framework of the lives they lived. We enter, in the fourteenth and fifteenth centuries, on an age when the welfare of Christian states began to matter more than the welfare of Christendom as a whole.

17

The Hundred Years War

WE have said that the fourteenth and fifteenth centuries were a
period when the welfare of Christian states began to matter more
than the welfare of Christendom. The history of the great struggle
between France and England, which is called the Hundred Years
War, is a demonstration of this point. When it began, King
Philip VI of France was assembling his fleet and forces for a great
crusade to the east, after the manner of that of his predecessor
St Louis. Later kings of France entertained similar projects, but
none afterwards got as far forward as his. Henry V of England
(1413–22) too dreamt of the reconquest of Jerusalem and so did
his ally Philip the Good, duke of Burgundy; but neither of them
ever came anywhere near to setting out for the Holy Land. All
through the course of the Anglo–French war, except during the
Great Schism, the papacy laboured with the two belligerent
kingdoms, to restore to them and to Christendom the peace
which was a necessary prelude to a crusade. Yet their war was
fought out to the bitter end notwithstanding, lasting more than
one hundred years, from 1337 to 1453.

Between the two principal combatants, the two most important
issues at stake in 1337 were the conditions of the overlordship of
the French king in Gascony, and the claim of Edward III of England to the crown of France. Both matters require some explanation. Gascony was an old bone of contention between the two
countries. Eleanor of Aquitaine had brought the duchy to Henry
II of England when she married him. When his son John lost
Normandy, this other French duchy remained in his hands; in
1259 his son Henry III did homage for it to St Louis, thus formally acknowledging that he held it as a fief from the king of
France. This meant that, as feudal overlord, the king of France
was entitled to hear in his *parlement* appeals lodged by the duke's
subjects against the decisions of the ducal courts. The officials of

the king of France encouraged such appeals, in which they saw a means to assert effective royal supervision over the government of the province. These appeals soon became so frequent as to make it difficult for the English officials in the duchy to discharge their duties effectively. As they saw it the king of France seemed to be supporting every subject of the duke in Gascony who sought to evade his obligations. As the French saw it, the duke and his officials seemed determined to obstruct their king's authority at every possible turn. If the duke backed up his officials and refused to abide by the decisions of his royal overlord, the king of France could treat him as a recalcitrant vassal, and confiscate his duchy by judicial sentence. This happened in 1294, again in 1324, and again in 1337. This sentence had then to be enforced: and as the Duke of Gascony had all the resources of his independent kingdom of England to aid him to resist, this meant war.

Edward III's claim to the French crown had nothing to do with all this: it arose out of accidents of heredity. When Philip IV of France died in 1314 he left three sons: none of the three had male issue that survived him. When the eldest, Louis, died in 1316, it was decided that a woman was incapable of succession to the crown; his daughter Jeanne was passed over, and Philip, the next brother, became king. When Charles, the youngest of the three, died in 1328, the two candidates with the strongest claims to the succession were Count Philip of Valois, and Edward III of England. Philip was the son of Philip IV's younger brother, Charles of Valois: Edward's claim came from his mother Isabella, Philip IV's own daughter. He was therefore a generation nearer to the crown than Philip of Valois, and, though his claim came through the female line, it could be argued that while a woman could not succeed to the throne, she could pass on her right to a male child. Two other points, however, in the event told definitely against Edward, the tradition of hostility between France and England and the fact that in 1328 he was a minor. It was Philip who was crowned at Rheims in May. (See Appendix, page 327.)

Edward at the time was in no position to press his claim. His age apart, the insecurity of his position in England precluded any

step to further his candidature. His father had been deposed a
bare year before, after a series of civil struggles which had bitterly
divided the English nobility. Edward's position was improved,
however, in 1330, when he personally assumed the government
of his kingdom, and his early victories in the Anglo–Scottish war,
which broke out anew in 1332, immensely strengthened him.
When the Gascon troubles reached a new peak of crisis in 1337
and Philip declared the duchy confiscate, he replied by declaring
that Philip's throne ought to be his. He sent Philip his defiance,
and proclaimed to the world that he was fighting not just to
defend his rights as duke in Gascony, but for the kingdom of
France, of which he had been unlawfully disinherited when he
was a child.

It will probably never be known how far Edward seriously
believed he might be able to make good his claim to the French
crown, which he certainly believed to be valid. Whatever the truth
about this matter, simply by claiming the crown he altered the
whole status of the war. From a quarrel between a vassal and his
overlord it was transformed overnight into a confrontation of
two rival royal dynasties. The old problem of feudal relations
dropped out of the picture as regarded Gascony: there was no
room left for friction between royal and ducal authority, because
Edward did not accept that Philip was king. From this time on
neither Edward nor his successors were ever prepared to accept
less than sovereign rights in the duchy. Though it took the French
a time to realize it, this left them with a clear alternative: they
must either surrender the duchy outright, or drive the English out
of it. The compromise of divided authority would no longer
suffice: it was becoming clear that it was not worthwhile for kings
as powerful as those of France and England to fight over rights
that were less than sovereign. This reflects the beginnings of very
important shifts of attitude towards problems of foreign politics
and governmental right; adjustments of the respective rights
of lords and vassals can no longer provide the key to their solution.

The course on which Edward had embarked should have
implied, therefore, total commitment of his resources in the war

and a fight with France to the finish, with the object of bringing
Philip of Valois to a point where he would be willing to surrender
at least all his right in Gascony, perhaps his crown too. In fact,
after twenty years of fighting, Valois France was brought to her
knees, by a war fought on French soil which in its effects was virtually total. The effort which achieved this, however, was not that
of Edward's England. Twenty years of war effort was far beyond
the resources of his state, or indeed of any state in the mid fourteenth century. Dependent on his subjects for taxation, with only
a rudimentary national administration, and no standing army,
Edward had to fight his war with resources very largely other
than his own. For this reason his success was less complete than
it seemed, and he was unable, as we shall see in due course, to
make it lasting.

*

The main obstacle to sustained national war effort in this period
was expense. The secret of Edward's success was the discovery of
diplomatic and military expedients for waging war on the cheap.
In the quest for allies, he had, as was to be expected, early success
in Flanders. True, the embargo which he imposed on the export
of wool from England did not succeed in bringing the count
round to the English side. But it brought round the weavers of
Ghent, led by Jacques van Artevelde, who made himself effective
governor of a large part of the county, and remained such until he
was assassinated in 1345. Inspired probably by the support he
found here among the king of France's subjects, Edward abandoned his original costly effort to build up by subsidies a German
confederation against France. He embarked instead on a new
diplomatic strategy, of remarkable ingenuity, whose object was
to persuade the king of France's own subjects to fight and largely
pay for the war against him.

The outlines of this strategy are clear in the great manifesto
which Edward issued from Ghent in 1340. In this he set forth the
details of his claim to the French crown, and also explained the
manner in which he proposed to rule when he had recovered his
rightful inheritance. The meat of the manifesto is in this second

part. The promises which Edward held out to his future subjects were based on the very demands which, earlier in the century, the leagues of discontented nobles in the French provinces had made of Philip IV and Philip V. By promising to soften the yoke of royal government, which he knew to be resented, Edward hoped he might be able to make Philip VI's position impossible by rallying support for himself inside his adversary's kingdom.

He gauged rightly where the real potential of discontent with French royal absolutism lay, in the provinces. His first success was in Brittany, where in 1341 the succession to the duchy came into dispute between the families of Blois and de Montfort. Charles of Blois, backed by the judgement of Philip's *parlement*, appeared as the candidate of royal intervention; and a powerful group among the nobility, backed strongly in the Breton-speaking areas where provincial solidarity was strongest, had come over to de Montfort and Edward by 1344. Edward's next success was with Normandy, where consciousness of separate local traditions had always been strong. Norman support for Edward acquired great significance, when in 1354 King Charles of Navarre, who was also Count of Evreux in Normandy, fell out with King John of France (who had succeeded his father Philip in 1350) and made common cause with the English and the discontented among the Norman nobility. By this time a large part of northern France had effectively withdrawn from allegiance to the Valois, who found themselves consequently engaged on too many fronts. By playing on provincial grievances and provincial separatism, Edward had exposed the Achilles' heel of the French national monarchy, which had seemed so powerful in the days of Philip IV.

In the circumstances, specifically English war effort did not need to be more than what it was, intermittent and ill coordinated. The fortunes of war favoured Edward when he did exert himself. In 1346 he undertook a great march with an English host through Picardy: at Crécy he met the army of King Philip, and the English long-bow proved its worth against a series of French cavalry charges. The Crécy army, having defeated the enemy in the field, settled down to besiege Calais, which fell in 1347. Ten years later, in 1356, the same tactics won for an army led by the Black Prince, Edward's eldest son, a still more overwhelming victory at Poitiers. King John of France was himself taken prisoner. A third great raid into France, carried out by an English royal host in 1359, was much less successful: the French had learned their lesson and did not risk an engagement in the field. Edward's losses, in heavy expenses and manpower, were very far from crippling, despite the successful harrying of his columns by the French. Yet the comparative failure of the English expedition solved only a fraction of the French military problem. This had by then become overwhelming, for other reasons which must be explained.

Twenty years of hostilities on French soil had created something like a vested interest in the war. The great raids that the English had carried out from time to time had proved very nearly to pay for themselves, with the plunder of towns and villages sacked, and the ransoms of rich prisoners. At the end of an expedition Edward and his lieutenants usually paid their men off and shared out the loot. It became clear enough soon to many of their 'cashiered' soldiers that they did not need to be paid in order to make a profit out of war service. A band of soldiers, with a fortress for a base and an effective captain to lead it, could live quite well by terrorizing the countryside into paying them tribute, waylaying prisoners on the highways and ransoming them, and occasionally joining with some other band to swoop on an ill-defended city and put it to the sack. The attractions of a rich life swelled the ranks of such bands (or 'free companies', as they were called), with adventurers from all parts, from Italy, Spain, Germany and Languedoc as well as from England. In the 1350s the whole of the *massif* of central southern France, where strongholds among the precipitous hills were virtually impregnable, was overrun by such soldiery. So were much of Normandy, and all the Breton frontier. Over large areas in France, the people were bled white by their raids, and the prosperity of the entire countryside was ruined.

Contemporary ideals of chivalry lent a colour of spurious romance to the activities of these men. Fighting had always been held to be a noble occupation. The pages of chivalrous romances were full of stories of high-born champions who, when not fighting the infidel, did service in the cause of wronged princes: the leaders of the free companies, who took up Edward's cause, aped their noble manner. Between them and their followers and the men of the same breed who fought in name for the Valois, a kind of freemasonry of arms grew up, superficially attractive. This was what enabled Jean Froissart to weave out of the history of their 'honourable enterprises, noble adventures and deeds of arms, performed in the wars between England and France', a chronicle that was almost itself a romance of chivalry. Edward III saw the potential of such sentiment, and sought to glamorize the fighting in the chivalrous ceremonial of his court. The order of the Garter was founded by him, a kind of secular version of a crusading order with something of Arthur's round table in it too, composed of knights devoted to his personal cause. It is important not to let this veneer of chivalry obscure the hard facts of the war, however. The sort of ideals which the men of the free companies understood was well put by Merigot Marchés, a Limousin captain of free soldiers who fought for the English. 'He had done,' he he claimed, 'all those things which a man can and ought to do in a just war, as taking Frenchmen and putting them to ransom, living on the country and despoiling it, and leading the company under his command about the realm of France, burning and firing places in it.'

Battered at all points by war bands too small and numerous to cope with, with the provinces shaken in their allegiance and the king a prisoner, the French monarchy faced a crisis which reached a climax in the mid 1350s. When the Estates General met in 1356, disaster had driven together the third estate and a section of the nobles and clergy, dominated by friends of Charles of Navarre, who was King John's prisoner at the time. Led by Charles's intimate, Robert le Coq, bishop of Laon, and by Etienne Marcel, provost of the merchants of Paris, they demanded for the Estates a share with the royal administrators in the collection of taxes, and that a number of their nominees should be associated with the king's council. Marcel and the citizens of Paris made contact with the discontented townsmen of Flanders. The misfortunes of war seemed to have transformed the Estates General at last into the instrument of communal resistance to royal absolutism. In 1356, to crown this crisis for the monarchy, John the Good was taken a prisoner of war at the battle of Poitiers.

What saved the monarchy was a sudden rising of the peasants of Champagne, Picardy and the Beauvaisis in 1358. Their patience had snapped with masters who gave them no protection against the ravages of war bands which were reducing them to starvation, and who were often, indeed, in league with them. The rising of the 'Jacques' swung back the nobility to the royal cause. Marcel found himself deserted and was assassinated: and the regent for King John, his son Charles, was able to gather just sufficient force to be ready for strictly defensive operations when Edward III appeared in force in Picardy in 1359. Edward's campaign over-stretched his always limited resources. At the end, he was ready to listen to negotiations which eventuated in the 'great peace' of Bretigny in 1360.

The conditions of this peace were hard for the French. They had to promise to pay a huge ransom, three million *livres tournois*, for King John. They had also to surrender to the English sovereignty in a Gascony enlarged by more than half the other provinces of the south-west. In the circumstances they were lucky to retain the sovereignty over Brittany and Normandy: two years before they could not have had much hope of keeping it. After the defeats, the crisis with the Estates, and the social turmoil of the *Jacquerie*, they were in a pass where the need for a breathing space was desperate.

The terms of Bretigny gave Edward a great deal of what he had fought for. But this was not so much due to his achievement as to the disintegration of government in France, caused by the ravages of the free companies, and the virtual secession of a series of provinces. It was beyond Edward, in consequence, to make the peace meaningful. Fighting continued in Brittany and in Normandy, and on the borders of English Languedoc, in which the 'English' companies were always aligned against French royal troops. In 1369 the war formally broke out again. It had never really ended, slackening after 1360 rather than ceasing altogether.

Charles V, who succeeded King John of France in 1364, was an able ruler. The reforms he instituted in taxation, and to steady the value of the coinage, helped to restore something of the country's broken prosperity; and by reinforcing the territorial authority of members of his own family, Louis, duke of Anjou, John, duke of Berry, and Philip, duke of Burgundy (whom he married to the heiress of Flanders), he made a beginning of dealing with the problem of provincial separatism. Unfortunately, the re-opening of the war in 1369 exposed the kingdom to too much strain when his efforts were still only half complete. He was able to restore an even balance of success to the fighting, but could not turn the tide of victory definitely in favour of France. As a result by 1380, the year that Charles died, the strains of war were becoming for France almost as intolerable as they had been in the late 1350s. There was this difference however. Now they were telling heavily on the English too. Edward III's grandson, Richard II, succeeded in 1377 to a kingdom over-taxed where government was in decline, and discontent rife. After forty years of hostilities, neither side had much to show for its efforts.

*

The thirty-five years between Charles V's death and the battle of Agincourt in 1415 form a period when, though there was much fighting in France, there were few serious campaigns. Both sides were suffering from exhaustion. In this interlude, domestic events of great importance took place in both England and France.

In England, heavy taxation, combined with the social distress caused by a series of plagues and bad harvests, led to a peasants' revolt in 1381. Taxation again, and a consistent record of naval and military failure in every new war effort, led to a series of outbursts of indignation from the Commons in Parliament, which made it nearly impossible for the king's councillors to maintain any consistent policy. Finally, the intrigues of noblemen anxious to turn this indignation to their own profit and secure greater influence in the council culminated in the deposition of Edward

III's successor, Richard II, in 1399. Henry IV of Lancaster, who unseated him, was also a grandson of Edward III, so the English claim to the crown of France did not lapse. But it was not until after Henry IV was succeeded by his son Henry V that an English king was strong enough to devote himself once more to large scale operations in France.

Internal disorder during this period prevented the French as well as the English from making any great effort. Charles VI was a child when his father died in 1380: he was barely a man when, in 1392, he was seized with the first fit of a recurrent madness which continued to incapacitate him for long intervals until he died in 1422. While the king was ill, the government of the country was virtually controlled by the great princes of the royal house. These were men whom, as we have seen, Charles V in his time had rewarded well. So great had he made them, indeed, with grants of territory, title, and privilege, that they were able to entertain ambitions beyond the frontiers of France. Louis, duke of Anjou, Charles V's first brother, hoped to win a crown for himself in Naples, as the adopted heir of Queen Joanna, who was deposed by her cousin Charles of Durazzo in 1381. Louis of Orleans, Charles V's younger son, married a Visconti princess and also hoped to win himself an inheritance in Italy, in parts of the papal patrimony which, after the outbreak of the great schism (1378), the Avignon pope had promised to make into a kingdom for him – if he could win them from the Roman pope's allies. Philip of Burgundy, the youngest brother of Charles V, having added Flanders to his duchy, was bent on enlarging his territories by incorporating with them the small principalities on his borders in the Rhineland and the Low Countries, such as Luxembourg, Brabant, Hainault and Guelders.

To further their ambitions, these princes strove each for himself to dominate the court and government, so as to retrench his authority in his French lands and divert royal resources to maintain his own diplomacy. Louis of Anjou died in 1384: Philip and Louis of Orleans were, in the 1390s, virtually sole rivals. Philip was by far the more successful. By the time he died, with the additions he had made to his inheritance, Burgundy was begin-

ning almost to constitute a state of itself. The problem of provincial separatism was beginning to be raised again, in a new,
dangerous form, with the royal princes themselves fostering
it.

Philip's son, John the Fearless, was a man more reckless in
politics than he. In 1407 his rival Louis of Orleans was assassinated at his orders in Paris. This was the signal for the outbreak
in France of a terrible civil war. To revenge his father, Charles of
Orleans allied with the Count of Armagnac, who had taken
advantage of the disorders of the times to build up his lordship
in Languedoc to near independence, and who brought to
Charles's support what was left of the old free companies. Their
savagery gained them a frightful reputation in the district around
Paris. John of Burgundy saw this as an opportunity to pose as the
champion of reforms long demanded by the Paris burgesses and
the third estate. So the mantle of the old court party among the
king's councillors fell to the Armagnacs, with the Dauphin,
heir to the Valois throne, among their supporters. The alliance
of the Dauphin and the Armagnacs combined with the
strong economic links between England and Flanders to drive
Burgundy into the arms of Henry V. It was an Armagnac army
that was defeated with such terrible slaughter in 1415 at
Agincourt.

When in 1419 Duke John in his turn was murdered by the
Dauphin's servants, Burgundy committed herself to England completely. Burgundy brought with her Brittany, whose duke had
always been John's ally: Henry V's forces had already overrun
Normandy. The situation was very like that of 1359, only more
desperate for France. As then, peace was the issue of it, but the
terms were still more humiliating. The Treaty of Troyes in 1420
gave the whole inheritance of Charles VI to Henry of England,
as soon as the former should die, a day which could not now be
far off. It gave Henry all he had been fighting for, not just part of
it, as the terms of Bretigny had given to Edward III. There was,
however, one still more important difference between the two
treaties. That of Troyes did not end the war even in name. The
Dauphin, whom it disinherited, and the Armagnacs were not

254

parties to it and remained in arms, with all the country south of the Loire, except Gascony, in their obedience.

*

The war in fact was not ending but entering on a new phase, its final one. Charles VI and Henry V both died in 1422: to succeed the former, the infant English prince Henry VI was proclaimed king of France in Paris, the Dauphin Charles at Bourges. Their reigns saw the long war through to its close. For thirteen years its fortunes looked uncertain; then they began to run definitely in Charles's favour. The key factor was Burgundy, for Henry V's success, like Edward III's, was built not on England's effort alone, but on the divisions of France also. When in 1435 Burgundy withdrew from the English alliance, which had proved to give insufficient advantages to hold her, Henry VI was in a weak position. It was still nearly twenty years before the English were finally driven out of all France (except Calais), after their two great defeats, at Formigny in Normandy in 1450, and at Chastillon near Bordeaux in 1453. But after 1435 the issue was never really in doubt. The English only managed to hold on for so long because of the great efforts which they put into the war. These efforts were symptomatic of a change which came over the whole aspect of the Anglo–French struggle in this its last phase.

The house of Lancaster waged war in a very different way to Edward III. The armies of Henry V and Henry VI were raised in England, and paid out of English taxes. They had siege trains of artillery, and troops of engineers; and in the towns taken from the French, standing garrisons were established which were regularly paid and supplied at royal expense. In the time of the Duke of Bedford, regent for Henry VI in France until he died in 1435, an efficient system of inspection was instituted to make sure that companies and garrisons were paid regularly and kept at full strength. This meant in England frequent summonses of Parliament to raise the necessary taxation, and careful explanation to its members of the king's necessities. For England the war had become what it had not really been in Edward III's day, a sustained national enterprise.

As such, it had profound effects socially in England, especially on the very important class of country gentry, from among whom most of the representatives of the Commons in Parliament were drawn. Many of their families sent sons to fight in France: some indeed owed their whole prosperity to spoils won in the French war, and soundly invested in manors and properties. The part they played in the war itself, the frequent meetings of Parliament, and the constant necessity of paying taxes, combined to habituate such people to thinking not in local, but in national terms. The signs that they were doing so grow clearer as time passes. In 1376 we hear for the first time of members of the Commons denouncing the failures of the government in a set debate in their own house. In the 1380s and in the 1450s they sought to hold royal councillors who had mismanaged military endeavour responsible to the nation. In the fifteenth century, numerous broad-sheet ballads and manifestos, official and otherwise, concerning public affairs show that these were exciting a really living interest. Family correspondence begins to be full of requests for 'tidings' of great matters, and of comment on them.

'Today it is heard that Cherbourg is gone, and we have now not a foot of land left in France.' In this sentence from a letter written to one of the Pastons of Norfolk by a London correspondent in 1450, the significant word is 'we'. The effort of the war had brought together, in a way perhaps nothing else could have done, the classes in England capable of taking a responsible and vocal attitude to government. General bewilderment, when men found at the end of the war that the efforts which they had made came to nothing, helped, it is true, to bring about the political turmoil of the wars of the Roses. At the end of them, however, and more importantly, the solidarity and sense of common interest of the English gentry was the foundation on which the strong monarchy of the Yorkists and the early Tudors was built. Separated at last from continental dominions, their kingdom was English in language, outlook and customs, with a pride in its purely native history. England was beginning her career as the island realm of future history.

In France at the end of the Hundred Years War the same sort

of national self-awareness began to show itself. In the gloom and confusion following the treaty of Troyes the signs of it can be hard to find; but feelings were latent under the surface, which the amazing career of Joan of Arc startled into life. The time when her voices were speaking to her in the woods of Domrémy, of a mission to deliver her people, was in fact the darkest hour of all, just after the treaty of Troyes. Her appearance in 1429, heading an army to save beleaguered Orleans from the English, caught the imagination of the Dauphin's war-weary troops, and stirred them to achievements which a year before they had not considered worth attempting.

She told them to bring me a glass of wine, and said we should soon drink together in Paris. And what she had done seemed to me a miracle of God, as it was to see and hear her.

That is how the soldier Guy de Laval remembered her, in the camp after Orleans was relieved. Her victories in the ensuing campaign gave men like him what they had never had before, victories in a national cause round which memories and myths could gather. The coronation which Joan, the child of the people, won for her 'gentle Dauphin' in Rheims cathedral at the end of the campaign of 1429, cast a new glamour on the line of the Valois, whom God had seemed to have deserted. From this time forward there was a new spirit abroad among the French which the terrible end that Joan met at the hands of the inquisition could not allay.

After Joan's death all the French needed was a leader to inspire them as she had done. They found one in Charles VII, who had thrown away the lethargy of his days as Dauphin (though it was not Joan who stirred him: it was not a saint but a sinner, his mistress Agnes Sorel, who roused him). In 1436 his troops entered Paris. As they began to press into Normandy there was an upsurge of enthusiasm to greet them, and Charles began to show that he could make a ruler who was worthy of it.

The French war effort was from now on put on a much more effective basis. Charles's great ordinance of 1439 laid down arrangements for the organization of a standing army, and the manner in which money was to be raised to pay for it by annual taxation (the *taille*). This did much to relieve the country of the depredations of the wild, undisciplined, and usually unpaid bands which had hitherto passed for an army. The care Charles took to safeguard the prosperity of town and countryside as he won them back from the English enhanced his reputation, and paid dividends in the future. In the weakened state of the realm, few among the common people wished for perilous liberties: they were glad to welcome a king who 'took year by year from his subjects as much as he needed to guard them'. The people of France had suffered infinitely from the endless fighting on her soil, and it needed a strong hand to restore prosperity. Royal absolutism gained strength in step with military success and the awakening of national spirit.

The full benefits of Charles's victories were reaped by his son, Louis XI. His reign saw the beginning of a new French commercial prosperity, the fruit of the effective protection which he and Charles gave to the mercantile interests of such great towns as Rouen, Bordeaux and Lyons, and of a close alliance of the monarchy with their great *bougeois* families. It saw the league 'for the public weal' of the princes, formed to protect the privileges which they and the high nobility had won or usurped in the wars, fall apart for lack of unity and popular support. It saw the refurbished monarchy able to stretch its sovereignty further, to the Rhone and the Pyrenees, and at the end of the reign into Burgundy, after the downfall of her last Valois duke, Charles the Bold. The horror of the war had, in the end, burned out the force of that provincial separatism, which had threatened during its course to undo France: so much so that she could now stretch out beyond old limits. If the wars with the English had not wrecked so much, Charles VII and Louis XI might not have been able to lay such strong foundations as they did. What they built was at the core of the power of France, as it endured to the end of the *Ancien Régime*.

Both England and France emerged from the Hundred Years War independent and self-contained national entities, aware of themselves as such. This was a direction in which their history had long been tending: signs of what was to be were clear long before their great war, in their development in the days of Philip IV and Edward I, back in the thirteenth century. Since then the pressures which the war created had immensely strengthened the sense of internal solidarity among their populations. It had also accustomed their rulers to thinking of policy in terms appropriate to this condition, allowing high priority to the demands of their subjects' secular prosperity, if only because their own power depended on it. This had virtually obliterated from their statecraft the kind of universal considerations which coloured it so deeply in the days of, say, St Louis in France or Henry III in England. Royal policy had become geared to playing a new kind of part in a different Europe. As we shall see in the next chapter, the repercussions of the Anglo–French war had, in fact, helped to make Europe different at the end of it.

18

Politics and Political Society
in an Age of Wars

WE have seen how, in the fourteenth century, though neither the king of France nor the king of England had the financial resources to organize and maintain a sustained military effort, their struggle nevertheless brought into being substantial standing military forces. As the crusades had done in an earlier period, the Anglo–French war attracted soldiers from all over Europe, who saw their chance, in the service of one side or the other, to win both renown and booty, perhaps even an inheritance for themselves in conquered lands. The 'free companies' into which these adventurers formed themselves were formidable and highly independent war bands. They proved by their conduct that they were prepared to serve any master who would offer them fair terms of service. In the absence of regular employment they were quite capable of sustaining themselves by organized brigandage. 'Without war you cannot live and do not know how to': that is what Sir John Chandos, the Black Prince's lieutenant, told a group of their captains who had come to consult him. When hostilities ceased formally, these soldiers usually carried on fighting until they found other employment, because they had no other means of living. Their depredations could be quite as serious a menace to prosperity as plague or famine.

Service with such a company offered chances both of adventure and of making a fortune, in an association in which both the risks and the profits of war were shared. This, however, was not the only attraction of such service. Because of the high social esteem with which contemporary chivalrous ideas endowed the profession of arms, it provided an outlet for the natural energies and inclinations of a whole class of persons on the insecure periphery of the aristocracy; knights, for example, whose patrimony was inadequate, younger sons and bastards of seigneurial families, and aspirants to a status which was not quite theirs by birth. As we have seen, writers like Froissart described their activities in terms of 'noble deeds and honourable enterprises', and this was how they thought of their profession themselves. 'With his bacinet on his head, a man at arms is noble, and of fit condition to combat with a king': that was the proud boast of one such soldier. The free companies were more than a by-product of war in an age when there were no standing armies: they were a social phenomenon. They played a significant part not only in the Anglo–French war, but in almost all the great wars of the fourteenth and fifteenth centuries.

Because they had no means of living except by war, such companies were very hard to disband. Princes, who could not afford to maintain standing armies, could not afford to pension off whole bands of soldiers whom they had employed on a purely temporary basis. The supply of soldiers seeking regular terms of service thus nearly always exceeded demand. The result of their quest for employment was a condition the opposite of what has been normal in more modern periods of hostilities. Instead of other powers being drawn into a central struggle, say that of France and England, the human and military effort involved in any given war tended to spill outwards into struggles unrelated to the central issue, or related with it only indirectly. This was because in contemporary conditions of political development the ready availability of military manpower, and the anxiety of rulers to find some other employment for soldiers than brigandage which they were powerless to control, greatly enhanced the possibilities of what is probably best described as 'dynastic adventuring'. The nature of these conditions of political development requires a little explanation, if one is to grasp their significance, and that of the military effort which they helped to canalize.

It was only in its closing stages that even the Hundred Years War of France and England began to be recognizable as a struggle of two nations. For most of its duration, it would be more correctly described as a 'dynastic' war. The concepts of a 'nation' and of its 'government', as we understand those terms, were not very familiar when the Anglo–French war broke out, in the fourteenth century. Men thought and spoke rather in terms of what they called 'lordships' and 'lordship' (or 'dominion'). 'Lordship' implied at once a proprietary right to territory, the piece of territory in question, and a right to govern the people who lived on it. Like property, lordship could be transferred, even (within certain limits) bought, and sold. It did not necessarily imply what we now call sovereignty. A duchy or a county, whose ruler was himself a subject, was a 'lordship' just as a kingdom was, though of a less exalted order. This was a legacy of earlier, feudal conditions, in which local noblemen had usurped the right to exercise a good many of the functions of public authority in dealing with those who lived on their estates. Another legacy of older conditions was the right, which a greater lord enjoyed, to create a lesser lordship for another within his own dominions, by a gift recorded in his charter or bull. He could also grant lordship to a corporation, as the emperors of the past had done for the city communes of Italy. Lordship was thus not necessarily a personal right, but most often it was so. Most lordships were the hereditary tenures of individual royal and noble families, passed on from father to son in accordance with a customary law of succession.

It was the reasonable policy of every great lord to retrench and increase his inheritance of power by a carefully managed dynastic policy, and to look for rewards for his service and alliance in the shape of grants of lordships which would round out the integrity of his existing dominions. Such policies made for ferocious competition. Two lords might obtain grants, perhaps, to some valued town or territory from two rival superiors, who both claimed that it lay lawfully in their gift. An advantageous marriage was another means of acquiring new rights, but there were sure to be many aspirants for the hand of an heiress, and he who won the prize might then find her right of inheritance questioned on the ground of some flaw in her pedigree. Such accidents as the extinction of a direct line of succession could precipitate acute political crisis. A great lord, very naturally, was seldom inclined to surrender his interest in such a matter as a disputed succession without a struggle. Contemporary opinion regarded the prosecution of hereditary claims, on the part of the great, as entirely justifying the use of force. To make war for such reasons was, men believed, to put the affair to the arbitrament of God, whose judgement should not fail. The result was an endless proliferation of hostilities, engendering conditions of great social and political insecurity, and much economic misery. They were conditions, however, in which men at arms could nearly always find employment. This is why the effects of the vogue of military adventure, which attracted men to the life of the free soldier, and of competitive dynastic policies were combined, and have to be considered together.

The companies of soldiers, which such great wars as that of France and England brought together, were constantly drawn away to serve in other wars, in which the great men of neighbouring territories became involved. The history of the fourteenth and fifteenth centuries is crowded with stories of such men and their adventures in pursuit of dynastic ambitions. Edward III, with his claim to the French throne, is just one example of a recurrent type. Successive dukes of Anjou led soldiers repeatedly into Italy, in efforts to win the inheritance of the kingdom of Naples, which Queen Joanna had bequeathed to Duke Louis in 1380. Louis, duke of Orleans hoped to win a kingdom of Adria in the papal patrimony, which in the time of the schism the pope of Avignon promised to set up for him in territory controlled by the pope of Rome; John, duke of Lancaster in England, coveted the crown of Castile in right of his wife, daughter of a deposed king, and spent a fortune in military and diplomatic effort, almost literally 'to build castles in Spain'. These are only a few examples, which it is not necessary to multiply. What is important is to remember that bids for power made by men such as these could have consequences quite unrelated to the success or failure of their original enterprises. The armies which followed them did not always go home when their leaders did. More often they remained where the end of the war or campaign left them, thereby introducing a new factor of confusion into the political struggles of yet another locality. It could take a long time for the full consequences of just one episode in a dynastic war to work themselves out.

The only way to understand more about the way in which the vogue of military and dynastic adventure affected the history of Europe in the later Middle Ages, is to look at examples in detail. Three may suffice, the stories of the 'overspill' of wars and their consequences in Spain, in Italy, and in Burgundy.

*

In Spain, two powerful kingdoms had emerged as a result of the wars of reconquest from the Moslems, Castile and Aragon. The later history of Castile furnishes the most straightforward example to illustrate most of the processes we have been examining so far. In this kingdom the Christian reconquest of Moorish territory had reached a limit for the time being in the mid thirteenth century. This left only a part of Andalusia, the kingdom of Granada, in Mohammedan hands. After this Castile's history until the middle of the fourteenth century was mainly a tale of struggles between the crown and a proud and overbearing nobility, in which both parties from time to time sought alliance with the Moors. In the reign, however, of Alfonso XI, who defeated in 1340 a great invading host of Moors from Africa at Rio Salado, the monarchy began at length to gain once more in prestige and power. His son, Pedro II (1349–69) endeavoured to take a stronger line with the nobility than any of his royal predecessors. This gave him a reputation for ruthlessness which was deserved, and for reliance on the Jews and the Moriscos among his subjects. It also embroiled him with his bastard brother, Henry, count of Trastamara, whom he finally succeeded in driving out of the kingdom in 1361. As it proved, he drove him into the hands of new and powerful allies. Henry found refuge in France. Thence, in 1366, he returned at the head of a great army of free companies, led by the famous Breton captain Bertrand du Guesclin, and paid by the king of France, who was glad enough to spend his coin on Henry if he would rid the land of these adventurers.

For twenty years after this, the struggle for the Castilian crown and the military efforts of the Anglo–French war remained seriously entangled. Pedro could not himself put any force into the field which would match du Guesclin's veterans; he appealed therefore to their natural opponents, the English of Gascony. So another army of free companies, led this time by Pedro and the Black Prince, marched into Castile, and overthrew Henry and du Guesclin in a great battle at Najera in 1367. Pedro, however, could not pay his ally's soldiers, and they soon fell out with one another. Henry and the French were able to return the next year, to defeat and kill Pedro at Montiel in Andalusia. This unfortunately was not the end of the matter, for Pedro left two daughters. John, duke of Lancaster, the Black Prince's brother and the richest nobleman in England, married the elder, Constanza, and in her right proclaimed himself king of Castile. His efforts to pursue this claim were not abandoned until 1387, when he had conquered Galicia with an English army, but lost so many men and spent so much money that he knew he could not press his cause any further. So he was ready to settle with Henry's successor, John of Trastamara, and waive his claim in return for the marriage of Constanza's daughter to John's heir. For her at least he won a crown, even if not for himself.

On the face of it, this sounds a confused and not very pointful story. It was much more important than that, for Castile at any rate. A series of campaigns on her soil, fought by foreign soldiers who lived off the country through which they passed, had impoverished the common people of the realm and damaged the whole economy. In addition, in order to retain the loyalty of the nobles, both Henry and John of Trastamara had been forced to woo them with grants of important privileges and great estates. Turbulent before this time, these nobles remained so: but they were now more formidable, and the crown's resources less than in the past. The monarchy had to struggle long to reduce them to order. The consequences of the dynastic war and the overspill of foreign armies into Castile in its course was, in sum, the eclipse for the time being of the power of this kingdom, which had led the way in Spain in the age of the reconquest from the Arabs. Not until the time of her union with Aragon under Isabella and Ferdinand did she begin to show that she had recovered from the misfortunes which befell her in the fourteenth century, in consequence of the competition of three men for her crown.

Ironically, factors very similar to those which were the ruin of Castile were the secret of the power and prosperity of Aragon in much the same period. In the war of Aragon against the Angevins of Naples, which followed the rising of the Vespers in Sicily, many companies of soldiers raised chiefly in Catalonia found employment. When Aragon herself withdrew from the war, they remained in the service of Frederic, the Aragonese royal cadet who became king of Sicily. When in 1302, by the treaty of Calta-bellotta, he finally made peace with Charles II of Anjou, they found a new outlet for their energies in the service first of the Byzantine emperor, then of the duke of Athens. They ended by overrunning his duchy for themselves, and making the Frankish Peloponnese an apanage of Aragonese Sicily. Thus, as a result of the largely independent efforts of these soldiers, Aragon found herself the focus of a formidable Mediterranean confederation of territories. She came to play a more significant part in the politics of the Levant than any other European power. Her merchants from Barcelona began to play an important role in Mediterranean commerce: they established trading depots at Messina in Sicily, at Modon in Greece, in Alexandria and in the Syrian ports. The country became richer, the power of her rulers one to be reckoned with.

Interestingly, the principal weakness of this Aragonese 'empire' arose out of the manner of its foundation. Brought into being in consequence of the independent and largely uncoordinated efforts of Aragonese soldiers, the government of its component territories remained independent and uncoordinated. Athens was lost to the Acciaivoli of Naples in 1386. Even in the time of the great Alfonso, who in 1443 added Naples to his other dominions, the coordination of government in Spain and Italy remained inadequate. Aragon's expansion was not truly national: her 'empire' was a flimsy structure produced by haphazard if successful military adventuring. Important as the results of such enterprise could be, they nearly always made for political insecurity.

This is immediately apparent in the case of Castile: it is not so at once for Aragon, but becomes clear as soon as the domination which had been won for her in the Mediterranean was put under pressure.

*

In Italy in the fourteenth and fifteenth centuries the activities of free soldiers were even more important than they were in Spain. At the beginning of this period the whole country was torn by internal wars, which the amateur armies of the city communes and the local nobility could never win finally. This provided an ideal context for military adventuring. In the middle of the fourteenth century the Italian chroniclers are full of the doings of the great bands of German mercenaries, who had appeared in their country, such as that of Count Werner of Urslingen. There were also native companies, such as that of Fra Moriale, who helped the visionary Cola di Rienzo to restore the ancient tribunate in Rome for a second time in 1354, and was afterwards put to death by him. In the years immediately following this, the numbers of the independent soldiery in Italy were swelled enormously by the overflow of free companies from the south of France during the Anglo–French war. French princes adventuring into Italy, as for instance Louis of Anjou, brought more men of the same stamp in their train. Captains from England like John Hawkwood and from Languedoc like Bernardon de la Salle mingled with the German and native Italian leaders, teaching the latter something of both their skill and their savagery. Italy came to know, almost in the same degree as France herself, what a bane men could be who would fight for anyone who would pay them, and, if no one would, lived on the land until someone paid them to leave it.

The numbers and professional skill of these soldiers, or *condottiere* as they were called in Italy, had a revolutionizing effect on the wars of the Italian cities and their parties. To employ forces on the scale they represented was something which only the richest and most powerful cities could afford. The republican governments of the communes were besides far too disorganized to direct the efforts of such substantial and independent armies.

The results of these facts were twofold. The great cities, as Florence, Milan, and Venice, began, with the aid of the *condottiere*, to absorb their lesser neighbours into their dominion. Within the communes meanwhile republican institutions gave way under war's pressure. Despotism had already often provided a temporary solution to the problem of directing energies in times of crisis: in new conditions it gained a firm hold, for none but an individual ruler, and preferably a hereditary prince, could give the clear and consistent direction to city policy which they necessitated. In some cities *condottiere* themselves became despots; in some others, despots became *condottiere*, and maintained the independence of their states by hiring out their armies to powerful neighbours.

The authority of the despots of Italy usually had at least a colour of legality. Some despots obtained this through the grant of a vicariate from either the pope or the emperor, as did the Visconti in Milan, which the emperor Wenceslas erected into a duchy in 1395. Others obtained it through a grant of power from their fellow citizens or subjects, as ultimately the Medici did in Florence. In reality the key to despotic power was always the same, the ability to pay and control troops, and so direct policy. This was the secret of Cosimo de Medici (1389–1464) in Florence, who managed her forces and diplomacy through his immense wealth, without officially even holding an office in the city's government. Milan came in the end to be actually ruled by a *condottiero*, Francesco Sforza (1401–66), who had served the Visconti well and married the daughter of their last duke. These are just two examples, which may give a false simplicity to the picture. The rise and fall of individual despots in individual cities is a story infinitely complicated, in which local and family rivalries, the tergiversations of mercenaries who had been offered better terms of service by enemies, and foreign interventions all play a part. The uncertain conditions in papal territories during the Great Schism were another disturbing factor in a history confused, personal and so intricate as to be all but impossible, at times, to follow.

Twice during the period of the schism rulers appeared so powerful that it looked as if their military might could overrun all Italy. By 1401 Giangaleazzo Visconti of Milan had brought all Lombardy under his control, and if he could have taken Florence the whole of central Italy would have lain open and defenceless before the conquering Milanese *condottiere*. Ladislas, king of Naples, just over a decade later, had taken Rome and ruled in the patrimony as far as the border of Florentine territory, and was openly said to be planning 'to bring all Italy into serfdom'. Sudden death cut off both these men at the height of their careers, Giangaleazzo in 1402 and Ladislas in 1414. The *condottiere* armies with which they had made their conquests broke up on the deaths of their paymasters. Out of the confusion of the next thirty years there emerged a kind of equilibrium of five great powers. They were Venice and Milan in the north; Florence in Tuscany; and further south the papacy with its patrimony, and the kingdom of Naples (reunited in 1443 with the island of Sicily, under Alphonso of Aragon). As far as external relations were concerned there was little difference in the nature of the power of these states; it depended on money and the military (or naval) forces that it could buy. Like the great states of northern Europe, but in miniature, those of Italy had come to constitute self-contained centres of secular power, based ultimately on local prosperity and military force.

Machiavelli, looking back over their history in this period, diagnosed as the chief weakness of the Italian states their dependence on unreliable mercenaries. This certainly was one of the reasons why victories such as those of Giangaleazzo and Ladislas, who sought to overrun the whole or a large part of the peninsula, proved so ephemeral. It is equally certain that the *condottiere* armies were no match for those of the king of France when, in Machiavelli's own day, he invaded Italy. In the meantime, however, these soldiers and their way of living exercised a profound influence in Italy, where their existence became an established feature of the social and political scene. Their leaders lived like noblemen, and acquired their cultivation of manners. Jacopo Sforza, the father of Francesco and never more than a mercenary, had books translated from Greek and Latin to engage his leisure. In their turn, the *condottiere* taught the rulers of Italy to share their taste for chivalry and tournaments. Above all, their activities made political conditions competitive and desperately insecure. In all these ways, they helped to fashion the thought and attitudes of Italians in the Renaissance period. But for the experience of Italy in the days of the *condottiere* Machiavelli could never have seen the whole art of statecraft as a struggle of man against fortune: nor would the architects of the early Renaissance have been so preoccupied with the military demands of design.

*

The histories of Italy and Castile show how the Anglo–French war overflowed south and west beyond the frontiers of France, with ultimate consequences which had nothing to do with that struggle. That of Burgundy shows how something of the same order happened also to the east. The pattern of events here is, however, a little different, and better controlled. The prolonged crisis, which shook the allegiance to the French monarchy of so many provinces, very nearly brought about the complete secession of this one. It gave an essential opening to the skilfully managed territorial and dynastic policies of four successive Valois dukes. By incorporating into their dominion a series of lordships outside the French realm in the Low Countries and the imperial Rhineland, they built Burgundy into an inheritance which finally approached the status of an independent power. (For family tree, see Appendix, page 324.)

Philip the Bold, the first of the Valois dukes (1363–1404) and count of Flanders also in the right of his wife, originated this policy of eastern expansion for Burgundy. His reign saw Luxemburg linked to her ducal house by a marriage and Limburg by cession, and the inheritance of Brabant settled on his wife's descent. His son John the Fearless (1404–19) continued his policy, and secured the marriage of the heiress of Hainault and Holland into his own family. The need to maintain a controlling influence in the government of France, in order to further his own diplomacy, was one of the reasons behind his obduracy in the

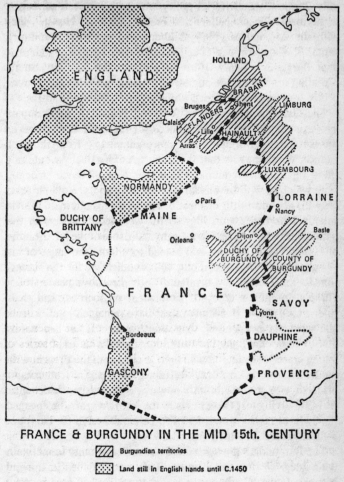

FRANCE & BURGUNDY IN THE MID 15th. CENTURY

///// Burgundian territories

::::: Land still in English hands until C.1450

■ ■ Boundary of the Kingdom of France

struggle with the Armagnacs in Charles VI's reign, and for his
tentative alliances with Henry V and the English. He was able,
in the course of the civil wars of this period, to make himself a
power in France, but virtually independent of her. It was not

only Burgundian territorial policy which, in John's time, began to be markedly independent of French interests. His struggles with the Armagnacs gathered about him a group of military captains, whose companies began to form the core of an independent Burgundian army. Here we see the now familiar pattern repeating itself, with the pursuit of dynastic ambitions by a great prince serving as a magnet to military manpower and talent.

The divisions of France in the years following the Treaty of Troyes enabled John's son and successor Philip the Good to sever the fortunes of Burgundy still more completely from those of France. Wisely he saw that the resources of his duchy would not stand full military commitment in the Anglo–French struggle, from which he withdrew as far as possible; almost totally, in fact, after his abandonment of the alliance with England in 1435. His veteran companies won him useful victories, however, in the minor wars which he had to wage to make sure of the inheritances of Holland and Brabant, and helped to uphold the cause of his vassal, Antoine de Vaudemont, who was fighting for the succession to the Duchy of Lorraine. The comparative peace which Philip's dominions enjoyed made them prosperous, and their ruler rich. Indeed, Burgundy might have remained to all intents and purposes independent long after his time, if her last Valois duke, Charles the Bold, had not sought to press his ambitions too intemperately. His attempts to fight at once with the French, with the Swiss, and in Lorraine, overtaxed the financial resources of his territories, and his military power was exposed as inadequate. In 1477, having lost two armies in the last two years, he engaged the Swiss at Nancy with inferior forces, and died in the complete rout of his troops which ensued.

The Burgundian territories had not sufficient unity to maintain their integrity after this disaster. They were divided in the end between Louis XI of France, and Maximilian of Austria, who married Charles's heiress, Mary. Their fate revealed how insecurely founded was the power of Burgundy, which had seemed great while France and England were fighting out their war to the bitter end. A series of contiguous lordships, brought together by dynastic diplomacy rather than true interest, could not coalesce to form the true semblance of a kingdom: multiplicity of local customs and language differences, which made their government as a single unit impossibly difficult, kept the component territories too far apart. Here the story of Burgundy illustrates well why the dynastic politics of the late Middle Ages were so confused and can seem so confusing. Lordships brought together by family arrangements, and maintained by military force which was at best casual, could constitute a power which appeared to the moment to be imposing, but was really weak, because politically and socially incoherent. It is an uneasy condition of things in which a state, which men have for forty years reckoned as one of the great powers of Europe, can dissolve at the death of a prince. It is not surprising that Fortune is a figure often invoked by writers of the fifteenth century: in the insecurity of the times, her wheel could turn full circle swiftly.

*

For all this, Valois Burgundy had a much more important influence on European history than as an ephemeral political phenomenon. Through the life of the ducal court, it made a powerful impression on European culture and manners. The standard it set in ceremony was a still discernible influence in the Versailles of Louis XIV. There was more to its influence than ceremony, moreover, although much of its importance can only be traced through ceremonial. This is a point worth pursuing a little, for it illustrates how, in spite of what often appears to be their pointlessness, the dynastic rivalries and wars of the fourteenth and fifteenth centuries helped to generate a new climate, not only politically and socially but culturally too.

The atmosphere of the Burgundian court in its heyday, in the time of Philip the Good and the early years of Charles the Bold, reflects directly the political and military preoccupations of these dukes. These preoccupations prove indeed to be virtually inseparable, as may be seen in the history of the order of the Golden Fleece, which Duke Philip founded on the model of the English order of the Garter. Politically, association with it was a means of binding to the ducal interest the nobility of newly acquired provinces, and of cementing alliances with foreign potentates. At the same time, through the cult of chivalry, which its statutes were devised to preserve and which its meetings adorned, it gave expression to the military aspirations and traditions of the captains and commanders who served the ducal cause. This cult of chivalry found expression also in the great court tournaments which the dukes staged, and in which every device was employed to combine the flavour of romance with that of magnificence. The places at which they were held were romantically rechristened for the occasion; thus there was the tourney at 'the tree of Charlemagne', at 'the well of weeping', and at 'the pass of the Golden Apple'. Vast sums were spent on these entertainments: noblemen came from all over Europe to take part in them, and they were carefully described by the chroniclers of the ducal court.

This deliberate parade of martial and chivalrous values is highly significant. It serves as another reminder that it was not merely pay and gain which men at arms sought in the service of hereditary princes, but glory also. The military calling was held to be noble: to follow arms was in itself 'to live nobly'. Knights and soldiers looked on the service which they performed for princes such as Philip of Burgundy very much as their ancestors had regarded service on the crusade, as an effort to uphold true right, by which renown and riches could be fairly won. Some even spoke of the knights of Duke Philip's order as being 'of the religion of the Golden Fleece', as if it had been, like the Temple in crusading times, a partly monastic order. One must not, of course, carry the parallel here too far. The complicated chivalrous rituals of Burgundian courtly society were in part, almost certainly, a subconscious effort to conceal an awareness that the causes of the duke were of more questionable ethical status than a crusade. The effort, however, was very largely successful. The magnificent style of the duke's court really did associate glory with his service. Its display made a direct appeal to the pride of caste and the established values of the nobility, which served to focus both their social self-consciousness and their military traditions around loyal service to the ducal house. Here we can see at work the beginning of a process, by which values once associated with crusading were to be altered out of recognition, through their association with ends of a quite different order.

It was not only in the cult of chivalry that the style of the Burgundian court found its expression. The dukes were great patrons too of letters and the arts. A telling memorial to their splendid style of living can still be traced in the paintings of such artists as Jan and Hubert van Eyck, in the rich detail of brocaded robes and of luxurious interiors in the pictures that they executed for courtly patrons. The van Eycks, we should remember, had as court painters much humdrum work to do of which only the record survives, such as decorating armorial bearings for tournaments, and helping to prepare elaborate *tableaux-vivants* for court festivities. To such men the instinct to present beauty in the minute detail of dress and design came naturally, even when the subjects they were painting were religious. Their work is a witness to the manner in which the courts of secular princes were, in the fifteenth century, setting the fashion and standards of artistic expression, as well as the social and ethical values of the aristocracy.

It is no accident that the van Eycks were the contemporaries of the first great generation of the Renaissance painters in Italy. There, too, the courts set the pace for style of living and culture. In the atmosphere of frenetic political competition of Italy in this age of despots and *condottiere*, lavish display and patronage of the arts served, as they did in Burgundy, to give expression to the aspirations of those who sought to live 'nobly', and to associate glory with the service of individual rulers. The fashions of Italy were different from those of the north, of course, especially the Italian passion for antiquity. No one in Burgundy sought, as did Pico della Mirandola, to penetrate the secrets of neo-Platonic 'theology', or to delight their patrons, as did Botticelli, by weaving allegories drawn from Greek myth into the subjects of their paintings. The differences between north and south which are here reflected, are important, but what is common is equally historically revealing. The same forces, we see, lie behind the dominant role which princely courts played in setting the standards and fashions of culture in both areas.

This points the way to an important conclusion. It shows how the competitive political conditions of the fourteenth and fifteenth centuries, which served to channel the efforts of much surplus military manpower, did much more than this as well. The dynastic rivalries of the great engendered many wars, which were the occasion, as the history of Castile shows so clearly, of much misery and depression. They fostered, however, creative as well as destructive forces. This was largely because, although military prowess was one of the attributes on which the aristocrats of the late Middle Ages prided themselves most highly, it was not the only ground of the self-esteem of their class. They took pride also in their superior standard of life, their use of leisure and appreciation of culture, in all that went to make their style of living distinctively noble. Thus political competition served to direct a whole series of energies besides the martial one, and in the process brought about decisive changes of outlook. Rivalry, in the course of the wars, became the life blood both of aristocratic and martial ideology, and of new movements in thought and letters. In these conditions, the call to take arms on behalf of Christendom united in crusade could find no response. Equally, the ideal of Christian unity which had inspired writers and thinkers in the time of Dante and St Thomas Aquinas ceased to do so for those who sought patrons in the aristocratic courts, because it had become irrelevant to contemporary circumstances. A new Europe was coming into being, in which it was not only boundaries that were different from those of the past: the whole framework of political thought and allegiance was altering.

19

Upheaval in the Church; Avignon, the Great Schism and the Councils*

DURING the century and a half that the great war between France and England was raging, the church of the west was undergoing a drawn-out crisis in its affairs. At the end of the crisis the standing and religious authority of the Roman Church had suffered irreparable harm, and there was no force left in its system that could make it capable of maintaining orthodoxy universally in face of the pressures which the Reformation was to put on it. At the beginning of the period, however, all had been calm on the surface: signs of the dangers which lay ahead were only just beginning to show. The intervening crisis developed slowly, after its dramatic inception with the outbreak of the Great Schism in 1378. Its story is so long and complicated that it will probably be best understood if broken up into sections. In the first we shall look at the Church and its condition in the period before the schism. In the second we must examine the impact which the schism made, and the difficulties in the way of healing it. In the third we shall trace the history of the general councils which restored outward unity, and try to see what really lay behind the unity that they restored.

I The Avignon Papacy

When the Hundred Years War broke out, the Pope and his court were no longer at Rome, but at Avignon, on the banks of the Rhone just beyond the then frontiers of the kingdom of France. Clement V (1305–14), elected in France, never went back to Italy, and his successor John XXII (1316–34) chose Avignon as his residence. There he began to build the great papal palace, which still stands to remind one of the magnificent style of living for

---

* My views in this chapter owe much to the influence of Professor E. F. Jacob's *Essays in the Concilian Epoch* (M.U.P., 1943).

which the Avignon papacy is chiefly remembered. The savage contemporary attacks on the luxury of manners of this 'second Babylon' were not quite fair, however. Six popes governed the Roman church from Avignon. All were Frenchmen, and this was the reason why they were unloved by those who were not, particularly by the English who were at war with France, and by the Italians who felt their residence in Avignon to be a slight to their own patriotism. All six were able, upright and sincere men, genuinely concerned for the well-being of Christendom. Neglect was not the besetting fault of the Avignon popes, rather the opposite. In a period when the problems facing papal government were particularly severe, they found themselves obliged to intervene in affairs more often than was good for the reputation of their office.

The most important advantage which residence at Avignon secured for the papacy was deliverance from the turmoil of Italy and her wars. This was the chief reason why the popes remained there for so long. The security and tranquillity of the Rhone valley also gave them a golden opportunity to put their affairs in order. This was the reason for the development which is most characteristic of the Avignon period, in which papal administration reached its peak of all-embracing bureaucratic efficiency. This led to an expansion of all the business of the Curia; it was, however, on the fiscal side, and in papal control of ecclesiastical preferment that development was most marked.

At Avignon, papal control of presentation to ecclesiastical benefices was built into a system. The papal chancery developed different departments for dealing with petitions for preferment, with the examination of candidates, with preparing instruments of provision to benefices, and sealing them, and with the enregistration of the whole transaction. Each stage in the process of thus obtaining a benefice involved the payment of fees to the chancery. Through this system, the popes established such a monopoly of nomination (or 'provision') to important benefices, such as bishoprics and abbacies, as to undermine totally the traditional right of election vested in the chapters of collegiate churches. Patrons, officially entitled and otherwise, connived at the papal system, giving notice of the names of those they wished to see preferred, so that the chancery could 'reserve' benefices for them in advance of vacancies. There was severe competition, with royal influence frequently brought to bear; with the claims of cardinals' cousins and curial staff to attend to, and the universities pressing the popes for preferment to support scholars in their studies. This competition gave rise to a flood of litigation in the papal courts, which added the profits of legal expenses to those arising out of fees paid for letters of 'reservation' and for bulls of 'provision'.

Fees and legal expenses represented only a part of the profit the papacy drew from this system. When any benefice to which the Pope collated was vacant, he claimed the whole income from it. For the first year after collation, the whole income was again due to him from the incumbent: this charge was called 'annates' or 'first fruits', and was very lucrative. During the Avignon period, not only these charges but also levies on the annual spiritual revenues of the clergy (the old crusading tenths) became more regular. Large sums were also raised by the sale of indulgences, again originally an expedient to pay for the crusade, but now becoming a regular source of income. In each metropolitan province of the church, a papal collector was appointed, to whom all these monies were paid over. He usually deposited them with the agents of the popes' bankers (the Bardi in the early fourteenth century were the most prominent: later the Alberti superseded them). The bankers transferred the money to wherever it was needed. Some went to Avignon, to pay for the expenses of the Curia, for the upkeep of the households of the Pope and the cardinals, and for buildings such as the papal palace. Much more, however, was spent in Italy, in the endless campaigns fought on behalf of the popes to recover control in the territories of the patrimony of St Peter.

The effects of papal control of collation to benefices were probably on balance beneficial to the Church. It largely put an end to the frequent and unedifying quarrels to which disputed episcopal and abbatial elections had in the past given rise. In many collegiate churches prebends had become almost hereditary in local noble families, and the papal candidates were often better men. 'Christ himself would not have been admitted into this college without a [papal] dispensation,' Erasmus was later to remark of one German cathedral chapter. On the whole, papal supervision tended to raise and regularize standards, and to break the hold of the local secular aristocracy over ecclesiastical preferment.

Nevertheless, the papal system inevitably aroused opposition. It struck too hard at influential vested interests, especially at those of the clergy themselves. Kings and powerful noblemen could often see that the Pope preferred their clients, by exerting political influence, but bishops and chapters had to resign themselves to the loss of most of their patronage in the way of benefices. Besides, papal control of preferment made room for abuses, such as pluralism and absenteeism, since papal dispensation to hold several benefices, and to discharge their duties through vicars, were not hard to obtain. Such dispensations were most easily obtained for the relatives and clients of cardinals and persons of rank generally, as were also dispensations from ordination, or to be ordained in early youth. Men without influence, often perhaps worthier, had to abide by the rules. To local clergy, the system had the appearance of being organized to promote the interest of foreigners. They knew also that it was the means whereby large sums were taken out of their country to pay for wars in Italy, which were no concern of theirs. Their leaders, the archbishops and bishops, were unable to check abuses to which the system gave rise, since they were sanctioned by their lawful ecclesiastical superior. It is very hard to say that the outcry against it, labelling it abusive and dishonest, was without foundation, even though it was probably less open to abuse than any other system would have been.

In some countries opposition was so strong as to render the papal system ineffective. This was especially so in England, where many suspected that monies destined nominally for Avignon were actually being diverted to assist the national enemy, the French. Widespread complaint gave the English kings their opportunity to gain a share of control over presentation to benefices. In 1351 the Statute of Provisors permitted the monarch to intervene in any instance where the Pope sought to collate to a benefice, and prefer his own man. This statute did not end the system of papal 'provisions' in England, because, diplomatically, the kings did not regularly enforce it. It simply made the system unworkable, if the Pope did not regularly acquiesce in the king's wishes in matters of preferment. Exploitation by two masters instead of one did little to content the English clergy, but significantly, many seem to have preferred royal to papal interventions. In the 1370s the dangerous suggestion was heard that the right to tax the spiritual revenues of the English clergy was the king's alone. Over this a fierce paper controversy blew up, with the Benedictine scholars Binham and Boldon taking up the cudgels for the papacy. Answering them, John Wyclif now first caught public attention as a pamphleteer in the king's cause.

In Germany the opposition to papal provisions was even more disturbing. Some papal nominees were resisted so strongly that they could not take up their duties. The secular authorities were ineffective as well as uncooperative, and ugly incidents occurred, as when at Wurzburg three clerks who had come to announce a provision were thrown into the river Main. The situation in Germany was further complicated by the political difficulties between the papacy and the empire in Italy. These led to the excommunication by John XXII of the emperor Lewis of Bavaria, who would not abandon his alliance with the Ghibellines of Lombardy. Until his death in 1347, the section of the German episcopate which was loyal to him was virtually out of communion with Rome. Lewis's court also gave asylum to the Pope's Franciscan enemies, among them the great English philosopher, William of Ockham. Ockham put his pen to good use in Lewis's service, seeking to demonstrate that the administration of all the temporal goods of the church pertained to the office of the emperor, as also final jurisdiction in all cases involving temporal properties, whether the parties were laymen or clerks.

Ockham had an influence far greater than as a mere anti-papal polemist. As a master of logical method he outshone all his predecessors among the schoolmen. He could not see why individuals should accept as true what they could not understand through experience of things that could be specified and identified. The long accepted arguments of many earlier thinkers simply would not bear the test of this standard. Ockham's logical method had such obvious potential that its critical and exacting spirit dominated the approach of scholars in universities all over Europe for nearly a century after he was dead. Men working in this spirit looked for answers to contemporary problems which could be justified without appeal to superhuman wisdom. Though many did not wish to carry the attack on the existing order as far as Ockham had done, the intellectual atmosphere thus generated was sceptical of old claims for papal supremacy. Some, moreover, wanted to carry the attack further, even among those who like Wyclif rejected Ockham's logical method.

*

The works of Ockham and Wyclif and their disciples were intellectually formidable: they do not make attractive reading. The spiritual ardour and humanity of, say, the early Franciscan and Dominican scholars (as Bonaventura, and Aquinas) is lacking in them. These are qualities hard to find in the universities in their age, or in the Curia, or even among the religious of the monastic and mendicant orders. This is not a sign that the fourteenth century was an age lacking in spirituality. It is merely a sign that one is looking for it in the wrong place, in its traditional stronghold in the ranks of the clergy.

It is not in the high places of the Church that one must look to find spirituality in the late Middle Ages, but among the poor and obscure priests and the laity, who were touched by a great upsurge of popular pietism. This amounted almost to a new movement in religion, a *devotio moderna*, as contemporaries called it. Its most remarkable expression is to be found in the communities known as the Brethren of the Common Life, founded by the disciples of the Flemish mystic, Gerard Groote (1340–84).

About him in his house Groote gathered a small circle of younger clergy and teachers; together they maintained themselves, with the aid of schoolboys and other scribes, by copying books.

Gerard's home circle was the model for numerous small 'houses of brethren', founded in the little towns of the Low countries and Germany, whose inmates were for the most part pious laymen. They led a communal existence, and followed a rule, but they never developed into an order: their personal and introspective religion had no need of such a formal framework. 'It is not the charters of the Brethren that make their members share in the watchings and fasting, in discipline and prayer: it is the union of brotherly love.' So wrote John Wessel of the house of the brethren at Zwolle. Groote and his followers had no desire for rank and influence in the Church and did not attain it. Nevertheless through their example and through their meditative writings, and above all through their activity as teachers and schoolmasters, they had a profound influence among the laity. This was why John Vos was able to call Groote 'the apostle of his country, who kindled the fires of religion in the cold hearts of men'.

In the personal religion of the Brethren there was an element of revulsion from the riches and abuses of the contemporary church: 'A prelate has no power to make a man more pleasing to God,' one brother wrote. This revulsion is even more marked in the sermons of the popular preachers such as Thomas Stitny and Milic of Kromeriz, who were making something of the same impression among the laity of Bohemia as Groote in Flanders, and at about the same time. Stitny, significantly, was long a layman, and his great religious treatises were written in his own tongue, Czech. The German mystics, Eckhart and Tauler, also wrote in the vernacular: so did Richard Rolle the hermit in England, and William Langland, who wrote the famous mystical poem called *Piers Plowman*. This use of the vernacular is a sign of the growth of lay literacy, which in turn made the growth of a self-aware lay pietism possible. It also rendered the anti-clericalism, which so often went hand in hand with piety, more formidable; sophisticated satire of clerical manners, often shot through with flashes of genuine religious feeling, could find plenty of readers. The anti-clerical tendency of the movements Groote and Stitny inspired got them both into difficulties with the ecclesiastical authorities. The religious attitude of their followers was too reminiscent of older popular heresies, as that of Peter Waldo, for the papacy of Avignon to look on it with anything but suspicion. One cannot say the popes were wrong to do so: it was in the lands where popular mysticism laid the foundations in this fourteenth century of a lay religious attitude that Protestantism, much later, was to find ready converts. The strong current of religious feeling among the laity thus added to the problems of the governors of the church, rather than subtracting from them. These problems were, with time, growing more serious.

It was clear that, sooner or later, the papacy must return to Rome: at Avignon it could not command adequate respect outside France. But to make Rome a safe haven meant for the popes fighting wars in Italy, which meant making more demands for money, and straining a system which had already raised so much opposition as to damage its own effectiveness. The popes thus had to struggle to maintain adequate control of ecclesiastical government, while at the same time disquieting signs suggested that their efforts to do so were costing the priesthood their command over men's souls. The divisions of interest and reaction which this situation prompted in the period of the Avignon papacy produced strains which did not show their full measure until long after. A difference began to be apparent between the ecclesiastical outlook of France and Italy, where loyalty to the popes was strongest, and of England and Germany, where popular pietism was turning away from the outward union of the Roman Church, to the inner union of brotherly love and the spirit. The religious geography of the Reformation was here foreshadowed.

II The Great Schism

In 1376 Pope Gregory XI left Avignon to return to his Holy City in Italy. In 1378 he died there. The citizens of Rome were determined that the cardinals should not elect another Frenchman, who would take the papacy back to Avignon. The conclave to elect Gregory's successor had to meet in conditions verging on a siege, with a murderous crowd outside calling for an Italian pope. The choice on which the cardinals ultimately lighted was Bartholomew, archbishop of Bari, who took the name of Urban VI. It proved to be disastrous. It became rapidly clear that Bartholomew's ungovernable temper, 'which made his face scarlet and his voice hoarse', would make the position of the cardinals, and especially the French among them, quite unendurable. There was a series of terrible scenes: Urban had to be held back one day in consistory from laying violent hands on the Cardinal of Limoges: on another occasion he tried to shout down the Cardinal of Milan in the middle of a service. In the conviction that the Church could not long endure such a shepherd, all but three of the cardinals retired from Rome to Anagni. There they proceeded to take desperate steps. Claiming that Urban's election was not valid, because undue pressure had been brought to bear on the cardinals by the Roman mob, they declared the Holy See to be vacant. On 20 September a new election was held, and Cardinal Robert of Geneva, a Frenchman, was chosen. He took the name of Clement VII.

The cardinals duly notified the world of the action they had taken, and their reasons for taking it. Urban's election had, however, been earlier notified in the normal official manner. He did not withdraw: instead he protested, and named new cardinals to take the places of the rebels. It soon became apparent that those who had staged Clement's election at Anagni had created a situation which it was beyond them to control. There were now two elected popes, Urban at Rome, and Clement, who shortly removed to Avignon. The Great Schism had begun.

The situation was without true precedent. There had been rival popes before, during the struggle of the empire and the papacy in the twelfth century: but they at least had stood for different principles in church government. Urban VI and Clement VII did not. From Rome and Avignon they made the same claims and directed the same kind of administrations – there was not even much to choose between them personally, for neither was a man of very edifying life. It was this parity between them that made the schism so profoundly shocking. No deep issue divided these two men: the spectacle of the two of them counter-claiming oecumenical authority in Christendom was a straightforward demonstration that a common faith, common ideals, and common institutions were not enough to hold its Church together. The situation seemed to imperil a religious unity that men had been taught not just to respect, but to assume.

Among the reactions it called forth, three demand special notice. First, it forced men to think much more seriously about the role that the papacy, which now stood divided, was meant to play in the life of the single body of Christ's Church. Secondly, it highlighted discontent with the existing ecclesiastical system and promoted imperious demands for reform. Abusive practices which could be ignored or forgotten when one pope was responsible could no longer be when two were. Finally, while everyone agreed that the schism must be ended as soon as possible, they found themselves bewildered and in sharp disagreement as to how this should be done.

In fact, the schism was to endure for almost thirty years, outlasting long the lives of Urban and Clement. For this there were again three main reasons. One was human failing. With the exception of Urban's immediate successor at Rome, Boniface IX, all the popes elected during the schism by the colleges of cardinals of Rome and Avignon swore beforehand that they would resign the moment that it seemed clear that this would secure union. But when it came to the point, neither Benedict XIII, who succeeded Clement, nor Innocent VII and Gregory XII who succeeded Boniface, were prepared to do so; not, at all events, in favour of their rivals. Excuses can be made for them: they had supporters and relatives and clients to think of as well as themselves, but it is hard to avoid severe reflections. Their obstinacy made it impossible to end the schism by any form of mutual agreement. Recourse to arms was no real alternative, since political support for Rome and Avignon was evenly balanced. This left only one way out, the ending of the schism by action taken in a general council, the only institution of the Roman Church recognized to be legally capable of judging a pope or popes.

Here the second difficulty in the way of ending the schism

appeared, a constitutional one. It was put clearly and succinctly by Conrad of Gelnhausen in the very first days of division.

It is impossible for a general council to be held or celebrated without the authority of the pope. But to convene such a council in the present case the pope cannot step in, because no person is universally recognized as pope.

To this constitutional impasse there was no solution in law. The two colleges of cardinals did their best to persuade their pontiffs to come to some accommodation, such as the simultaneous summons of a council to an agreed venue, but to no avail. When finally the cardinals lost their patience and summoned a council to Pisa in 1409 on their own combined authority, it only made things worse. No one could be sure that the summons was lawful, and the response was insufficient. Nevertheless, the council proceeded to declare both popes deposed and to elect another. There were now three popes instead of two. When Alexander V, the pope of Pisa, died, his supporters elected a successor, Cardinal Baldassare Cossa, who became John XXIII. (For popes of schism, see Appendix, page 328.)

As Pisa showed, it was not so hard to bring together a council: what was so difficult was to make it general. If the rulers of Europe had been in agreement, they could easily have forced the clergy of their realms and principalities to come together, but they were not. Hence the third difficulty in the way of reunion appears. The schism had broken out at a moment when Europe was already politically sundered by the great struggle between France and England. Allegiance to Urban and Clement, the two original rivals, set along ready-made lines of diplomatic demarcation. France, Scotland and Castile all adhered to Clement: England, Flanders, and most of the Italian states were for Urban, and the emperor Wenceslas joined them. Very soon the problems of the schism became caught up in the internal as well as the external politics of these powers. In France, the lure of inheritances in Italy, held out by Clement and Benedict to the royal dukes Louis of Anjou and Louis of Orleans, attached the latter and their parties firmly to the cause of Avignon. In the empire, when Wenceslas fell out with Rupert of the Palatinate, who got himself elected as a rival king of the Romans, the Roman popes made unshakeable allies of Rupert and his supporters by recognizing him as king. Wenceslas and Philip of Burgundy, Orleans's rival, became in consequence ardent supporters of a council, and Rupert and Louis opponents of one. Before a council which was truly general could come together, a degree of diplomatic concord and internal political harmony was necessary among the states of Europe, which the schism itself made very hard to achieve. The schism had the natural consequence also of strengthening the hold of secular rulers over the clergy of their dominions, and this made reunion harder still.

III The Councils of Constance and Basle

In the end, however, diplomacy did prove to be the way out. The lull in the Anglo–French war paved the way: both countries sent representatives to Pisa. In 1411, after Rupert's death, Sigismund of Hungary was elected to the empire, and his brother Wenceslas resigned to him his claim thereto. The new king of the Romans proved a tireless worker for union. He was given a great opportunity when the invasion of the papal patrimony by Ladislas of Naples drove John XXIII to seek refuge with him, and he was able to force the unwilling pope to summon a council to Constance. The majority of the cardinals acted in concert with Sigismund: he could count also on France and England, and after Rupert's death Gregory XII's supporters in Germany had ceased to signify. When in 1415 Sigismund finally persuaded the kings of Aragon, Castile and Portugal to send their representatives to Constance, the triumph of council over schism was assured. By that time the Council of Constance had been in session for over a year.

Thirty years of schism had added to the depth and complexity of the two main problems facing the fathers at the council, the restoration of unity and the reform of abuses in the church. It had greatly weakened the solidarity of those institutions which had been in the past the strongest props of ecclesiastical unity. It had not only divided the secular clergy, who in their obedience followed usually the lead of their rulers, but the orders too. The organization of the orders as international bodies in a universal church had given the papacy intrinsic strength which had enabled it to ride out the crisis of the time of Boniface VIII and Clement V. The schism broke the unity of their international organization and habituated them to a much greater degree of obedience to local authority. The combined effects of the schism and the Hundred Years War damaged also the internationalism of the learned communities in the universities. The old links between Oxford and Paris, and between Paris and the German universities had been broken, and the outlook of their scholars had become much more parochial. The effects of these growing divisions in the ecclesiastical world were reflected in the procedure of the council. The representatives were organized for purposes of voting into national groups, English, French, German and Italian. On the decisive issues the orders, the universities, even the College of Cardinals, could not vote as such. This meant that the council's efforts continued to be dependent on the same degree of diplomatic unity that had brought it together. National divisions had become so important that it was not in the council's power, even had it wished to, to restore the papacy to that pre-eminence in ecclesiastical government which it had enjoyed before the schism.

From the beginning the schism had concentrated attention on the views advanced by such writers as Ockham and Marsiglio of Padua about the powers of general councils. The great French churchmen, whose influence in the early days of Constance was decisive, Jean Gerson, Cardinal Pierre d'Ailly and Cardinal Fillastre, were all deeply influenced by Ockham, whose logical teaching emphasized human reason in a way which seemed to demand more room for the expression of individual opinion than the old system had allowed. The Church cannot be separated from her bridegroom, Christ, Gerson wrote, but from his vicar she can be: the council represents the whole Church which is always one with Christ, the Pope only the supreme human magistracy in it. D'Ailly was clearer still in his representative views on Church government. All terrestrial authority, he believed, derived ultimately from the community. He wished to see the cardinals become the elected representatives of the metropolitan provinces of the Church, so as to make the sacred college a kind of parliament about the Pope.

Views of this colour found expression in two of the council's most famous and significant decrees. The decree *Sacrosancta* (1415) laid down that, in matters of faith, a general council was the supreme authority in the Church. The decree *Frequens* (1417) made arrangements for the regular summons of general councils, at intervals of not more than ten years. Thus, the council produced the outline of a new scheme of ecclesiastical government, with a constitutional papal monarchy working within a representative conciliar system. Unfortunately it was an outline plan only: no rules for procedure, and no specific system of representation such as d'Ailly had suggested were laid down. It was not clear what the scheme would in practice entail or how it would work.

Most of those who advocated conciliar limits on papal powers saw as their necessary concomitant a far greater degree of local autonomy in the government of the Church. This offered really the only possible solution to the problems of papal taxation, papal provisions, pluralism, absenteeism, and the low standard of education of ill-remunerated parochial vicars – the whole assortment of abuses in the ecclesiastical system which had aroused such bitter criticism of the papacy in the days of Avignon. The schism had made these evils much worse. The rival popes were always desperate for money, and created new abuses to obtain it, as the new kind of letters of reservation which Boniface IX invented, which for an added fee were antedated to take priority over all previous reservations to the same benefice. 'Such things were done openly,' wrote Dietrich of Niem, an official of the Curia, 'all fear of God and shame of men set aside.' The popes were also too weak to resist patrons with political influence who pressed for preferment for unsuitable candidates. There seemed no answer to the evils which had become engrained in the papal system of patronage, except to take patronage away from the popes and restore to bishops their old rights of collation, together with full jurisdiction over all beneficed clergy in their dioceses, exemptions from the Pope notwithstanding. A great clamour for reform on these lines is a recurrent theme in the writings of the academic publicists whom the schism inspired with radical yearnings, as those of Gerson, Dietrich, Nicholas of Clemanges and John Wyclif.

To this problem of the control of benefices and of the pastoral clergy time had added a new dimension before the Council of Constance met. In England and Bohemia, alienation from Rome had provided a seed-bed for heresy. Wyclif went far further than others who denounced with him the abuses of the existing Church. Essentially academic though his views were they carried him to a position closer to that of popular pietists than that of his fellow dons. He was more radical than the conciliarists: for him there was only one final authority in theology, that of the Bible, which he believed must be translated into the native tongue, so that simple men could con the whole of its inspired truths. Rigidly predestinarian, he found the true Church not under any outward form, but in the union of hearts among those predestined to salvation. His philosophical views led him even further than this, into an attack on transubstantiation, an accepted and central dogma of the Church. In all these opinions, Wyclif was not very far from Martin Luther. The prompt action of the ecclesiastical authorities destroyed his following in the schools of Oxford, but his disciples there carried his doctrine into the country. For many years little groups of Protestant minded laymen in obscure places continued to disturb the peace of mind of English bishops, by their conventicles where they read and discussed the translations of the Bible and of Wyclif's own works which his disciples had prepared.

Wycliffite heresy in England remained scattered and proletarian, and was never really dangerous to the traditional authorities. In Bohemia his teachings acquired much greater influence, because of their enthusiastic reception among the Czech scholars of the University of Prague. The religious history of Bohemia was unique in this period, because it was the one country where academic anti-clericalism and popular piety really made common cause. The Bethlehem chapel at Prague provided a meeting place for them. The apostolate of Milic and Stitny inspired John of Mulheim and the burgher Kriz to found this chapel for the preaching of sermons in Czech to the townspeople: the preacher, they stipulated however, must be a Czech master of the university. This was the pulpit from which John Hus, who had adopted Wyclif's opinions while studying philosophy at Charles College, stirred his fellow-countrymen by his eloquence and gathered an immense following. In 1409, when he was chancellor of the university, the staunch defence of Wyclif's views by its Czech scholars became entangled with their quarrels with the Germans in the university: while about the same time Hus's attack on the riches and corruption of the clergy brought him up against the archbishop. His advocacy of communion in both kinds for the laity established a sharp difference of observance between his followers and their opponents. In 1413, while Hus was preaching in Czech among the peasants of southern Bohemia, the Germans and Archbishop John were preparing charges of heresy to lay against him before the forthcoming council. Thus the fathers at Constance found themselves faced with a choice between a champion of reform who was stirring the spirit of a whole people, and orthodox doctrine which he and they seemed to be preparing to abandon.

Until 1416 the Council of Constance was dominated in crucial decisions by the English and German nations, who always voted together and could usually bring the Italians to support them. The other determining force in this period was that of the leading French academics, who had been trained in a school which firmly rejected the whole basis of the philosophy on which Wyclif and Hus founded their teaching. This doomed Hus, who, although he had come to Constance under safe-conduct, was condemned solemnly as a heretic by French, Germans, and English alike, and was burned. It was an inauspicious step, as the powerful protest which the Estates of Bohemia shortly lodged with the Council indicated; one which militated against the unity which up to that point the Council had worked consistently and successfully to restore.

*

Pope Gregory XII, deserted by all but a handful of his erstwhile followers, had meanwhile at last put his resignation in the hands of the fathers. John XXIII, who had brought them together, lost what supporters he had when he tried to escape from Constance: after the passage of the decree *Sacrosancta* he was declared to be a promoter of schism, and deposed. The adhesion to the council of the kingdoms of Spain in 1415 left the third pope, Benedict XIII, without significant support. While he shut himself up in the fortress of Pensacola in the Pyrenees, he too was formally removed from office. The schism was ended. The council had cut through to the end of its first task, to restore the outward unity of the Church. It had also made a beginning, as we have seen, on a second, the extirpation of heresies which the schism had permitted to take a hold.

The adhesion of the Spanish kingdoms proved, however, not to pave the way to a fuller unity, but to be the end of what unity there was. At the same moment that, outside the council, a new offensive and defensive alliance of England and the empire against France (the treaty of Canterbury of 1416, between Sigismund and Henry V) upset the delicate diplomatic balance which had permitted its meeting, the addition of a new nation to the conciliar debates destroyed the working majority of the English and the Germans. The French now claimed that England ecclesiastically contained too few provinces to constitute a nation in her own right. In the furious scenes that followed all thought of unity in action was lost, and when the storm began to subside, the council was divided into two political alignments, determined to thwart one another. The English and Germans wished to proceed to the reform of local government in the Church. The French and Spaniards insisted that the election of a new pope should take priority over this. The Italians would not commit themselves, and there seemed to be an impasse. It was resolved by the despair of the English. A committee, composed of representatives of the nations and the cardinals, elected as pope an Italian, Odo

Colonna, since no other national could obtain a majority. He became Pope Martin V.

The English surrender was a symptom of the exhaustion which was becoming general among the fathers. The question of further reform was now shelved. A measure of local autonomy was granted experimentally for five years in a series of concordats agreed between the Pope and the lay rulers represented at the council. Everything else was put off to the future council, which the decree *Frequens* bound Martin to call in due course. The concordats proved in fact to be a dead letter: no sooner was the council dissolved than the old abuses began to creep back. Martin, a Roman noble, had been left to restore order to his patrimony without any outside military or political support. He needed every penny which his sovereign rights in the Church could bring him, and he soon found that most rulers were quite happy with the old system of provisions to benefices, if he would meet them by looking after their clients and servants adequately.

*

The Council of Constance dissolved, having at last restored to the Church a single spiritual father. It was about all it had done. In every other respect, its actions had added to the difficulties of the ecclesiastical situation. By postponing reform, it kept alive discussions of the critical issues, but made reform in practice infinitely hard to achieve, for there was now a lawful and universal pope, determined not to give away any right unless forced to do so. For him and his successors, the decrees *Sacrosancta* and *Frequens* were simply measures whose force it was a political necessity to evade. Constance made future compromise between pope and council almost impossible.

But the most disastrous step that had been taken was the burning of John Hus. It did not stifle heresy, but gave the Bohemians a martyr in the cause of national religion. When Sigismund tried to enforce orthodoxy by arms with Martin's blessing, he was crushingly defeated outside Prague by the one-eyed Hussite general John Zizka. The whole Czech nation rallied to the cause of 'the chalice', of communion in both kinds and the native liturgy. They appealed over the head of pope and emperor to a future council; and they found too a way of making sure that it met. The priest general Prokop led Zizka's army out of Bohemia, to ravage far and wide in Germany, into Prussia, and as far as the Baltic, where, their chronicle boasts, 'they watered their horses in the far sea'. While their victories seemed to threaten all Germany with heretic dominion, and tales of their atrocities were making men shudder in France, the invasions of the Ottoman Turks were pressing into the Balkans and threatening Hungary. The Greeks of Constantinople, all but encircled, appealed desperately to the west for aid, offering reunion with the Catholic church as their price for it. Martin V's successor, Eugenius IV, had no alternative in the circumstances but to yield to the pressure for another general council. It began to assemble at Basle in 1431, against a background this time not of schism, but of the threat of the infidel to Christendom, and of the need to find new compromises with Christian communities in Greece and Bohemia which were unorthodox in Roman eyes.

These issues gave a new colour to the hopes of the conciliarists, as they began to rise again. 'There cannot be concord without differences,' wrote Nicholas of Cusa,

Cyprian of old and the whole council of seventy bishops held different views within the faith of the church: yet they were not cut off, for they did not prefer their own opinion to fraternal unity.

In the mind of this great Christian Platonist arose the vision of a council which, bringing Bohemian and Greek and Catholic together in one representative body, should sink their differences in unity of the spirit. This was a far more grandiose idea of the possibilities of representation in ecclesiastical government than any that had been envisaged at Constance. Old issues meanwhile were not forgotten. For many sincere clergy new prospects such as Nicholas perceived were mingled with reawakened hopes for all that great programme of reform which the Council of Constance had contemplated and then postponed.

The seventeen years, during which the Council of Basle sat,

saw all these high hopes disappointed. In order to avoid the kind of quarrels which, so it seemed to the fathers, had ruined the efforts of Constance, the representatives were not divided into 'nations', but into five large committees or 'deputations'. This proved to be the council's undoing. Within the deputations the men who gained control were not those with real administrative responsibilities and experience, the cardinals, archbishops, and bishops, but the academics, above all the lawyers. By 1436 it was becoming clear that their rigid stand on the canonical superiority of council over pope, and their consequential flat rejection of the bulls by which Pope Eugenius sought to adjourn the council to another meeting place, in Italy, must imperil the proposals for Catholic union with the Greeks. The Greeks absolutely refused to come further than Savoy to meet the representatives of the west. The council had already achieved a formal reconciliation with the moderates among the Hussites. In this situation the most enlightened leaders at the council – among them Nicholas of Cusa and Cardinal Cesarini – felt that they could not remain at Basle. They withdrew with a substantial following, whom they claimed to represent the 'true' council, to obey the Pope's summons. At his council at Florence, which was theoretically the continuation of that of Basle, the Roman and the Greek communions were formally reunited in 1439.

After the withdrawal of Cesarini and his colleagues, what the Council of Basle did steadily dwindled in significance. The reconciliation with the Hussites, effected previously, ceased to be meaningful, because Eugenius did not accept its terms. This perhaps did not matter so much now, since the Hussites were so divided among themselves as to be no longer dangerous outside Bohemia. More serious was the fact that the sweeping series of reforms in ecclesiastical administration, which were at last approved by the council in 1438, were brought up after the departure of Cesarini and his supporters, when it had clearly ceased to be general. As a reforming body the fathers still at Basle were in a very tricky position. Not recognized by the Pope as a council, and short of funds to maintain themselves, they could achieve little without princely support. Their next effort, aimed to regularize their legal position, compromised such support very seriously. They declared Eugenius deposed, and chose as his successor Amadeus, ex-duke of Savoy. Amadeus was a layman, and his chief recommendation to the fathers was that he was rich: but as Felix V he cut no ice with the rulers of Europe, who had no desire to involve themselves in a new schism.

Without much guidance from Felix, the rump of the council struggled on through the 1440s, but the only thing which gave their moribund authority any significance outside Savoy was the political embarrassment of the emperor Frederick III in his relations with Eugenius. When, shortly after Eugenius's death, Frederick came to terms with the new pope, Nicholas V, the fathers took the only respectable course open to them. Felix laid aside his tiara: they elected Nicholas: then they dissolved themselves. This was in the year 1449. At last all the troubles to which the schism had given rise were over.

The long and inglorious years of its decline have done damage to the reputation of the Council of Basle. They must not lead us to forget the successes and high hopes of its early years, for these were important. If the Council of Constance stood alone, it would probably be remembered merely as an interlude in the story of the restoration of a single papacy. The early period of Basle shows how much more than this the conciliar experiment in Church government was. In a period when deep divisions were becoming apparent within the body of the 'one holy church' of the west, the two councils represent together a great effort to restore the unity of former times, by creating a new framework in which those divisions would cease to matter. It is his clear perception at this point that makes Nicholas of Cusa the greatest of the conciliarists: 'There cannot be concord without differences.' The quest for such concord does a great deal also to redeem the obduracy and dry legalism of the canonists who stood out against Eugenius IV in 1436 and 1437, on the issue of the superior authority of a council over that of the Pope. Surrender, as they saw it, meant the victory of the old ways of the papacy, the return of old abuses, and the appearance of deeper cleavages besides those already dividing Christendom. It is very hard to hold that they were short-sighted in their views, knowing, as we do, what was to happen shortly, in the lifetime of Martin Luther.

The failure of Basle was not a triumph for the papacy, though it seemed such at the time. What had then decided the issue in favour of Eugenius was the fact that most rulers preferred him to Felix V. The real control in the affairs of the Church had passed to these rulers. The Council of Constance, whose fortunes were dictated by the diplomacy of princes and the quarrels of national deputations, had already shown this: the aftermath of Basle showed it even more clearly. The reforms in Church government which the council decreed in 1438 were circulated to all the provinces and princes of Christian Europe. The English took no notice, because the Statute of Provisors and other legislation dating back to the period of the Avignon popes already gave their king sufficient control over Church affairs. Charles VII of France assembled his clergy at Bourges in 1438, established the reforms of Basle on his own authority, and having, by this 'Pragmatic Sanction' brought their enforcement within his own jurisdiction, proceeded two years later to recognize Eugenius as pope. In the empire, the reforms of Basle were accepted, until Frederick III traded their abandonment to Nicholas V in return for the promise of an imperial coronation. Which popes and what councils should be recognized, and what reforms enforced, were matters which secular rulers had by now come to decide.

The universal Church of the west, as it emerged from the period of the schism and the councils, was really a confederation of churches national in all but name. What held it together in appearance was not the authority of the Pope as spiritual father, but his diplomatic skill in his dealings with secular powers. This was the result not just of the failure of the councils, but of causes which had been at work long before they met. The effective control of government and administration in the Church, which the papacy had established in the Avignon period and earlier, had so undermined the local autonomy of the provincial churches, that there was insufficient intrinsic strength in them. This left them, when the schism broke out and two rival popes found themselves dependent on political support, an easy prey to secular authority.

The councils could not put things right, because though they were able to express the universal anxiety for reform, actual reforms could only be made effective through administrative control of ecclesiastical government, which they did not possess and could not gain. Their efforts helped to reduce papal authority, but to the profit not of the clergy, but of princes.

'Bishops,' the Parlement of Paris judged in 1487, 'are held to obey the king more than the Pope in the matter of benefices.' This is how the long upheaval in the Church's affairs and the arguments over the manner of their government ended, in direction by the temporal power. Effectively, the whole reserve of wealth and influence, which was concentrated in clerical hands, was now at the disposal of the secular authority, to swell out its sovereignty in the temporal community into full national sovereignty. 'You are the right arm of the Church': that is how the chancellor Jean Juvenal des Ursins addressed Charles VII of France. It could have been said as well of Edward IV or Henry VII of England. Henry VIII made it the statutory position of the English crown.

A single body cannot have a multiplicity of right arms, any more than it can have two heads. When the monarchs of Europe became each the right arm of the Church in his own territories, the unity of Christendom was dead. The universal authority of the Church was no longer a living force, but a tool of power in the hands of secular sovereigns. The councils were only an epitaph on the ecclesiastical unity which had once existed, which showed that it did not pass away unmourned, or without a struggle.

20

Europe and the Infidel After the Crusades

THE history of the councils and the history of the Hundred Years War are so closely interwoven as inevitably to concentrate attention on those countries which were most affected by the war, England, France, Burgundy and Italy. Their story shows how these two great upheavals in Christian Europe splintered its unity, in so far as it depended on these lands. In telling of them we have partly lost sight of those territories at the fringes of Christian Europe, which were least affected by the Anglo–French war and had most frequent contact with Europe's non-Christian neighbours. Until something has been said of them our picture of Europe as she stood in the second half of the fifteenth century remains incomplete. In fact, as will appear, the story of Europe's political contacts with outside neighbours in the fourteenth and fifteenth centuries makes a very illuminating companion piece to the story of the councils and to the Anglo–French war.

After the fall of Acre in 1291 the crusade to the Holy Land ceased to be a practical venture. Men still talked of plans for a great expedition to recover Jerusalem, but there was no more fighting in Syria. This is not a sign that Europe's contacts with the Mohammedan world were less important than they had been. It is a sign that Egypt and Syria, though still commercially important, had ceased to be the significant points of political contact with Islam. These were now on the soil of Europe itself, in southern Spain and, far more important, in the east beyond the Danube. Here in the middle of the fourteenth century the threat of the Ottoman Turks began to develop.

The Ottoman Turks first appear in history in the early thirteenth century, among the many nomad tribes driven from their Asian pastures in the course of the Mongol expansion. They found refuge from Genghis Khan in the territories of the Seljuk sultanate of Iconium, where they settled around Angora, and did notable service for the sultan against the Greeks. At the dissolution of the Seljuk sultanate in 1300 their leader Osman declared himself an independent prince. Under his son Orkhan (1326–59) the Ottomans began to make powerful inroads into the Asian territories of the Byzantine empire. Between 1326 and 1338 Orkhan took Brusa, Nicaea, and Nicomedia, and finally reached the shores of the sea of Marmora. He was a ruler of gifts, who built his conquests into a powerful hegemony in what had once been Byzantine Anatolia. It was Orkhan who first formed the famous corps of Janissaries, recruited among Christians who were taken from their parents in early childhood to undergo a rigorous education in the Moslem faith and the art of fighting. They formed a celibate, devoted standing army, drilled to a high point of expertise and to absolute obedience to the sultan.

When Andronicus Palaeologus, emperor of Constantinople, died in 1341, his general, John Cantacuzene, planned to supplant his young son Manuel. Cantacuzene appealed to Orkhan to help him. This it was that first brought the Turks into Europe, and the immense spoils which Orkhan's son brought back from his campaign with Cantacuzene in the Balkans determined them to return there. In 1354 they seized Gallipoli. From then on the west had to take note of them. In 1366 the Venetians and Genoese sent a fleet to help the Greeks in an attempt to retake Gallipoli, but the old enmity of these two cities was so strong that they were soon fighting on opposite sides. Meanwhile, Orkhan's son Murad began to advance further into the Balkans. Adrianople and Philippopolis fell to him. This brought him up against a much more serious Catholic enemy, the kingdom of Hungary.

At this time Hungary was prospering greatly under kings of the house of Anjou. Charles the Lame of Naples, son of the great Charles of Anjou, had married the daughter of King Bela of Hungary, and after the native Hungarian line died out his grandson Charles Robert succeeded to the Hungarian throne in 1308. He ruled until 1342 and was followed by his son Louis the Great (1342–82), who in 1372 became king of Poland also by the choice of the nobles and on the advice of their late ruler, Casimir the Great. Robert and Louis of Hungary were able kings. They protected the nascent bourgeoisie of the towns of their kingdom and invited immigrants into them from Italy and Germany. They fostered commerce by reorganizing the coinage and doing away with tolls on the highways, and increased the production of Hungary's gold mines by their new laws for miners. They also strengthened the kingdom's military resources by protecting the hereditary integrity of the estates of the great noble families, whose retinues formed the army, and by increasing their own standing bodyguard. Casimir the Great in Poland largely modelled his policies on those of the Angevins in Hungary because they were so successful: it was in the hope that his country would gain further by their enlightened rule that he urged the choice of Louis as his successor.

Louis of Hungary in the fourteenth century began to revive the imperialist tradition of the Angevins. King of Hungary and Poland, he began to cast envious eyes at the family's crown of Naples, and but for the Turks he might have also coveted Constantinople, as Charles of Anjou had done. Before the Turks established themselves in Europe, Louis had already been seeking to extend Hungarian hegemony over the independent Slav tribes of the Balkans. Here the militant catholicism of the Angevins created difficulties for them. Most of the Slavs, and the other Balkan peoples too, were Greek Christians, and the orthodox of Roumania, Moldavia, and Bulgaria put up a stout resistance to the Angevin advance. For this reason Louis gave them little help when the Turks began to press them. In 1389, seven years after his death, a great confederate army of Roumanians, Serbs and Moldavians was overthrown by the Turks at Kossovo, and this defeat ended their independence. Angevin policy thus ended by helping to build an empire in the Balkans not for Hungary, but for the Turk, with whom the Hungarians now found themselves face to face.

It was not a happy moment for a confrontation from Hungary's point of view. Louis the Great's death in 1382 had left his throne in dispute between his daughter Mary and Charles of Naples. The former succeeded in the end, but it was with weakened resources that she and her husband King Sigismund had to face the Turkish peril. Poland was lost to them; there Jadwiga, Mary's younger sister, had been chosen by the nobility as their 'king'. It was to the west that they appealed for aid, and in response the last great crusading army to be organized in France marched east under John, the eldest son of the duke of Burgundy. This crusading army and that of King Sigismund were defeated and cut to pieces almost to a man by Sultan Bajazeth at Nicopolis, beyond the Danube, in 1396. Hungary was defenceless.

Immediately after Nicopolis the Turks turned away to attack the Greeks. From Constantinople the emperor Manuel sent desperate appeals to the west, but no new force was sent. Hungary and Constantinople must both in fact have succumbed soon had it not been for the appearance, far away in Asia, of a new enemy for the Turk. In Tamburlaine of Samarkand the Mongols had found a new leader of the stamp of Genghis, who led his conquering hosts all over Asia and into India. On his return thence he overran Syria, and began to harry the Ottoman frontier. Bajazeth marched against him, and in 1402 in a great battle near Angora the Turks were completely overthrown. Bajazeth's power was broken with his army: the Mongols overran Anatolia and reached Smyrna on the Aegean. After this Tamburlaine turned home to Samarkand where he died in 1405, 'leaving behind him ruined cities, wasted countries, mountains of spoil, and pyramids of skulls'. It took the whole lifetime of Bajazeth's son Mohamed to restore something like his father's authority and empire. He died after a laborious and successful reign in 1421.

Sigismund of Hungary had had a long interval in which to prepare for the renewal of the struggle with the Turk. He was not idle. The motive behind his tireless activity to bring together the Council of Constance was his hope after it to head a crusade of all reunited Christendom against the Ottomans. In 1410 the electors of the empire chose him to be king of the Romans. He should therefore have been in a strong position when, after Mohamed's death, the Turkish attacks began anew. To explain why he was not we shall have to turn back and examine the foregoing history of the empire of which Sigismund was now ruler.

*

Sigismund's father, Charles IV, had been emperor before him, and so had his elder brother Wenceslas. Charles was of the house of Luxemburg, and his father had become king of Bohemia, having married the heiress of the native rulers in the time of the first Luxemburg emperor, Henry VII (d. 1313). Charles was chosen to be king of the Romans by some of the electors in 1346, in the lifetime of his predecessor Lewis of Bavaria, and under papal auspices. Lewis's death the next year marked the end of the long alliance between the empire and the Italian enemies of the Pope. Charles's undisputed accession in 1347 marked the beginning also of a new imperial policy in Germany.

Charles's first care was for his kingdom of Bohemia, where he ruled most successfully. 'There was such peace in his time,' an admirer declared later, 'as had not been seen in the memory of man, nor even read of in the chronicles.' His courts gave a newly effective protection to the common people against the oppression of the nobility. He spent large sums on the building of the great cathedral of St Charles at Prague, and founded a university there (the model for Casimir's university at Cracow in Poland). So prosperous did Prague become that Charles began to lay the foundations of a new town across the river Vltava to house a host of immigrants from the country. He also took steps to incorporate the outlying territories, which he had inherited in Lusatia and Silesia, fully into the Bohemian kingdom, and to exclude for the future all possibility of imperial interference in her internal affairs. To do these things he had to have the cooperation of the electors of the empire, whose constitution they affected. The price he had to pay for this may be seen in the terms of his Golden Bull of 1356, which became a law of the empire.

Its chief object was to protect Bohemian interests. This may be seen from the fact that it gave the king of Bohemia pride of place among the four secular electors, and established that, whereas other electorates on falling vacant were in the emperor's disposal, the Estates of Bohemia had the right to choose their own ruler if their hereditary royal line failed. Other privileges, however, Bohemia had to share with the other electorates. The bull confirmed to electors all mining and metal rights in their territories, and the right to issue coinage, and made it high treason to plot against an elector's life. No subject of an elector was to be entitled to sue, or be sued, outside the territories of his native electorate. Effectively the Golden Bull thus gave the electors sovereign rights in their own dominions. This made it virtually impossible for any emperor in the future to restore an efficient imperial administration in Germany.

Charles, however, was not really interested in Germany. In 1376, in order to obtain the election to the empire of his son Wenceslas in his own lifetime, he was ready to make more concessions to the electors in return for their complaisance. He alienated the sovereignty over a number of the imperial cities of the Rhineland, hitherto directly dependent on the empire, to various princes. This won him the support he needed; but it also led to the formation of the Swabian league among the towns in order to resist their new masters, and to its long war with the princes. Thus Charles strengthened the authority of the Bohemian crown, and kept the imperial office in his house, but at the price of strengthening electoral independence, and of promoting internal disorder in the empire.

Charles's son Wenceslas was to suffer for his father's policies. The peace leagues which he tried to organize in order to restore some sort of quiet in Germany were a failure; and he ran up against very severe trouble when he fell out with the Elector Rupert of the Palatinate. Rupert showed what electoral independence could achieve by obtaining from the imperial Diet in 1400 a sentence of deposition against Wenceslas, and his own election as counter-king. Wenceslas also had troubles in Bohemia, where his reign saw the beginning of social and religious upheaval during the apostolate of John Hus. He took to drinking hard (on a visit to France in 1397 he is said to have been splendidly drunk on champagne every night before supper) and his policies became less and less certain. At his death in 1419 the nobles and common people, who were beginning to accustom themselves to communal action as a result of the ineffectiveness of their ruler, confederated to uphold a national church and a national faith. As Wenceslas had no child, Sigismund became heir to Bohemia and to its problems: he had already, in 1411, inherited Wenceslas's problems in the empire. He had other difficulties on hand too, at this moment when he needed to be free to attend to the new Turkish threat.

All the chief territories of Sigismund's house were in the east. Here his lifetime had witnessed what was virtually a diplomatic revolution. The fourteenth century had seen the power of the Teutonic knights to the north-east of the empire at its height. This crusading order had made great conquests in the thirteenth century in the lands of the heathen Livonians and Prussians. After the fall of Acre their Grand Master had transferred his headquarters to their great fortress of Marienburg in Prussia, whence they began a crusade of wild savagery against the pagans of Lithuania. The knights allied with the Hanse, to whose league most of the towns of their territories attached themselves, and with the Poles, using their alliance in this instance to extend their lordship into Poland. Their whole position, however, was altered suddenly by the conversion of Jagiello, the Grand Duke of Lithuania, and his marriage in 1385 to Jadwiga, the daughter of Louis of Hungary whom the nobles of Poland had crowned in Cracow a year before.

The Teutonic knights thus found themselves faced with a new, formidable, and Christian enemy. Sigismund, whose wife Mary was Jadwiga's elder sister, also had an interest in the succession to the Polish throne, and, besides, Jagiello's power appeared clearly to threaten the territories of his own house at the eastern fringe of the empire. This threat became still more clearly apparent when the Hussites of Bohemia, having defeated the 'crusade' which Sigismund had led against them at the Vitkov in 1420, offered their crown to Jagiello. Sigismund managed to prevent this by abandoning his previous support for the Teutonic knights in return for a promise that neither Jagiello nor his cousin Witold would accept the Bohemian crown. This diplomatic success did not however solve his problem, which was raised again in a new form. The probability was now that the defenceless knights would strengthen their alliance with Frederick of Hohenzollern, Margrave of Brandenburg and hitherto Sigismund's ally against the Poles. Together they could constitute a power on the borders of Bohemia no less frightening than Jagiello's, and probably equally ready to exploit the revolutionary Bohemian situation to their own advantage.

The consequence of all these diplomatic complications was to leave Hungary hideously isolated in face of the new wave of Turkish attacks. In Germany, where Sigismund's authority had been weakened by the concessions of his father and the failure of his brother, he was embroiled with Frederick, who was one of the most powerful of the German princes. His most powerful non-German neighbour was Poland, whose assistance he was afraid to seek. In Bohemia he had, as the result of the Hussite rising, lost all control. It was with the forces of Hungary alone that Sigismund fought the Turks, with the varying fortunes of war always a little in their favour. During his long absence from the empire, imperial authority was further weakened: in fact, under the pressure of the great raids of the Hussite armies virtually all authority was beginning to disintegrate in Germany. The Poles meanwhile began again to advance into the territories of the Teutonic knights. Frederick of Hohenzollern was now too busy protecting himself against the Bohemians to do anything much to help them.

Sigismund died in 1437. The inadequacy of his unaided efforts against the Turks had by then permitted them to re-establish themselves unshakeably in the Balkans. His reign had also created such a confusion in Germany that there could be little hope, henceforward, of aid for Hungary from that quarter; especially after the election in 1440 of Frederick of Austria to be king of the Romans, which separated Hungary and the empire once again. Perhaps worst of all, Sigismund's difficulties had also produced a structure of diplomacy in the east which made it very difficult for Hungary to find allies against the Turk among the Slavs. The old entanglements with Bohemia and Poland nearly provoked disaster at the death in 1439 of Sigismund's successor Albert. Frederick III and Albert's relict Elizabeth invaded Hungary with an army of Hussite mercenaries to secure it for her infant son, while the Hungarian nobles offered the crown to Ladislas of Poland who they believed would give them better protection. If it had not been for the intervention of the papal legate Cardinal Cesarini, Hungary might have been destroyed by civil war and the Turk simultaneously.

Cesarini's intervention led to the brief alliance of Poland and Hungary against the Turk, led by Ladislas and the great Hungarian nobleman, John Hunyadi. The alliance ended after the terrible defeat of Varna in 1444, in which both Cesarini and Ladislas fell. Hunyadi, who fought on against the Turk all through his lifetime, did so alone. At Kossovo in 1448 he suffered a second tremendous defeat from which he was barely able to rally. After his son Matthias Corvinus had become king of Hungary in 1458, the old system of alliances was resuscitated, to exercise once more its baneful influence. Matthias knew that he must find assistance by some means, but every means he tried was beset with difficulties which Sigismund's reign had bequeathed. He was encouraged to attempt intervention in Bohemia and to seize the throne of the Hussite king, George Podebrady. George in self-defence fell back on the traditional alliance with the Poles, and this time the entente of Hungary and Poland was broken finally. Matthias had then to turn to the Teutonic knights to keep the Poles occupied. He even thought of attempting to make himself emperor in place of the weak Frederick III, in the hopes thereby of obtaining German support. This came in the end to nothing and served only to weaken further the crumbling authority of the most impotent of all the medieval emperors.

Matthias Corvinus was a great king of Hungary. He recodified her laws, established a standing army, and fought many campaigns against the Turks. If he had not had to waste so much effort in unfruitful enterprises in Bohemia, in the empire, and against the Poles, perhaps his country might have avoided the disaster of Mohacz, where in 1526 the Hungarians were defeated by the Turks, who overran their kingdom afterwards. Most of Matthias's difficulties were legacies from the time of Sigismund. It was what happened in Sigismund's reign that committed Hungary to isolation against the Turk. In a crucial period of her struggle she was disastrously alienated from her Slav neighbours, Bohemia and Poland, while in Germany authority and order had disintegrated so far that there was no hope of help from the empire. It is unfair, however, to blame Sigismund himself too much. The failures of his reign had a very long history behind them in which the over-ambitious schemes of Louis the Great of Hungary, the neglect of Germany by Charles IV and the territorial avarice of the Teutonic knights all played a part, not to mention John Hus.

*

There was one power besides Hungary which, all through the confusion of Sigismund's reign and its aftermath, was untiring in its efforts to organize a grand alliance against the Turk. That power was the papacy. Even in its darkest hours, when the patrimony was threatened on all sides by hostile *condottiere*, and when the Council of Basle was at the height of its successes, the popes never forgot the defence of Christendom. Through the difficult latter years of Martin V, negotiations with the Greeks for union were kept alive, always with the thought of a crusade against the Turks in the background. Eugenius IV worked tirelessly to bring these negotiations to fruition, even when his authority was most profoundly shaken by the successes of the fathers of Basle. At his council of Florence he showed himself ready to persevere in face of all obstacles and the obstinacy of Greeks and Catholics, and to make concessions at the right moments. When the union was finally achieved, his first prayer was that 'He who has thus begun the good work will perfect it, and by these endeavours of ours will be propitious and merciful to snatch the Catholic flock from the yoke of miserable servitude.' The yoke of servitude that he spoke of was Turkish.

It was not only with the Greeks that Eugenius laboured. It was he who sent Cardinal Cesarini to reconcile Frederick III and Ladislas of Poland when they were struggling for the inheritance of Hungary. The alliance of Poland and Hungary that went down at Varna was his creation. His successor Nicholas V could not after that help John Hunyadi much, or prevent the second defeat at Kossovo: nor could he, with Hungary so hard pressed, do anything for the Greeks. The union of 1439 had been abandoned by them in their disillusion long before the Turks closed in on Constantinople, which fell to them in 1453. Even after that the papacy did not despair. The whole of the pontificate and energies of Pius II (1458–64) were occupied with plans and negotiations for a new crusade. But the promises of support that he received from the Sforza of Milan, from Venice, and from the two most consciously chivalrous princes of France, Philip of Burgundy and René of Anjou, proved to be no more than expressions of good will. Pius's last attempt to shame men into activity by putting himself at the head of the crusade ended in tragedy. He was carried out of Rome in a litter, dying, at the head of a motley force, most of which had deserted by the time he reached Ancona on the Adriatic. Waiting for him there was the crusading fleet – two galleys and a septuagenarian cardinal. Pius never went aboard because he never recovered strength to do so. He died at Ancona in 1464.

The continued and strenuous efforts of Eugenius IV and Pius II to organize crusades proved one thing clearly and finally, that the popes' calls to Holy War could no longer evoke in Christendom a general response, even with the Turk in Europe. They proved more than that too. Even in eastern Europe, whose rulers were aware of the measure of the Turkish peril, such combinations as the popes did bring together depended, for their continued effectiveness, entirely on the political convenience of the rulers involved. Holy War took second place consistently to diplomacy. Sigismund could not work with any ally who might acquire interest in Bohemia. Frederick III was readier to fight Hungary in order to keep the heir to its throne in his care than to aid John Hunyadi. Matthias Corvinus was ready to use his prestige as a champion against the Turks to obtain papal support against Christian Poland. The policy of the Teutonic knights, crusading order though they were, was governed entirely by their determination to save what they could of their territorial power. They never thought of turning their arms against the Turk.

The pattern of development in eastern Europe in the time of the Turkish invasion, with powerful states emergent in Poland, Hungary, and Bohemia, in consequence not so much of war with

EASTERN EUROPE IN THE LATE MIDDLE AGES

Shaded area shows the approximate extent of Ottoman conquest by C. 1480

the infidel as of war with one another, has a striking parallel in the far west, in the Iberian peninsula. This was the only other area in Europe where there was direct contact with the Mohammedan world, for the Moorish kingdom of Granada survived in Andalusia until 1492. Iberia in the fourteenth and fifteenth centuries was the scene of many wars, and here too three strengthened kingdoms emerged at their close, Castile, Aragon and Portugal. It was not, however, combination against the Saracen which conditioned their development. The Portuguese fought indeed against the Moslems, but more often in Morocco than in Andalusia, and

311

the discoveries of Henry the Navigator fixed their attention more
firmly on Africa than anywhere else. The chief wars of Aragon
were fought in Italy, and in the Mediterranean for the conquest
of the Balearic islands. Castile was long disturbed by civil wars,
during which her kings looked often for aid from the Moors of
Granada rather than fighting them. In the fourteenth century,
indeed, Castile made greater efforts to conquer Portugal than
Granada. It was not until the marriage of Isabella of Castile and
Ferdinand of Aragon brought the two kingdoms together in 1479
that the offensive against the Moors really began to be pressed.
Confederation, ending political rivalry among the Christians, was
necessary before the last stage of the *reconquista* could be accomplished. If a similar confederation of, say, Poland and Hungary
had been feasible in the east, it might have made itself very formidable against the Turks. In both areas the war against the
infidel and its fortunes were governed by politics, not religion.

There is one great difference between the struggle against the
Moors in Spain and the Turks in the Balkans. The Moors were
not strong enough to be a real threat to the Spanish kingdoms.
The Turks threatened directly the kingdom of Hungary, and not
the kingdom of Hungary only. Advancing up the eastern coast of
the Adriatic through Serbia the menace of the Ottomans against
Italy was clear. The desperate situation of the Christians of Constantinople before 1453 was discussed in every chivalrous court
of Europe. The absorption by the Turk of the possessions of
Venice and the order of the Hospital in the Aegean, and of the
remnants of the Frankish lordships in Greece spelt danger for
Christians all over the Mediterranean world. The advance of the
Ottomans was not a local and limited problem, as the survival of
the kingdom of Granada was; its scale was European.

This is what gives such significance to the failure of Christian
Europe to respond to the Ottoman menace. Both the universal
authorities in Christendom, the emperor in Sigismund's time and
the popes continuously, made tremendous efforts to rouse Christian Europe to united activity in self-defence. Both failed totally.
This is a touchstone of the emptiness of their universal authority.
Go back two hundred years to the days of Innocent III and

Frederick II and one will find both these authorities playing on the universal response which the call to crusade surely evoked in order to maintain their oecumenical status. The contrast with the fifteenth century reveals a change greater than the decline of papal and imperial authority. The sense of unity on which popes and emperors had both played in the past was now no longer a living force. Even the threat of the infidel marching into Europe failed to fan the embers of it into an active flame. That consciousness of Christian union, in matters political as well as religious, which marks off medieval from modern Europe, did not exist any more.

21

Epilogue: The Break With Traditional Attitudes

ABOUT the middle of the fifteenth century, a number of very important events coincided very closely. The final dissolution of the Council of Basle in 1449 marked the end of the attempt to restore unity to the western church by conciliar means. In 1453 Constantinople fell, and the last vestige of Christian empire in the eastern Mediterranean disappeared. In 1453 also, the French won at Chastillon the great victory which set the seal on the outcome of their long struggle with the English, which had done so much in its course to form the character of the two kingdoms involved. The near coincidence of these events makes the middle of the fifteenth century a point at which it is possible and useful for the historian to pause in his task, to turn back and take stock of change.

In the first chapter of this book we began by looking at the map of Europe in the Middle Ages, and compared it with the map of Europe of Roman times. We saw then that the most striking point which these maps have in common is that for both the Mediterranean basin provides the focal centre. It was the highway of commerce, the lands about its shores were the nurseries of culture and traditions of government. This remained true in the medieval as well as the classical period, until at least the fourteenth century. France, it is true, in and after the time of St Louis seemed to have become the dominant power in Europe: but what were the outward and visible signs of this dominance? French leadership of the crusades; the power of the Frankish states in Greece, and of the house of Anjou in Italy – French dominance, in other words, in the Mediterranean world. By the middle of the fifteenth century there had been drastic alteration here. The conquests of the Turks had carried into Europe an authority neither Christian nor European, and had made the eastern Mediterranean the headquarters of the infidel threat to the west. Politically, the most formidable Catholic power in the Mediterranean was now Aragon, at its western extremity. The Levant was ceasing to be the most significant area in which Europe stretched out beyond her own confines. With Portuguese sailors feeling their way along the African coast, the Atlantic seaboard was assuming a new importance well before the voyage of Columbus.

In these circumstances, the political ideal of some kind of revival of the empire of Rome was bound to lose much of the sway which, from the time of Charlemagne onward, it so long exercised over men's minds. Only once indeed, after the mid fifteenth century, did the so-called empire of the west look formidable, and that was when, in the time of Charles V, the emperor was king of Spain also. In the thirteenth century, in the time of Frederick II, possession of the city of Rome still seemed a prize which could add lustre and significance to the title of emperor. In the middle of the fifteenth century it could not matter quite so much, because Rome was now too far from the true centres of political power in Europe. As the seat of the papacy and the ecclesiastical capital of the west, Rome was still an important place, and veneration for the classical tradition of ancient Rome was as powerful a force as it had ever been. But the connexion of these facts or factors with political conditions was no longer very important. This reflects a change of outlook with important implications.

The nature of this change of outlook is perhaps best illustrated by example. We spoke in the first chapter of the view of classical and biblical history which the early Middle Ages inherited from the Christian fathers. It was a view which considered the whole past in relation to divine intention, and which saw the incarnation as the common climax of both these histories. It endowed the Roman empire with a specific historical mission, to bring peace and unity to the world in preparation for the coming of the redeemer. The association of a religious significance with the political role of the empire was a chief reason for the eager interest in some sort of restoration of its authority. This way of looking at things still held good for Dante, writing soon after the year 1300; it provided, indeed, the essential historical framework for his great poem. It explains for us why he chose Vergil, the poet of imperial Rome, who, before the coming of Christ, had foreseen her grand destiny, as his guide to the underworld, and why he placed Caesar's assassins, who had attempted to thwart that destiny, with Judas Iscariot in the nethermost pit of hell. His attitude to the past coloured his view of the present also. For the evils of his own day he saw only one remedy: the restoration to Christendom of a single directive authority, such as the Roman empire had once been in the world. He saw this as a means not towards civil tranquillity only, but towards human salvation also, as it had been, he believed, in the classical past. The one without the other had no value or meaning for him. This was the reason for the depth of his bitterness against his own native city, Florence, which, by her uncompromising resistance to the emperors, had sought to prevent the restoration of peace to Christendom.

If we compare the views of Dante with those of Leonardo Bruni, who wrote also both of the Roman past and the Florentine present just a hundred years later, we find that the Christian framework of providential design, essential to Dante, has dropped out of the picture. The two men's lives are divided by an age of discovery, pioneered by Petrarch, among manuscript works of classical authors. Bruni in consequence had not only a surer knowledge of the facts about the classical past than Dante, but also knew more about the way in which men at the time had explained them; and had learned thus to view not only the events of the past but those of his own day too, as the classical historians had done, in terms of purely human effort. For Brutus, who by the assassination of Caesar had sought to preserve the traditions of the Roman republic, he had nothing but admiration, seeing in his career a historical echo of the struggle of Florence in his own youth to maintain her republican liberty, threatened by the might of Giangaleazzo of Milan. The providential role ascribed to the Roman empire by tradition had no meaning for him. So, when he writes of Florence, to praise her constitution, we find his views untinged by religious and providential theories of history. He admires it as a human artefact, designed to achieve a certain human end, the preservation of liberty together with security. Bruni points the way here towards an idea of statecraft as a human skill, which helps men to achieve their ends by sound estimates of the way in which people will react. This is the idea of statecraft which was given its classic expression later, in the work of another Florentine, Macchiavelli. In his book, *The Prince*, one will seek in vain for the notion of the unity of Christendom as a valid political ideal, or of political endeavour serving as a means toward human salvation.

As this comparison between the ideas of Dante and of Bruni helps to illustrate, something more important was taking place in the fifteenth century besides a change of attitude towards Rome and the Roman past. A framework of thought in which religious and political ideals were not separated, which saw the work of priests and princes essentially as complementary means toward the same end, was losing currency. Men were beginning to experiment with guiding principles to thought and action which ignored these associations. With their passing, the concept of Christendom, of Europe as a kind of Christian super-state, ceased to be meaningful. From the time of Charlemagne until the time of the Councils, the belief that the unity of Christendom was not only meaningful but of the highest value in political and religious terms, had led men not only to think and write but to act also. There is a real change here which provides justification for treating the period when this belief ceased to bear fruit in practical effort as the end of an era.

In accepting it as such, we must observe great caution with regard to one matter. In no sense, it must be emphasized, did the growth of a divorce between religious ideas and political ideology, which is the essence of the change we have been discussing, reflect a decline of genuine religious feeling. It did not even mean that religion ceased to be accepted as a guide to political action. The wars of Catholic and Protestant in the sixteenth century were not fought on paper only; they were fought with sword and powder in the field, with the bloodthirsty valour of conviction. The principle enunciated at the end of these wars, *cujus regio ejus religio*, directly associated religion and politics. It was a principle, however, of regional coexistence, not of religious and political unity. In this respect it is illuminating: it helps us toward a fuller understanding of what the changes meant which were taking place at the end of the Middle Ages and which we have been examining.

It was not decline of religious feeling on which the unitary ideal of medieval Christendom foundered, but rather on regional differences in Europe, their development, and a growing sensitivity to their relevance. This is really what much of the history of the later Middle Ages, as we have studied it, has been about. We have seen how, in such kingdoms as France and England, there grew in this period, hand in hand with increased efficiency of government, a sense of corporate national entity. Institutions developed, such as the English parliament, which gave expression to the growth of such feelings, while at the same time the scope of government extended to include the regulation on a national basis of such matters as trade and social relations. We have also seen how, in this period, the divisions in Europe, which wars and the great schism fostered, weakened the influence of the clergy as an international body, and rendered their leaders less independent of regional secular authorities. With the spread of lay literacy, the local vernaculars came into their own, and Latin began to lose its influence as a living language, the *lingua franca* of all educated men: thus the learned world too became less cosmopolitan. All these factors worked together to make regional separation a more important social force at the end of the Middle Ages, especially for the dominant classes, the clergy, the men of letters, the military and mercantile aristocracy.

In order to obtain as full an understanding as we may of the change of outlook, which we are seeking here to elucidate, we must set beside this growing importance of regional separation what some historians have called 'the growth of a lay spirit'. Really the two were part and parcel of the same process. The ecclesiastical system of the Middle Ages was international. In contrast, personal and local connexions, then as always, provided the focus of purely secular loyalties. As long as the laity continued to look to the clergy for much leadership and direction, the ideal of unity in Christendom, which found its classical exposition in the writings of ecclesiastical thinkers (especially those of the twelfth century), and for which a unitary system of ecclesiastical government seemed to provide a foundation, could be actively and generally influential. In times when nothing that was secular was safe, unless it could be defended, and when even the most powerful laymen lived in castles, dwelling places in which the demands of fortification came before all considerations of beauty and comfort, it is not surprising that the laity did look to the clergy for advice and leadership. In all matters connected with the things of the mind, the standards of the clergy seemed and were superior. These were conditions which discouraged questioning of the secular implications of ideals by which the clerical authorities set great store.

By the mid fifteenth century these conditions were a thing of the past. The fashions of thought and artistic expression were being dictated in the courts of secular princes. The splendid houses which the nobility were building for themselves – the ducal palace at Urbino, for example, or the Pitti palace in Florence – testify to the extent to which secular life had by this time freed itself of its old circumscriptions. So do the treasures, manuscripts, and paintings, which in this period great collectors among the secular nobility, like Jean de Berry and Humphrey, duke of Gloucester, brought together. There were no longer the same good reasons for secular men to look on the living of the clergy as superior to their own. Even as concerned direction in spiritual things, the pre-eminence of clerical authority seemed less absolute. The educated laymen, who were drawn by the teaching of such men as Gerard Groote and Master Ekkehart, could find God in their hearts in their own houses, as well as they could through the ministrations of a priest in church. With the decline in the influence of the clergy, the idea of building upon the foundation of the Roman ecclesiastical system a unity which should be social and political as well as religious, lost inevitably both its appeal and its practical point. In a world in which laymen played a much more independent part in the direction of affairs, this was an end towards which it no longer seemed necessarily desirable to strive.

Once again, example may be the best way to illustrate an important point. Buildings always provide a useful guide to the tenor of life in the past, and its changes, because they are its visible and tangible monument. The buildings of the Middle Ages afford a kind of palimpsest of their history. In the early Middle Ages, all over Europe, we find one style predominant, the Romanesque. The rounded arch, the apse, and the dome, which are its hallmarks, remind us of its derivation from the Roman style of the late classical period and of Byzantium. Almost all the best Romanesque work in the west is ecclesiastical, the church of St Mark in Venice, such cathedrals as Moissac and St Gilles in France, and Durham in England. This is true also of the style which, in the twelfth century, began to replace it almost universally, the Gothic, whose name calls to mind such great churches as Notre Dame in Paris, the cathedrals at Salisbury or Exeter in England, or Burgos in Spain. The homeland of Gothic was northern France: and the rapid predominance which it achieved as a style all over Europe reminds us at once of the unity of European ecclesiastical culture from the twelfth century to the fourteenth, and of the pre-eminent influence of France in this same period. But perhaps the most important thing we can learn from the design of the best Gothic churches is how inevitable the dominance of the clergy was, in an age when ordinary people learned most of what they knew about religion and the meaning of life not from books but by what they saw and heard in church. There is hardly a detail in a great Gothic church without its purpose, structural, devotional, or didactic.

Between the Gothic and the style of the Renaissance which began to oust it in the fifteenth century, two significant differences may be remarked. One is the greater preoccupation of the Renaissance architects with effects which are purely aesthetic. There is a tendency in this direction already in late Gothic: it is a sign that the demands of religious instruction were becoming less strenuous for the designer. The other difference is a much more important one. We no longer have to look so exclusively to ecclesiastical buildings to trace the triumphs of the style of the Renaissance. Italian palaces and the villas of their owners in the countryside, and French *chateaux* such as Blois and Fontaine-bleau, show clearly that secular architecture has come into its own. The world has learned at last to house its princes no less magnificently than its priests. The testimony here is to a change not just of architectural style, but in the whole tenor of living.

The buildings which are our evidence here of a great change give us an indication of its nature, and some measure of its importance. It does not bring us up against conditions which we can properly call modern, by the standards of the mid twentieth century. It was not a change, clearly, which affected all classes of men, not equally at any rate: nothing suggests that anyone in the fifteenth century bothered very much about how the poor were housed. Nevertheless, it was a very important change, reflecting an alteration not merely of the outlook of men of influence, but in the circumstances which conditioned their outlooks. It is a pointer to significant change when we find that a privileged lay-man can hope to live in comfort and with a fair standard of culti-vation, even in the countryside, without having to choose between the security of either a fortress or a cloister. What made this possible for him was the increased efficiency of regional secular government. He did not have to worry, in the way his ancestors who lived in a fortified castle had to, about the activities of enemies, who lived in other castles not so many miles away. This local security, the secret of his comfort, he shared now with many whose predecessors could not have afforded to build a castle. This change, however, would not have mattered so much if it had not been accompanied by a rise in the standard of education and culture among the laity, if the secular upper classes had not acquired an increased ability to reason for themselves in broad and general terms about their situation. The two changes taken together were enough to break the spell of social, religious, and political ideals characteristic of the Middle Ages.

APPENDIX

Tables of the Royal Houses
and Popes

THE VALOIS DUKES OF BURGUNDY AND DYNASTIC MARRIAGES (cf. page 270)

Philip the Bold,
Duke of Burgundy, 1363–1404,
m. to Margaret, heiress of
Flanders, who was recognized
as heiress of her aunt Joanna
of Brabant in 1390

John the Fearless,
Duke of Burgundy, 1404–19,
m. Margaret of Bavaria

Anthony, Duke of
Limburg and
Brabant, 1406–15,
m. Jeanne, heiress
of Luxemburg

John, Duke of Brabant m. Jacqueline, Countess of Holland
etc.   and Hainault

(this marriage had
no issue)

Margaret,
m. William,
Count of Holland
and Hainault

Catherine,
m. Leopold
of Austria

Marie,
m. Duke
of Savoy

Philip the Good,
Duke of Burgundy,
1419–67, acquires the
family interests in Flanders,
Brabant, Limburg,
Luxemburg, Hainault
and Holland

Charles the Bold,
Duke, 1467–77

Mary, m. Adolf,
Duke of Cleves

Catherine,
m. Louis
of Anjou

Anne, m.
John, Duke
of Bedford

Agnes,
m. Charles
Duke of
Bourbon

THE HOUSE OF ANJOU AND ITS CONNEXIONS (cf. page 187)

CHARLES I of Anjou
(1266–85), m. Beatrice,
heiress of Provence

- CHARLES II (1285–1309), m. Mary of Hungary
- Robert, d. 1266
- Blanche, m. Robert, Count of Flanders
- Isabella, m. Ladislas IV of Hungary
- Beatrice, m. Philip de Courtenay, titular LATIN EMPEROR of Constantinople

CHARLES II (1285–1309), m. Mary of Hungary:

- Charles Martel, d. 1296
  - Charles Robert, King of HUNGARY (see Chapter 20)
- Philip, m. Isabella Villehardouin, heiress of ACHAEA
- ROBERT (1309–42)
  - JOANNA (1342–82)
- John, Count of Durazzo
  - Charles
    - CHARLES III (1381–6)
  - Lewis
- 10 other children

325

THE HOHENSTAUFEN AND THE ARAGONESE OF SICILY (cf. pages 173 & 188)

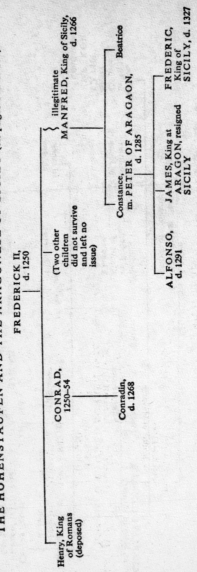

FREDERICK II,
d. 1250

Henry, King
of Romans
(deposed)

CONRAD,
1250–54

Conradin,
d. 1268

(Two other
children
did not survive
and left no
issue)

{ illegitimate
MANFRED, King of Sicily,
d. 1266

Beatrice

Constance,
m. PETER OF ARAGAON,
d. 1285

ALFONSO,
d. 1291

JAMES, King at
ARAGON, resigned
SICILY

FREDERIC,
King of
SICILY, d. 1327

THE FRENCH SUCCESSION PROBLEM, 1328 (cf. page 245)

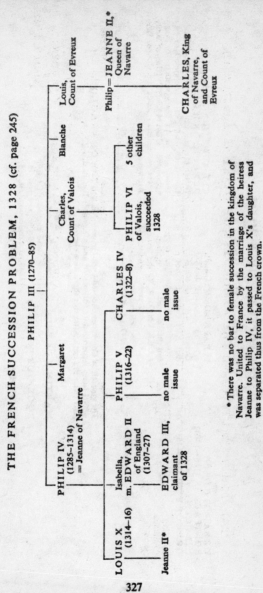

PHILIP III (1270-85)

PHILIP IV (1285-1314) = Jeanne of Navarre

Margaret

Charles, Count of Valois

Blanche

Louis, Count of Evreux

LOUIS X (1314-16)

PHILIP V (1316-22)

CHARLES IV (1322-8)

Isabella, m. EDWARD II of England (1307-27)

PHILIP VI of Valois, succeeded 1328

5 other children

Philip = JEANNE II,* Queen of Navarre

Jeanne II*

EDWARD III, claimant of 1328

no male issue

no male issue

CHARLES, King of Navarre, and Count of Evreux

* There was no bar to female succession in the kingdom of Navarre. United to France by the marriage of the heiress Jeanne to Philip IV, it passed to Louis X's daughter, and was separated thus from the French crown.

327

THE POPES OF THE SCHISM

Gregory XI – d. 1378

Rome

URBAN VI (1378–89)
BONIFACE IX (1389–1404)
INNOCENT VII (1404–6)
GREGORY XII (1406–15)

Pisa

In June 1409 the Council of Pisa deposed both Gregory XII and Benedict XIII (who did not recognize its authority), and then elected:
ALEXANDER V
who was
succeeded by
JOHN XXIII

Avignon

CLEMENT VII (1378–94)
BENEDICT XIII (1394–1423)
(After his deposition, by the Council of Constance, Benedict still claimed to be pope, and at his death a successor was appointed, CLEMENT VIII; he was never recognized outside the County of Armagnac.

The council of Constance deposed both Gregory XII and John XXIII (who recognized its authority): and afterwards Benedict XIII (who did not). After this there were elected:

MARTIN V (1417–31)

EUGENIUS IV (1431–47) { deposed by the Council of Basle, who elected FELIX V in 1439: he resigned in 1449, and the council elected NICHOLAS.

NICHOLAS V (1447–55)

Basle

Bibliography

Note: I have divided this bibliography, like this book, into sections. In a general paragraph, at the beginning of each section, I have tried to name one or two books, which examine broad aspects of the problems of the period in question, and which seem to me to discuss them in a particularly illuminating way. No historians' book, however, can bring a reader into direct contact with the life and ways of thought of a period, in the way that accounts which men wrote down at the time can do. I have therefore tried to list, in each section, a few original sources, of which translations can be found, by means of which those readers who wish to may start to form their own first hand impressions of the life of medieval Europe. After this, within each section, I have tried to give some indication, chapter by chapter, of the books through which the subjects discussed in each chapter may most easily be pursued further.

Section One: 800–1046

General: The general problems of this period are discussed in two outstanding works by English scholars: R. W. Southern, *The Making of the Middle Ages* (London, 1953), and J. M. Wallace Hadrill, *The Long Haired Kings* (London, 1962). A third work which combines scholarly distinction with a broad approach is Marc Bloch, *Feudal Society* (London, 1961, trans. L. A. Manyon). Among original sources perhaps the best introduction at first hand to the problems that these scholars discuss is Einhard's *Life of Charlemagne*, translated in A. J. Grant (ed.), *Early Lives of Charlemagne* (London, 1905). There is some very illuminating material too, in Theodore E. Mommsen's *Imperial Lives & Letters of the Eleventh Century* (Columbia, 1962). No one can really understand the ecclesiastical life of this age until he has read *The Rule of St Benedict*, which is translated by Justin McCann (London, 1960). The *Regularis Concordia*, translated by T. Symons (Nelson's Medieval Classics, 1953), gives an excellent impression of the way in which this rule was followed in a tenth-century monarchy.

Chapter 2. One of the most useful of the many discussions of the Carolingian age is M. Fichtenau, *The Carolingian Empire* (trans. P. Munz, Oxford, 1963). D. Bullough, *The Age of Charlemagne* (London, 1965) is a distinguished book, and splendidly illustrated.

There are some excellent books discussing various aspects of the barbarian invasions of the ninth and tenth centuries. A. R. Lewis has contributed two admirable works in his *Naval Power and Trade in the Mediterranean A.D. 500–1100* (Princeton, 1951), and *The Northern Seas A.D. 300–1100* (Princeton, 1958). On the Vikings, there are T. D. Kendrick, *A History of the Vikings* (London, 1930), and the challenging work of P. H. Sawyer, *The Age of the Vikings* (London, 1962). On the rise of the German empire, the best introductory books are G. Barraclough, *The Origins of Modern Germany* (Oxford, 1957), and F. Dvornik, *The Making of Central & Eastern Europe* (London, 1949).

Chapter 3. The classic modern discussion of the origins and nature of feudalism is M. Bloch, *Feudal Society* (London, 1962). Also useful is F. L. Ganshof, *Feudalism* (trans. P. Grierson, London, 1964). The chapter on the 'Bonds of Society' in R. W. Southern's *Making of the Middle Ages* (London, 1953) is particularly illuminating, and approaches the problems in a rather different way. The European economy of the period is examined and interpreted by H. Pirenne in his famous posthumous book *Mohamed & Charlemagne* (trans. B. Miall, London, 1954). His challenging thesis has been heavily criticized, and a selection of the views of his critics are collected by A. F. Havighurst (ed.), *The Pirenne Thesis* (Boston, 1958).

Chapter 4. There is vast literature dealing with the monasteries and the monastic ideals of the early Middle Ages. Two, which should be mentioned because they are outstanding, are C. Butler, *Benedictine Monachism* (London, 1919), and D. Knowles, *The Monastic Order in England* (Cambridge, 1949). On Cluny and her influence, L. M. Smith, *The Early History of the Monastery of Cluny* (Oxford, 1920) is useful.

On the other hand, there is no single and satisfying general account, in English, of the political ideals of this period. P. E. Sehramm, *Kaiser Rom und Renovatio* (Darmstadt, 1957), has not been translated, in spite of its importance. There is useful comment in O. Gierke, *Political Theories of the Middle Age* (trans. F. W. Maitland, Beacon paperback, 1958). E. Kantorowicz, *The King's Two Bodies*, and G. Tellenbach, *Church, State, and Christian Society* (Oxford, 1958, trans. R. F. Bennett) have much that is interesting and illuminating to say about the ideas of this period, but their scope is chronologically much wider.

Section Two: 1046–1216

For this period, as for the preceding one, R. W. Southern's *Making of the Middle Ages*, and M. Bloch's *Feudal Society* are outstanding among the works which discuss broad problems. There is a richer supply of contemporary sources than there is for the Carolingian period, and they throw fresh and exciting light on the fabric of life and events. A good many translations have been made. There is, for instance, C. C. Mierow's translation of Otto of Freising, *The deeds of Frederic Barbarossa* (New York, 1953); a number of good crusading memoirs, as the *Deeds of the Franks*, the memories of an unknown soldier on the first crusade, translated by Rosalind Hill (Nelson Medieval Classics, 1951); and the chronicle of the fourth crusade written by Geoffrey Villehardouin, translated by M. R. B. Shaw in *Chronicles of the Crusades* (Penguin Classics, 1963). *The Chronicle of Jocelin of Brakeland* (trans. H. E. Butler, Nelson Medieval Classics, 1951) gives a vivid picture of life at a quite different level, in an East Anglian cloister and about the estates which the monastery of Bury St Edmunds possessed.

Chapter 5. G. Tellenbach, *Church State and Christian Society* (Oxford, 1958) is an outstanding and up to date discussion of the problems raised by the conflict of the papacy with the empire. W. Ullman, *The Growth of Papal Government* (London, 1955) is a work of immense scholarship, based on very wide reading among the sources for the period and subject. J. P. Whitney, *Hildebrandine Essays* (Cambridge, 1932) reviews usefully the work of men who influenced Pope Gregory VII, as Cardinal Humbert and Peter Damian, and discusses the Pope's troubles over the archdiocese of Milan. There is a very considerable further literature on the subject matter of this chapter, as the bibliographies of these books will indicate. No list, however, could be complete without mention of the work of the great continental scholar A. Fliche, *La Réforme Grégorienne* (3 vols., Louvain, 1924–37).

Chapter 6. The best introduction to the topics discussed in this chapter will be found in the relevant sections of the *Cambridge Economic History of Europe*, Vols. I and II (ed. J. H. Clapham and E. Power, Cambridge, 1941–52). Some very interesting ideas are put forward by Lynn White Jr., *Medieval Technology and Social Change* (Oxford, 1962), but not all his arguments are convincing. On the growth of towns and trade,

H. Pirenne, *Medieval Cities* (trans. F. D. Halsey, Princeton, 1925), a brief and masterly survey, has become a classic. On the Normans and their conquests, C. H. Haskins, *The Normans in European History* (Boston, 1915) is an excellent guide. The German expansion eastward in the twelfth century is well described by J. W. Thompson in *Feudal Germany* (Chicago, 1928).

Chapter 7. C. H. Haskms, *The Twelfth Century Renaissance* (Harvard, 1927) is the best general treatment in English, and especially illuminating about the re-awakening of interest in classical studies. Also very valuable, in spite of its age, is R. L. Poole, *Illustrations of the History of Medieval Thought and Learning* (London, 1920). But the best works on the intellectual history of the twelfth century, which have appeared in the twentieth, have been those of French scholars, as J. de Ghellink, *Le Mouvement Théologique au XIIme Siècle:* (Paris, 1948) and G. Paré, A. Brunet and P. Tremblay, *La Renaissance du XIIme Siècle: les écoles et l'enseignement* (Paris, 1933).

On new ideas and motifs in literature, there is much valuable comment in W. P. Ker, *Epic and Romance* (London, 1908), an established classic. C. S. Lewis in the *Allegory of Love* (Oxford, 1936) pursues exciting themes, and the Arthurian legend is examined in great detail in R. S. Loomis (ed.), *Arthurian Literature in the Middle Ages* (Oxford, 1959).

Chapter 8. There is no single work which offers a general survey of the subjects discussed in this chapter. Sicily in the first half of the twelfth century is well described in E. Curtis, *Roger II and the Normans in Lower Italy* (New York, 1912). There is a considerable body of work on English institutions in the period 1066–1216; two works which survey the problems broadly are A. L. Poole, *From Domesday Book to Magna Carta* (Oxford, 1951), and J. C. Holt, *Magna Carta* (Cambridge, 1965), the latter especially lively and well presented. R. Fawtier, *The Capetian Kings of France* (trans. L. Butler and R. J. Adam, London, 1960) is the best brief treatment of French history. On conditions in the Empire, G. Barraclough, *The Origins of Modern Germany*, and *Medieval Germany* (2 vols., Oxford, 1961) are both useful. R. L. Poole, *Lectures on the History of the Papal Chancery* (Cambridge, 1915) gives an excellent account of the growth of bureaucratic method in church government.

Chapter 9. Two excellent guides to the narrative history of the crusades are Sir S. Runciman, *A History of the Crusades* (3 vols., Cambridge, 1951–4), and the collaborative *History of the Crusades*, ed. K. M. Setton, (2 vols., Pennsylvania, 1958–62): the former immensely readable, the latter detailed and scholarly. Two other outstanding works dealing with specific and important aspects of the crusades are R. C. Smail, *Crusading Warfare* (Cambridge, 1956), and J. L. La Monte, *Feudal Monarchy in the Latin Kingdom of Jerusalem* (Cambridge, Mass., 1933). The relations of the crusaders with the Greek empire are discussed by both A. A. Vasiliev, *History of the Byzantine Empire* (Oxford, 1952) and G. Ostrogorsky, *History of the Byzantine State* (Oxford, 1956). The best general discussion of the commercial interests involved in the crusades is W. Heyd, *Histoire du commerce du Levant au moyen âge* (Leipzig, 1936).

Chapter 10. A really good biography in English of Pope Innocent III has yet to be written. For an overall appreciation of his life and work one must turn to A. Luchaire, *Innocent III* (6 vols., Paris, 1905–8). Of specific aspects of his pontificate there are, however, excellent studies. C. R. Cheney and W. H. Semple, *Selected Letters of Pope Innocent III Concerning England* (Nelson Medieval Classics, 1953), with a valuable introduction, gives a fine insight into Anglo–Papal relations. C. C. Bayley, *The Formation of the German College of Electors* (Toronto, 1949), gives an excellent account of Innocent's dealings with Germany and the candidates for empire. Sir S. Runciman, *The Medieval Manichee* (Cambridge, 1955) is illuminating on the nature of the dualist heresy in Languedoc, and there is a useful chapter on the Albigensian crusade in K. M. Setton's collaborative *History of the Crusades* (Vol. 2, Pennsylvania, 1962). The best general account of this aspect of the pontificate is P. Belperron, *La Croisade contre les Albigeois* (Paris, 1959).

Section Three: 1216–1330

The book which, for me, stands out among discussions of the thirteenth century, and which catches the spirit of the times in a special degree, is E. Gebhardt, *Mystics and Heretics in Italy* (trans. E. M. Hulme, London, 1922).

There are some excellent English translations of contemporary sources. Three seem to single themselves out for special notice. One is the autobiography of the Franciscan friar Salimbene, perhaps the best gossip of the Middle Ages, which is translated by G. G. Coulton, under the title *From St Francis to Dante* (London, 1906). The memoirs of the Seigneur de Joinville in the form of a biography of the great French king St Louis, with whom the fortunes of crusading made the author intimate, are translated by M. R. B. Shaw in *Chronicles of the Crusades* (Penguin Classics). The third author who must be mentioned is of course Dante. There are a great many translations of the *Divine Comedy* available; perhaps the best is that of G. Bickersteth (Oxford, 1965).

Chapter 11. In this chapter in particular, all that I have written is heavily influenced by E. Gebhardt, *Mystics and Heretics in Italy*. For a study of the rise of the universities, of their organization and influence, one should turn to H. Rashdall, *The Universities of Europe in the Middle Ages*, ed. F. M. Powicke and A. B. Emden (3 vols., Oxford, 1936). On the philosophers and their teaching the most useful works are those of E. Gibson, *A History of Christian Philosophy in the Middle Ages* (London, 1955), and *The Philosophy of St Thomas Aquinas* (trans. E. Bullough, Cambridge, 1924).

Two biographies by French scholars, of St Francis and St Dominic respectively, are outstanding: P. Sabatier, *The Life of St Francis of Assisi* (trans. L. S. Houghton, London, 1904), and P. Mandonnet, *St Dominique: l'idée, l'homme, et l'œuvre* (Paris, 1937). On the Franciscans, R. B. Brooke, *Early Franciscan Government* (Cambridge, 1959) is readable and illuminating; and D. L. Douie, *The Nature and the Effect of the heresy of the Fraticelli* (Manchester, 1932) is an excellent study of the spiritual Franciscans and their fortunes.

Chapter 12. There are two excellent books on Frederick II and his age. E. Kantorowicz, *Frederick II* (trans. E. O. Lorimer, New York, 1957) is an important book, which really catches something of the colour of the emperor's story. Georgina Masson, *Frederick of Hohenstaufen* (London, 1957), a shorter and less ambitious account of events, is eminently readable. There is some penetrating comment on the period and its problems in A. L. Smith's *Church & State in the Middle Ages* (Oxford, 1913).

Useful on specific topics are D. Waley, *The Papal State in the Thirteenth Century* (London, 1961), and once again C. C. Bayley, *The Formation of the German College of Electors* (Toronto, 1949) which is valuable especially for discussion of the problems which arose in Germany after Frederick's death. Much the best guide to the complicated politics of Italy at the end of his reign and after it is that of E. Jordan, in *Les Origines de la domination Angevine en Italie* (Paris, 1909). Also useful in this respect are Sir S. Runciman, *The Sicilian Vespers* (Cambridge, 1958), and, in spite of its age, P. Villari, *The Two First Centuries of Florentine History* (2 vols., trans. L. Villari, London, 1901).

Chapter 13. For the history of the crusades in the thirteenth century, as the twelfth, the best guides are Sir S. Runciman, *A History of the Crusades* (Vol. III), and the collaborative *History of the Crusades*, ed. K. M. Setton (Vol. II, Pennsylvania, 1962). Some of the changes of attitude, which are important in this later period, are discussed by P. A. Throop, *Criticism of the Crusade* (Amherst, 1940); and by R. W. Southern, *Western views of Islam in the Middle Ages* (Harvard, 1962), which includes a brilliant chapter on the contacts of the westerners with the Mongols. The career and the vast oriental ambitions of Charles of Anjou are described by Sir S. Runciman in his exciting study of *The Sicilian Vespers* (Cambridge, 1958).

Chapter 14. In English history, the period discussed in this chapter is fully treated by Sir Maurice Powicke in his two great books, *King Henry III and the Lord Edward* (2 vols., Oxford, 1947), and *The Thirteenth Century* (Oxford, 1953). There is a good biography of *Simon de Montfort*, by C. Bemont (trans. E. F. Jacob, Oxford, 1930). The best introduction to French history is R. Fawtier, *The Capetian Kings of France* (London, 1960). A good modern biography of St Louis is badly needed: H. Wallon, *St Louis et son temps* (Paris, 1875) is still valuable. The general problems of French history are ably reviewed by Ch. V. Langlois in E. Lavisse (ed.), *Histoire de France* (Vol. III, pt. II, Paris, 1911).

Chapter 15. It is surprising that the able and eminently readable study by T. S. R. Boase, *Boniface VIII* (London, 1933) has not been reprinted. It is the most useful work on this pontificate in English. Two excellent discussions by continental scholars are J. Riviere, *Le Problème de l'église et de l'état au temps de Philippe le Bel* (Louvain, 1926) and J. Digard, *Philippe le Bel et le saint siège* (Paris, 1936).

The career of the empeor Henry VII, of whom Dante had such high hopes, is studied by W. M. Bowsky, *Henry VII in Italy* (Lincoln, Nebraska, 1960). The story of Dante's own life is told by Paget Toynbee, *Dante Alighieri* (London, 1910), a biography which has stood up to the test of time. A. Gewirth's volume introducing his translation of Marsiglio of Padua, *The Defender of Peace* (Columbia, 1956) is the best modern study of that thinker.

Section Four: c. 1330–c. 1460

The two books which seem to me to convey most illuminatingly the unsettlement of this period, and the problems which unsettled the men who lived in it, are J. Huizinga, *The Waning of the Middle Ages* (trans. F. Hopman, London, 1924), and E. F. Jacob, *Essays in the Conciliar Epoch* (Manchester, 1963). Huizinga's *forte* is his sensitivity to the reactions of the secular aristocracy, Jacob's his appreciation of the preoccupations of Christian thinkers and scholars.

There is a great wealth of original writing of this period which may be read in English. There are numerous translations of Froissart's *Chronicles* of the Hundred Years War, of Boccaccio's *Decameron Nights* – and of course there are Chaucer's portraits of English life in the *Canterbury Tales*. To this list one might add the translations of three eyewitness accounts of the Council of Constance, less well known but equally illuminating, which have recently been published by L. R. Loomis in *The Council of Constance* (New York, 1961). The diary of the great Cardinal William Fillastre in particular makes excellent reading.

Chapter 16. For a general introduction to the subjects discussed in this chapter see J. W. Thompson's *Economic and Social History of Europe in the Late Middle Ages* (New York, 1960). On urban life and its development, C. Gross, *The Gild Merchant* (Oxford, 1890) is useful for England; H. Pirenne, *Histoire de Belgique* (Brussels, 1948–52) includes important discussion of the troubles of the towns of Flanders; and Gene A. Brucker, *Florentine Politics & Society* offers a thorough examination of the social history of a great Italian commercial and industrial city in the fourteenth century.

The late medieval aristocracy has not been as fortunate as the *bourgeoisie* in attracting the attention of great historical writers in the recent past: J. Huizinga's *Waning of the Middle Ages* (London, 1924) is not a systematic study of their way of life, but tells one more about them, perhaps, than any other single work. Something similar may be said, with reference to agrarian life, of G. G. Coulton's book *The Medieval Village* (Cambridge, 1931): it is an illuminating work, but it is not a coherent study of peasant life, because it was not meant to be such. *The Black Death*, by the same writer (London, 1929) is the best introduction to the history of the great plagues. Sir C. Oman, *The Great Revolt of 1381* (Oxford, 1906) is a well presented study of the English peasants' revolt.

Chapter 17. E. Perroy, *The Hundred Years War* (trans. D. C. Douglas, London, 1951) surveys the whole course of the Anglo–French struggle in a masterly study. The English attitude to the war and its fortunes in the fourteenth century is well portrayed by M. McKisack in

The Fourteenth Century (Oxford, 1959), E. F. Jacob, in his *Henry V and the Invasion of France* (London, 1947), gives a clear account of the course of the war in the first half of the Lancastrian period. Covering roughly corresponding periods from the French point of view are J. Calmette, *Charles V* (Paris, 1945), and A. Buchan, *Joan of Arc and the Recovery of France* (London, 1948). The purely military aspects of the war are vigorously discussed by A. H. Burne in two books, *The Crécy War* (London, 1955), and *The Agincourt War* (London, 1956).

Chapter 18. The subjects reviewed in this chapter can most profitably be explored further through works which deal with the history of the countries mentioned in it. There is a considerable literature on the history of Burgundy in the Valois period: J. Calmette, *Les Grands Ducs de Bourgogne* (Paris, 1949), and O. Cartellieri, *The Court of Burgundy* (trans. M. Letts, London, 1929) deserve special mention. R. Vaughan has written excellent biographies of two of the dukes, *Philip the Bold* (London, 1962), and *John the Fearless* (London, 1965).

It is less easy to find books dealing with the history of Spain. R. B. Merriman, *The Rise of the Spanish Empire* (New York, 1918), and H. J. Chaytor, *History of Aragon and Catalonia* (London, 1933) are probably the most helpful introductions. There is an old but quite useful biography of *Prince Henry the Navigator* by C. R. Beazley (London, 1895).

There are so many outstanding works dealing with the problems of Italy and the Italian Renaissance that it is difficult to know which to mention. But, despite its age, J. Burckhardt, *The Civilisation of the Renaissance in Italy*, written in the nineteenth century and the starting point for most subsequent discussion, must take pride of place (paperback translation by S. G. C. Middlemore, Harper, New York, 1958). Another old book, J. A. Symonds, *The Age of the Despots* (London, 1880) is a useful guide for political history. Denis Hay, *The Italian Renaissance* (Cambridge, 1961) is among the best recent studies of the subject and its problems, and includes some discussion of the challenging views put by H. Barron in *The Crisis of the Early Italian Renaissance* (Princeton, 1955).

Chapter 19. The history of the papacy in the Avignonese period is very well described by G. Mollat in *The Popes at Avignon* (author's translation, London, 1963). M. Creighton, *A History of the Papacy from the Great Schism to the Sack of Rome* (6 vols., London, 1897) covers the period after 1378 in great detail. W Ullman, *The Origins of the Great Schism* (London, 1948) and G. Barraclough, *Papal Provisions in the*

Late Middle Ages (Oxford, 1935) are useful studies of particular subjects. The series of papers included by E. F. Jacob in his *Essays in the Conciliar Epoch* (Manchester, 1963) cover a wide range of topics: I have found them especially illuminating, and they have influenced my views heavily. There is an excellent chapter on the Brethren of the Common Life.

Chapter 20. A very useful study of the early Ottoman period is P. Wittek, *The Rise of the Ottoman Empire* (London, 1938). The final collapse of the Byzantine Empire is vividly described by Sir S. Runciman in *The Fall of Constantinople* (Cambridge, 1965). The best English accounts of the efforts of the papacy to organize resistance to the Turk are to be found in two biographies, J. Gill, *Eugenius IV* (London, 1961) and C. Ady, *Pius II* (London, 1913).

On the affairs of Eastern Europe the following works are useful: F. L. Carsten, *The Origins of Prussia* (Oxford, 1954); F. G. Heymann, *John Zizka and the Hussite Revolution* (Princeton, 1955); C. A. Macartney, *Hungary* (Edinburgh, 1962).

Index

Alfonso XI 264,
al-Hakim, 182
Al-Kamil, Sultan of Egypt, 169, 184
'allodial' estates, 53, 58, 59
Alphonse of Poitiers, 142
Alphonso V, King of Aragon, 269
Alphonso VI, King of Leon, 87–8
Alpine passes closed, 169
Amadeus, 297
Amaury, King of Jerusalem, 127
Anagni, 216, 285
Ancona, 310
Andalusia, 264, 311–12
Andronicus Comnenus, 130, 131
Andronicus Palaeologus, 301
Angelo Clareno, 160
Angelus, Isaac, 131
Angevin dominion, 175
Angevins, 174, 266, 302
Anglo-French War *see* Hundred Years War
Angora, 300
Anjou, 59, 110
An-Nasr, Sultan of Damascus, 169
anointing at coronation, 67
Anthony of Padua, 158
Antioch, 119, 123, 127, 130–31, 143
Antwerp, 232
Apocalypse, beast of the, 171
Abbo of Fleury, 47
Abelard, 97 ff.
Achaea, 180, 189
Acre, 119 ff., 133, 169, 178 ff., 300, 306
Adhemar of Le Puy, 118, 119
administration, professional, 110, 200
Adolph, Count of Holstein, 200–201

Adria, kingdom of, 263
Adrianople, fall of, 301
Adso of Montier-en-Der, 68
Agilbert of Lyons, 34
Augues Mortes, 185
Ain Jelat, 182
Aix, 30, 35
Albertus Magnus, 155
Albigensian heresy, 139–40
Alcataym, 164
Alcuin of York, 66
Aleppo, 124, 182
Alexander II, Pope, 77
Alexander III, 113, 115
Alexander IV, 173, 193
Alexander V, 287
Alexandria, 18
Alexius Angelus, 131
Alexius Comnenus, 117 ff., 125
Alfonso X, King of Castile, 173
Apulia, 45, 170
Aquinas, St Thomas, —, 153 ff., 276, 282
Aquitainians, 31, 35
Arabs, 16, 124, 125
Aragon, 175, 192, 205, 208, 264
Aristotelian studies, 151 ff.
Aristotle, 96, 152 ff.
Armagnac, Count of, 254
Armagnacs, 271, 272
armour, 239
Arnold of Brescia, 114
Arnulf, Emperor, 40
Arsuf, 119, 129
Artevelde, Jacques van, 247
Arthur, King, 101
artillery, 239
artisans revolt, 230
Ascalon, 178

FOR THE BEST IN PAPERBACKS, LOOK FOR THE 🐧

In every corner of the world, on every subject under the sun, Penguin represents quality and variety – the very best in publishing today.

For complete information about books available from Penguin – including Puffins, Penguin Classics and Arkana – and how to order them, write to us at the appropriate address below. Please note that for copyright reasons the selection of books varies from country to country.

In the United Kingdom: Please write to *Dept E.P., Penguin Books Ltd, Harmondsworth, Middlesex, UB7 0DA.*

If you have any difficulty in obtaining a title, please send your order with the correct money, plus ten per cent for postage and packaging, to *PO Box No 11, West Drayton, Middlesex*

In the United States: Please write to *Dept BA, Penguin, 299 Murray Hill Parkway, East Rutherford, New Jersey 07073*

In Canada: Please write to *Penguin Books Canada Ltd, 2801 John Street, Markham, Ontario L3R 1B4*

In Australia: Please write to the *Marketing Department, Penguin Books Australia Ltd, P.O. Box 257, Ringwood, Victoria 3134*

In New Zealand: Please write to the *Marketing Department, Penguin Books (NZ) Ltd, Private Bag, Takapuna, Auckland 9*

In India: Please write to *Penguin Overseas Ltd, 706 Eros Apartments, 56 Nehru Place, New Delhi, 110019*

In the Netherlands: Please write to *Penguin Books Netherlands B.V., Postbus 195, NL–1380AD Weesp*

In West Germany: Please write to *Penguin Books Ltd, Friedrichstrasse 10–12, D–6000 Frankfurt/Main 1*

In Spain: Please write to *Alhambra Longman S.A., Fernandez de la Hoz 9, E–28010 Madrid*

In Italy: Please write to *Penguin Italia s.r.l., Via Como 4, I-20096 Pioltello (Milano)*

In France: Please write to *Penguin Books Ltd, 39 Rue de Montmorency, F-75003 Paris*

In Japan: Please write to *Longman Penguin Japan Co Ltd, Yamaguchi Building, 2–12–9 Kanda Jimbocho, Chiyoda-Ku, Tokyo 101*

SOME FURTHER READING IN PENGUINS AND PELICANS

The Penguin Book of the Middle Ages
Morris Bishop

Medieval and Tudor Britain
Valerie Chancellor

The Waning of the Middle Ages
J. Huizinga

Montaillou
Emmanuel Le Roi Ladurie

The Penguin Atlas of Medieval History
Colin McEvedy

English Society in the Early Middle Ages
(The Pelican History of England: Volume 3)
Doris Mary Stenton

England in the Late Middle Ages
(The Pelican History of England: Volume 4)
A. R. Myers

A Distant Mirror: The Calamitous Fourteenth Century
Barbara Tuchman

Medieval Political Thought
Walter Ullmann